1997 EDITION

Annual Report of the United States of America

★ 1997 ★

*What Every Citizen Should Know About
the REAL State of the Nation*

Meredith E. Bagby

McGraw-Hill

New York   San Francisco   Washington, D.C.   Auckland   Bogotá
Caracas   Lisbon   London   Madrid   Mexico City   Milan
Montreal   New Delhi   San Juan   Singapore
Sydney   Tokyo   Toronto

1 2 3 4 5 6 7 8 9 0   MAL/MAL   9 0 1 0 9 8 7

ISBN: 0-07-006286-2

The sponsoring editor for this book was Allyson Arias. It was designed and produced by Melinda Letzing and Tiffani Francisco, New York, NY.

McGraw-Hill books are available at special quantity discounts to use as premiums and sales promotions, or for use in corporate training programs. For more information, please write to the Director of Special Sales, McGraw-Hill, 11 West 19th Street, New York, NY 10011. Or contact your local bookstore.

10/97

Annual Report of the
United States of America
★ 1997 ★

Table of Contents

Where Your Tax Dollar Goes

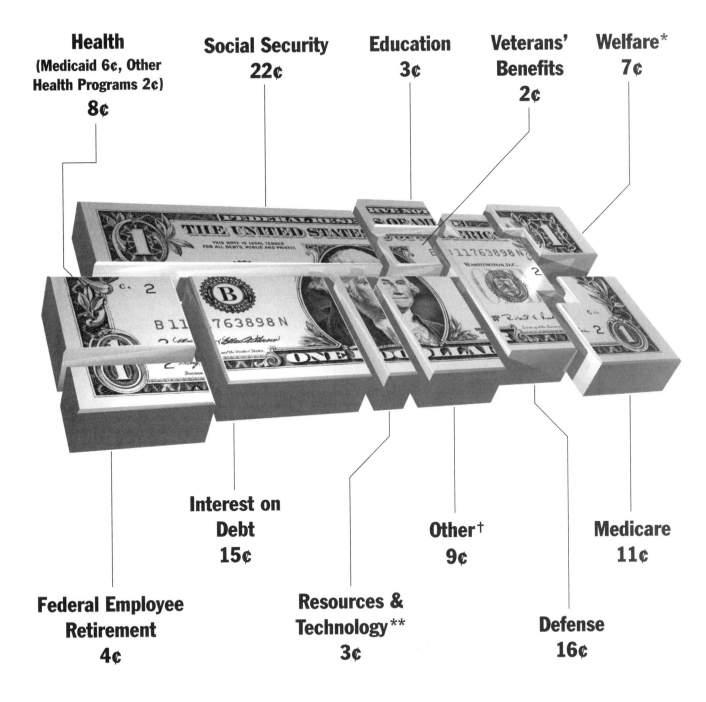

Health
(Medicaid 6¢, Other
Health Programs 2¢)
8¢

Social Security
22¢

Education
3¢

**Veterans'
Benefits**
2¢

Welfare*
7¢

**Interest on
Debt**
15¢

Other†
9¢

Medicare
11¢

**Federal Employee
Retirement**
4¢

**Resources &
Technology***
3¢

Defense
16¢

* Includes Unemployment Compensation, Food & Nutrition Assistance, Family Support Assistance, Supplemental Security Income and Earned Income Tax Credit.

** Includes spending on Energy, Natural Resources, Environment, Agriculture, General Science and Space Technology.

† Includes Transportation, Community Development, Administration of Justice, International Affairs, and General Government—each of which makes up less than 2% of the budget.

Special Thanks

My greatest appreciation to **Ross Perot** for inspiring me to seek accountability from government and for taking the *Annual Report* before the U.S. Congress.

I would like to thank my parents, **Joseph and Martha Bagby**, and my grandmother, **Louise Green**, for their support and encouragement.

Many thanks to **Melinda Letzing**, **Tiffani Francisco** and **Tony Tharae** for their constant help in design and production, to **Bonnie Cazin** for her research, and to **Chrissy DeNitto** and **Claire Johnson** for their continued contributions to this work.

Much appreciation to **Doe Coover** and to **David Conti** for believing in the content. At McGraw-Hill I would like to recognize my editor, **Allyson Arias**, for her care in preparing this report.

Special acknowledgment goes to **Dr. Dan Feenberg** of the National Bureau of Economic Research for his guidance in the art of research and to **Dr. Martin Feldstein**, Harvard professor of economics, for inspiring me in economics.

I thank the many people who continue to offer me their endorsements and comments. As always, I need your advice to make this publication better in future editions.

Also, thanks to the members of the *Harvard Political Review* who contributed their work to this report. The *Harvard Political Review* is a non-partisan, undergraduate journal on politics and public policy. For more information, please contact:

Harvard Political Review
79 John F. Kennedy Street
Cambridge, MA 02138
(617) 495-1360

Annual Report of the
United States of America
★ 1997 ★

Listening to American Voices

DEAR FELLOW AMERICANS,

This is the third year of *The Annual Report of the United States,* which began as a college project. Since the first report was published in 1995, I have received thousands of letters from many concerned citizens. For this reason, I have dedicated this report to "**American Voices**." The report includes many of your comments and concerns from letters that you have sent.

This report is meant to be an interactive tool for citizens to learn in plain English how the government is managing their money. It is also designed to be a summary of the year in politics, international relations, economics, social issues and business.

In 1996, America witnessed the most expensive Presidential and Congressional elections ever. With a low voter turnout, we re-elected President William Jefferson Clinton and reaffirmed a Republican majority in both the House of Representatives and the Senate.

Our legislators passed significant reforms that liberalized the telecommunications business, authorized the line-item veto for the President, made health insurance more portable and increased the minimum wage. Perhaps the most sweeping reform was this year's Welfare Bill, which replaces all federal welfare programs with block grants to states, limits time on welfare and requires states to put welfare recipients to work.

The quality of our lives made gains and losses as crime in cities was down along with unemployment. The stock market was up, breaking records, thanks to low interest rates and increased productivity. Our budget deficit was the lowest in 15 years. On the other hand, teenage drug use was up. Our trade deficit for 1996 was still one of the largest in history, as deficits with Mexico and China grew. We were told that Medicare would go bust by 2001 and that Social Security would be in trouble when the baby boomers started retiring. Meanwhile, our public education system still did not measure up to other industrialized countries.

The international front was fraught with ethnic and civil turmoil. Delayed elections in Bosnia, bloodshed over Hebron in the Middle East and mass migrations of people in Western Africa kept our State Department busy. We still battle with questions over extending the power of NATO, trade policy with China and protecting our own borders from terrorism.

These are only some of the issues that Americans faced this year, and next year will be no less challenging. As new Congressmen, Senators, governors, and members of the Cabinet settle in, the issues they face—from entitlement reform to constructing our foreign policy to re-energizing our cities and our schools—are fraught with controversy.

I hope that each citizen will join in answering some of our most difficult questions through participation in the political process. I am deeply grateful to each of you for sharing your ideas with me. I can only continue to write the *Annual Report* with your support. Please continue to write and send your ideas for next year's *Annual Report*, the theme of which is "**Solutions for America**."

Sincerely,

Meredith Bagby

Meredith Bagby

Meredith Bagby
c/o Allyson Arias, McGraw-Hill
Business Books
11 West 19th Street
New York, NY 10011-4285
Web Site: http://www.arusa.com

I. Who We Are

Our Population

The United States of America is a nation of approximately 265 million in a world of 5.7 billion people. By the year 2000, our population is expected to climb to 276 million, and to reach 326 million by 2020. Sixty-five percent of this rise in population will be the result of more births than deaths, with the remainder from immigration.

The U.S. is comprised of more than just the 50 states and the District of Columbia. It includes many other territories as well: American Samoa, Baker Island and Jarvis Island, Guam, Howland Island, Johnston Island and Sand Island, Kingman Reef, Midway Island, the Northern Mariana Islands, Palmyra Island, Puerto Rico, Trust Territory of the Pacific Island, the Virgin Islands of the U.S. and Wake Island.

More Racially and Ethnically Diverse

America's population is becoming increasingly racially and ethnically diverse. In 1995, African-Americans numbered 33 million, while 22.8 million Americans were of Hispanic origin. The U.S. Census Bureau estimated that 9.2 million of us are Asian or Pacific Islander, while 193.3 million people considered themselves non-Hispanic white.

African-American, Hispanic and Asian populations are becoming an increasingly important part of America's demographic makeup. These minority groups currently represent about 25% of the population, but this number is predicted to rise to 38% by 2030 and to just under 50% by 2050. The Hispanic population is expected to increase rapidly over the next quarter-century to become the number one minority by 2020.

More than 31 million Americans speak a language other than English at home (more than half of these speak Spanish), up from 23.1 million (11%) a decade earlier. In addition, four in 10 New Yorkers over the age of five speak a foreign language at home.

Immigrant Population on the Rise

The United States contains a higher proportion of immigrants within its borders today than at any time since before World War II. In 1990, approximately 20 million (8%) of us were not born in the U.S. This figure is at its highest since 1940, when it stood at 9%. More than four million immigrants came from Mexico, making it the most common country of origin. In 1994, immigration accounted for 30% of our population growth. In some cities, like New York, the population would actually have decreased without regular immigrant inflow.

Population Ages

Between 1960 and 1994, the total U.S. population grew 45%. In comparison, the segment of the population aged 65 and older climbed a remarkable 100%. In fact, the most rapidly growing group of Americans is made up of those 85 and older. The elderly population rose from 17 million (1 in 11 people) in 1960 to 33 million (1 in 8) in 1994. At the same time, the proportion of Americans 18 years of age or younger declined from 36% to 26%. These changes are reflected

The Changing Face of the U.S.

Population distribution of the U.S. by race and ethnic origin

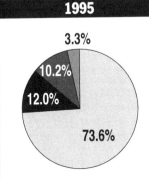

1995

3.3%
10.2%
12.0%
73.6%

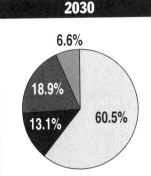

2030

6.6%
18.9%
13.1%
60.5%

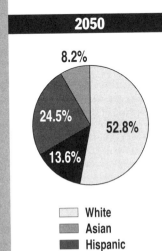

2050

8.2%
24.5%
13.6%
52.8%

- ☐ White
- ☐ Asian
- ☐ Hispanic
- ■ Black

Numbers do not add up to 100 because of rounding and because Native Americans are not shown.

Source: U.S. Census Bureau, 1994

in our median age, which increased from 24 in 1960 to 34 in 1996. In addition, the 45 – 64 age group is expected to jump to 25% of the population by 2020, up from 20% today. The states with the largest number of elderly citizens are California, Florida, New York, Pennsylvania, Texas, Illinois, Ohio, Michigan and New Jersey.

South and West Grow

Between 1980 and 1994, the population of the South grew 20%, while the population of the West increased by 32%. Birth rates in these areas are well above the U.S. average of 15%. As a result, these two regions combined contained 57% of our population in 1994, up from 52% in 1980. California, Texas, New York and Florida are our most heavily populated states. Since 1980, our fastest-growing states have been Nevada, where the population has increased 82%, and Alaska, where the population has increased 51%.

Americans Less Mobile

U.S. residents are not moving from place to place as often as they did in the mid-1980s. Between 1983 and 1984, 20% of the country's residents changed households. Between March 1993 and March 1994, 43 million Americans moved, about 17% of the population. However, most did not travel very far; 62% changed residence within the same county and only about 7 million pulled up roots and went to another state.

Urban and Rural Populations Rise

As recently as 1980, only 76% of Americans lived in metropolitan areas. Twelve years later, the percentage rose to 80%. Our five most popular metropolitan areas are scattered across the map: New York, Los Angeles, Chicago, Washington, D.C. and San Francisco.

Even so, rural areas of the country are growing at the fastest rate in more than two decades. The U.S. Department of Agriculture found widespread and substantial gains in the rural population between 1990 and 1995. Overall, some 75% of the 2,300 rural counties are growing in population, up from 45% in the 1980s. The greatest growth occurred in counties that attract retirees and others in search of recreation, such as those in the western mountains, upper Great Lakes and parts of the South.

Church-Going Declines

Most Americans identify themselves as Christians. The largest single denomination is Roman Catholic, and the most widespread non-Christian religion is Judaism.

A recent sampling of main-line Protestant denominations shows that most have lost members since 1960. Church scholars cite a growing distrust of institutions and a reluctance to join large organizations as reasons for the departure. However, one must also consider the rise in formation of new church groups as well as an increased movement across religious lines.

Newsweek Poll

00 years from today, will the United tates still exist as one nation?

es, exist as one nation

LACKS	WHITES	HISPANICS
41%	61%	54%

o, not as one nation

LACKS	WHITES	HISPANICS
48%	26%	38%

urce: The *Newsweek* Poll, June 19 – 25, 1995

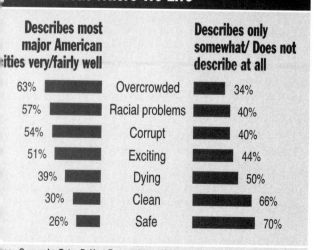

pinions About Where We Live

Describes most major American ities very/fairly well		Describes only somewhat/ Does not describe at all
63%	Overcrowded	34%
57%	Racial problems	40%
54%	Corrupt	40%
51%	Exciting	44%
39%	Dying	50%
30%	Clean	66%
26%	Safe	70%

ce: Survey by Peter D. Hart Research for NBC News/*Newsweek*, July 14–18, 1991

The Family

The Family Has Become Less Traditional

Families occupied 71% of our 97 million households in 1994. Married couples comprised approximately 78% of these families, down from 87% in 1970. In contrast, families maintained by a woman without a husband present in the household rose from 11% of all families in 1970 to 18% in 1994. These transformations can be explained by changes in marital status. Back in 1970, 75% of men and 69% of women were married; by 1994, the percentages had declined to 63% and 59%, respectively. Additionally, the number of persons who have never been married has doubled, growing from 21.4 million in 1970 to 42.3 million in 1994.

As a result of these changes, children are now less likely to live with two parents. About 73% lived with both parents in 1994, down from 85% in 1970. On the other hand, the percentage of children living with only their mother rose from 11% to 22% during the same period. Likewise, children who lived with only their father climbed from 1% to 3%. With more children living with only one parent, child support awards are now more commonplace.

Mom Works More

Mom is spending more time working and less time with her children and husband than her own mother did. However, she still spends about 45 hours a week with her family, compared to 36 hours working. Mom is now also more likely to raise a child alone. Nearly 30% of all family groups with children are maintained by single parents, usually mothers.

About 59% of women 16 years of age and older were members of the work force in 1994, up from 52% in 1980. As increasing numbers of women move into the work force, child care has become an even greater concern. In 1991, families with employed mothers and preschool-age children spent 7% of their income on child care. About two-thirds of these children were cared for in a home environment, usually by relatives or neighbors while their parents were at work. Another 23% received care in organized facilities, such as nursery schools or day-care centers. Virtually all of the remaining 9% were cared for by their mothers while they worked—and most of these mothers worked at home.

Dad Is Home Less

Dad spends more time at work (an average of 62 hours a week) than Mom and less time with his children (only 20 hours a week). Dad is also less likely to remain with his family. More families today are headed by single mothers, particularly in African-American communities. Nearly 70% of all black children are born out of wedlock. Statistics show that a father is less likely to remain an active part of his children's lives if he is not married to their mother. There is also evidence that many men do not pay adequate support for the children they father. Of all those owed child support from a father in 1995, less than half received the full amount they were due.

Divorce Rate High but Stabilized

The number of U.S. residents who are currently divorced has more than quadrupled since 1970, jumping from about four million to about 17 million. About 39% of the country's adult population has been divorced, up from 28% in 1970. In 1996, the chance of a marriage ending in divorce appears to have stabilized at 50%.

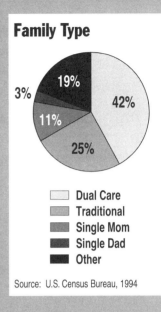

Family Type

19%
42%
3%
11%
25%

- ☐ Dual Care
- Traditional
- Single Mom
- Single Dad
- ■ Other

Source: U.S. Census Bureau, 1994

Percent of Children Born Out of Wedlock

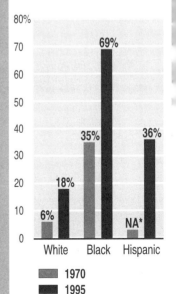

80%
70
60
50
40
30
20
10
0

White 6% 18%
Black 35% 69%
Hispanic NA* 36%

- 1970
- ■ 1995

*Hispanic not recorded in 1970.
Source: U.S. Census Bureau, 1994

Vital Statistics

Married Mothers in the Workplace

Percentage of married working women with children under age six

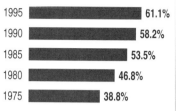

Year	Percentage
1995	61.1%
1990	58.2%
1985	53.5%
1980	46.8%
1975	38.8%

Source: U.S. Bureau of Labor Statistics

Child Poverty

Percentage of children living in poverty

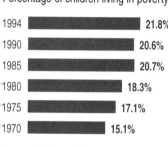

Year	Percentage
1994	21.8%
1990	20.6%
1985	20.7%
1980	18.3%
1975	17.1%
1970	15.1%

Source: U.S. Census Bureau

Juvenile Violent Crime

Violent-crime arrests per 100,000 juveniles

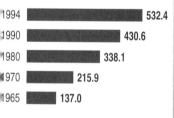

Year	Rate
1994	532.4
1990	430.6
1980	338.1
1970	215.9
1965	137.0

Source: F.B.I.

Most Non-Custodial Fathers Don't Pay Child Support

Percentage of non-custodial fathers who paid child support, 1989

62.5% — Paid nothing
25.5% — Paid full amount
12% — Paid partial amount

Source: U.S. Census Bureau

Meanwhile, the age at which Americans typically get married for the first time continues to creep upward. The median age of marriage for men was 26.7 in 1994 and 24.5 for women, an increase of more than three years for both since 1975.

Children Are Poorer

There are 70 million children under 17 in the U.S. About half of the nation's households contain children. Most families with children have both a mother and a father. Eight million families are headed by single mothers and one million by single fathers.

The total expenditures in 1995 dollars for raising a child born in 1995 until the child reaches age 17 ranges from $176,000 to $350,000, depending on the type of schooling and the income level of the parents, according to the Family Economics Research Group.

In 1996, about 16% of children under 15 did not have health insurance coverage. Twenty-two percent of children under 17 fall below the poverty line, comprising over 40% of the poor.

Grandparents Live Longer, Better

There were nearly 35 million people over the age of 65 living in the U.S. in 1996. Approximately 31 million lived either with a spouse, with relatives or non-relatives, or alone. The remainder lived in "group quarters," about half of which are nursing homes. Of those who lived alone, nearly eight in 10 were women.

The elderly poverty rate has declined dramatically, from 25% in 1970 to 12% in 1996, a rate slightly lower than that of the general population, thanks to Social Security and health care provided by Medicare.

Jobs and the Economy

About 66% of Americans 16 years and older (about 137 million people) are in the labor force. Seventy-six percent of men and 59% of women work. The number of women belonging to the labor force has been increasing steadily since 1960. The U.S. labor force, in general, is projected to grow by over 25 million workers by 2005, according to the Bureau of Labor Statistics.

Work Force More Technical and Service-Oriented

In 1995, the top three occupations were administrative support, professional specialty and executive and managerial positions. Approximately 21 million people are also employed by the retail sales industry—15% of the labor force.

Other important trends include the rise in the number of service-sector, high-technology and government jobs. Meanwhile, there has been little, if any, growth in the manufacturing sector since 1960. The new emphasis on high-skilled labor and the disappearance of blue collar jobs in the face of foreign competition and technological improvements has left many workers disenfranchised.

Foreign Trade Grows

Our economy has grown increasingly dependent on foreign trade. Nearly 40% of all our economic growth last year came from export growth. In addition, almost 30% of our entire economy is now dependent on trade. The fastest-growing export sectors are chemicals, pharmaceuticals, food and electronic equipment.

HOW MUCH DOES LABOR COST?

Average Weekly Manufacturing Wage

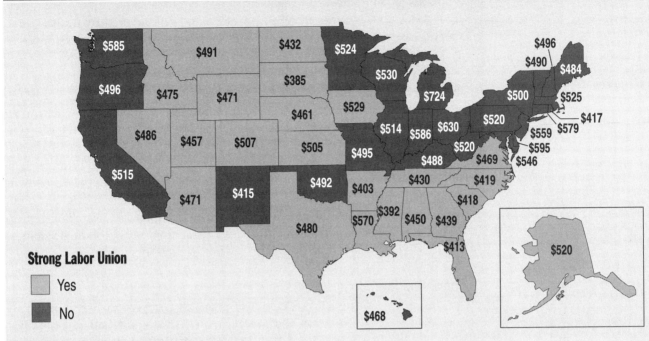

Strong Labor Union

☐ Yes

■ No

Source: *Expansion Management Magazine*

Big Business Is Largest Employer

Over 88 million people are employed by almost five million employer businesses in the U.S. Nearly 70% of these businesses had annual receipts of less than $500,000, but these smaller firms employed a relatively low number of workers, about 11 million (12%) of the total. The remaining 1.4 million businesses employed the other 77 million workers.

Income Depends on Education

The median household income in 1994, according to the U.S. Census Bureau, was $32,264. Economists tell us that 1996 median income is virtually unchanged in inflation-adjusted terms from the 1994 level. In 1989, income was about $2,200 higher than it is today. Some parts of the country are faring better than others; the West has the highest median household income at close to $35,000, but Southern incomes are increasing. The median income for the South, $30,000, jumped an estimated 3% between 1994 and 1996.

In 1994, the median salary of 25-year-old males with college degrees who were employed full-time year-round was $46,000. In comparison, the median salary for men just with a high school diploma was $27,000, and the median salary for men with a partial high school education was $21,000. For females, those numbers were $32,000, $19,000 and $15,000, respectively.

Health Care Costs High but Slowing

Household health care costs have soared in recent years. Between 1987 and 1993, health insurance costs increased 105% overall, and the amount each household spent on health care in current dollars rose 56%. By comparison, household income rose only 28% from 1987 to 1992. The good news is that early

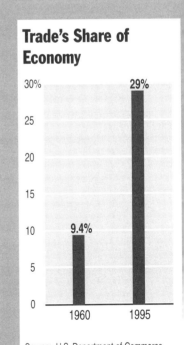

Trade's Share of Economy

Source: U.S. Department of Commerce

statistics from the Department of Labor show that increases in health care costs have slowed in 1996.

About 14% of the population (37 million people) do not have any type of health insurance. Not surprisingly, the poor were most likely not to have coverage—about 30% of those living in poverty were not covered by health plans. Sixteen percent of full-time workers did not have health insurance as opposed to 20% of part-time workers.

Housing Costs Up for Renters and Owners

In 1993, the U.S. had 107 million housing units, 95 million of which were occupied. Nearly two-thirds of these households were owned by their inhabitants. Of the 61 million owner-occupied housing units, 37 million had a mortgage. Owners with mortgages spent a median of $800 a month (22% of their income) on housing costs (including the mortgage payment), while owners without mortgages paid $250 (13% of their income). In 1975, housing costs averaged just over 10% of income. Occupants living in the 33 million renter-occupied housing units paid an average of $480 a month (29% of their income), whereas 18 years ago, renters spent only 23% of their income on housing.

Charitable Donations Up

Americans donated $23.5 billion to charities last year, giving most generously to the Salvation Army, the American Red Cross and Catholic Charities U.S.A., according to the Chronicle of Philanthropy. Donations were up 5% from 1994. Community foundations, which raise and distribute money in a single geographic area, saw the biggest gain in donations (93%). Donations to museums and libraries were up as well, to 25%, while the sharpest decrease was in donations to public affairs groups.

Basic Statistics

Gross Domestic Product (1995)	$7,246 billion
Per Capita Personal Income	$16,555
Median Family Income	$32,264
Civilian Labor Force	137 million

Source: U.S. Department of Commerce, U.S. Census Bureau, 1994

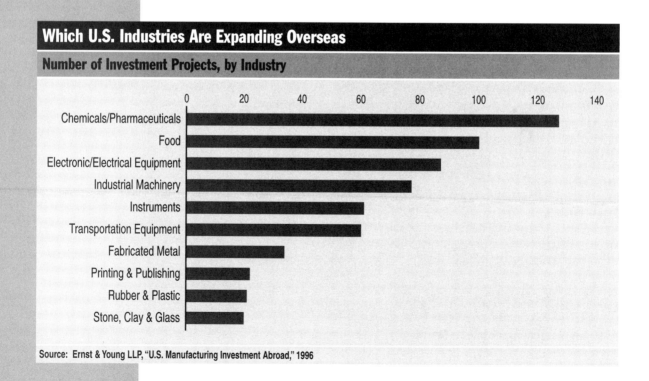

Which U.S. Industries Are Expanding Overseas

Number of Investment Projects, by Industry

Source: Ernst & Young LLP, "U.S. Manufacturing Investment Abroad," 1996

II. Financial Highlights

THE UNITED STATES BUDGET: Receipts by Source (Billions of Dollars)

Source	1995	Estimate						
		1996	1997	1998	1999	2000	2001	2002
Individual income taxes	$590.2	$630.9	$645.1	$683.4	$714.2	$748.7	$790.0	$834.5
Corporation income taxes	157.0	167.1	185.0	201.7	212.7	225.4	236.7	245.8
Social insurance taxes and contributions	484.5	507.5	536.2	560.9	589.4	618.8	647.0	679.5
Excise taxes	57.5	53.9	59.6	60.4	61.7	62.8	64.2	65.6
Estate and gift taxes	14.8	15.9	17.1	18.1	19.5	20.9	22.5	24.1
Customs duties	19.3	19.3	20.5	20.8	20.9	21.9	22.4	24.3
Miscellaneous receipts	31.9	32.1	31.8	32.7	34.2	35.3	37.1	38.4
Total receipts	$1,355.2	$1,465.4*	$1,495.2	$1,557.9	$1,652.5	$1,733.8	$1,819.8	$1,912.2

*Includes $38.7 billion of "extra" tax revenue not projected in the President's budget, but which was gathered due to strong economic growth.

Source: Budget of the U.S. Government, Fiscal Year 1997

Tax Receipts

Individual Income Tax

A tax levied on your salary and any other income you have (e.g., from the stock market or your savings account). The tax on income is a progressive tax, which means that the higher your income, the greater the percentage of that income paid as taxes to the government. Tax rates range from 15% to 39.6%.

Corporate Income Tax

A tax levied as a percentage of corporate income; a marginally progressive tax. Corporate tax rates range from 15% for corporations with income under $50,000 to 38%.

Social Insurance Tax

A tax taken out of wages before the funds ever reach the individual. The money is put into a fund to pay for the Social Security or Medicare benefits of the elderly, retired and disabled. The tax exists to ensure that people will have something to live on, as well as health care, once they become too old to work. U.S. payroll tax is just over 15% of income—half of which is paid by your employer and half of which is withheld from your income.

Excise Taxes

A tax imposed on certain commodities, like tobacco or alcohol. Excise taxes tend to be popular politically. For instance, it has been suggested that we increase taxes on cigarettes in order to encourage people to smoke less. We also have placed excise taxes on oil so that people will consume less gas.

Estate and Gift Taxes

Estate taxes are placed on personal property at the time of death. Gift taxes are levied on large gifts given from one person to another.

Tax Receipts

Fiscal Year 1997 Estimates

- Individual Income Taxes
- Social Insurance Receipts
- Corporate Income Taxes
- Borrowing
- Excise Taxes
- Other

Source: Budget of the U.S. Government, Fiscal Year 1997

THE UNITED STATES BUDGET: Outlays by Function (Billions of Dollars)

Function	1995 Actual	Estimate 1996	1997	1998	1999	2000	2001	2002
ENTITLEMENT PROGRAMS								
Medicare	$159.9	$177.6	$190.1	$204.9	$218.4	$231.1	$248.4	$267.0
Income security								
Federal employee retirement and disability	65.8	67.8	70.9	74.1	77.4	80.6	84.0	87.9
Unemployment compensation	21.3	23.7	24.7	25.3	26.1	27.0	28.1	29.2
Food and nutrition assistance	33.5	34.7	33.5	35.0	36.5	37.9	39.5	41.3
Supplemental Security Income	24.5	24.5	28.3	30.3	32.1	36.5	33.2	37.7
Family Support Assistance	17.1	17.4	18.0	18.4	19.1	19.7	20.4	21.1
Earned Income Tax Credit	15.2	18.1	19.3	20.1	21.0	22.0	22.9	23.8
Other**	43.0	42.1	42.0	41.7	41.2	40.6	41.2	40.6
Total income security	$220.4	$228.3	$236.7	$244.9	$253.4	$264.3	$269.3	$281.6
Social Security	335.8	350.9	368.1	386.2	404.8	424.4	445.0	466.7
Commerce and housing credit	(14.4)	(10.7)	5.6	6.4	7.0	6.7	4.5	4.6
Veterans benefits and services	37.9	37.7	39.9	39.4	37.2	37.4	36.4	40.2
Health								
Medicaid	$89.1	$94.9	$105.6	$111.3	$116.5	$122.3	$128.6	$133.2
Other**	26.3	26.3	29.0	30.0	30.1	29.8	27.8	29.0
Total health	$115.4	$121.2	$134.6	$141.3	$146.6	$152.1	$156.4	$162.2
SERVICE PAYMENTS								
National defense	$272.1	$265.6	$258.7	$254.8	$256.5	$262.9	$266.0	$275.5
International affairs	16.4	14.8	15.0	14.4	14.0	13.4	13.5	14.5
General science, space, and technology	16.7	16.9	16.6	16.6	15.6	14.9	15.3	16.5
Energy	4.9	3.2	2.2	1.9	1.9	1.5	1.6	0.3
Natural resources and environment	22.1	21.6	21.6	21.0	20.8	20.4	20.8	21.7
Agriculture	9.8	7.7	7.7	9.0	8.5	7.6	7.4	7.4
Transportation	39.4	39.8	39.1	38.9	36.9	34.8	34.1	35.5
Community and regional development	10.6	12.9	11.8	10.5	9.5	8.3	8.0	8.1
Education, training, employment, and social services	54.3	54.1	53.5	53.8	55.6	57.2	59.5	62.2
Administration of justice	16.2	18.8	22.0	51.0	24.9	25.6	26.1	25.4
General government	13.8	13.6	14.6	14.4	14.2	14.4	14.9	15.5
Net interest on debt	$232.2	$241.1	$238.5	$236.1	$234.6	$229.9	$227.0	$223.2
Allowances		(0.3)	(0.1)	(0.1)	(0.1)	(0.1)	5.1	9.0
Undistributed offsetting receipts	(44.5)	(42.3)	(41.0)	(42.4)	(43.4)	(45.5)	(47.9)	(68.7)
Total outlays	$1,519.1	$1,572.4	$1,635.3	$1,675.9	$1,716.9	$1,761.4	$1,811.5	$1,868.3
SURPLUS/DEFICIT	($183.9)	($107.0*)	($140.1)	($118.0)	($64.6)	($27.6)	$83.0	$43.9

* Adjusted to reflect more recent data. Does not match President's budget.
** Includes general administration expenses.

Source: Budget of the U.S. Government, Fiscal Year 1997

Customs Duties

Taxes on food and goods coming into the U.S. (for instance, the tax on Japanese cars).

Outlays

Entitlement Programs

When the government transfers money from one societal group to another, it is called a transfer payment or "entitlement." For example, the government can tax the general public in order to give money to the poor in the form of welfare; or, the government can give money from workers paying Social Security taxes to the elderly through Social Security.

Other forms of transfer payments include the Commerce and Housing Credit, which gives money to people who cannot provide housing for themselves, and Medicare, which provides health care for the elderly.

Service Payments

The government makes a service payment when it buys a particular service for the U.S. Examples include building roads, providing for our national defense or investing in science by financing a space shuttle. Service payments also include interest on the national debt.

Net Interest

The government must pay interest on the national debt. Interest is the price the government has to pay for taking out loans. Net interest equals the interest payments the U.S. government makes on its debt, less any interest it receives on foreign bonds.

Interest on our debt is the third largest expense for our federal government. It is paid to people, corporations and institutions who hold government securities. In 1997, the U.S. will pay $238.5 billion in interest. Because our debt is projected to grow well into the next millennium, the interest on the debt will continue to rise as well.

The Deficit/Surplus

The deficit (or surplus) equals total income minus total expenses, or the amount the federal government receives annually from taxes less its total expenditures. For the past 25 years, this number has been negative. However, in 1996 the deficit fell to $107 billion, its lowest level in 15 years.

Franklin Raines, Director of the White House Office of Management and Budget (OMB), attributed most of the deficit reduction to reduced spending and stronger than expected economic growth, which resulted in more tax revenues than anticipated. Other factors cited in the decrease in deficit were a drop in the growth of health care spending as well as increased capital gains tax revenue as people cashed in some of their stock market earnings. The new budget bill passed by Congress for fiscal year 1997 seeks to end the deficit and balance the budget within the next seven years.

The Debt

The U.S. began accumulating large deficits during the 1980s, when President Reagan initiated large tax cuts but was unable to pass equivalent spending cuts through Congress. This drove a wedge between income and expenses. To finance the deficit, the government has borrowed $5.3 trillion (as of January 1997) from its citizens and from foreign investors. This borrowing has transformed America from the largest creditor nation in the world to the largest debtor nation.

Deficit Projection (Billions of Dollars)

Surplus

Deficit

Source: Budget of the U.S. Government, Fiscal Year 1997

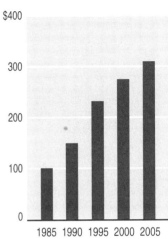

Net Interest on the Federal Debt*

(Billions of Dollars)

* Projections differ from the President's budget.

Source: 1985 – 1995: Budget of the U.S. Government, FY 1996; 2000 – 2005 Congressional Budget Office Projections

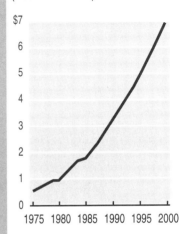

Total Federal Debt

(Trillions of Dollars)

Source: 1975 – 1995: Budget of the U.S. Government, FY 1996; 1996 – 2000 Congressional Budget Office Projections

America's Net Worth

In order to calculate the "net worth" of a company, one must subtract the company's liabilities from its assets. As you can imagine, it is extremely complicated to put together a balance sheet and calculate a net worth for an entity as large and as complex as the U.S. government.

The Treasury Department is responsible for compiling such a balance sheet. The Treasury's Consolidated Financial Statements for 1995 can be found in the "Financial Review," Section IX.

Assets

The 1995 report attempts to calculate the total assets of the federal government. The government's main assets consist of property and equipment, cash, investments and inventories. All totaled, the government has $1.298 trillion in assets.

Liabilities

The liabilities of the federal government were estimated to be $5.810 trillion. These liabilities include debt held as U.S. securities, federal employee pensions and actuarial liabilities, as well as other moneys owed.

Net Worth

Net worth is defined as assets minus liabilities. According to the 1995 report, the net worth of the U.S. government is a negative $4.513 trillion. Theoretically, if the government were to sell all of its assets to pay down its debt, it would not be able to pay its current obligations.

Future Obligations

According to a 1993 report commissioned by the Treasury Department and conducted by the accounting firm of Arthur Andersen & Company, the net worth figure does not take into account many of the future obligations of the U.S. government. Currently, the future liabilities of the federal government total $20.7 trillion. This translates to almost $80,000 owed for every man, woman and child in the U.S.A. These liabilities include:

1. $7.6 trillion, which represents the present value of Social Security payments
2. $5.9 trillion in contingent liabilities, such as rents on land, veterans' benefits, federal pensions and obligations to independent agencies
3. $3.6 trillion, which represents the present value of Medicare's (Part A) Federal Hospital Insurance Trust Fund
4. $3.2 trillion in public debt held as U.S. securities (excludes debt held by Federal Reserve)
5. $0.4 trillion in commitments or moneys owed for various other services rendered

Major Categories of Assets

Total Assets: $1.298 trillion

- Property and Equipment
- Inventories
- Receivables
- Cash and Other Monetary Assets
- Investments and Other Assets

39% — 20% — 16% — 15% — 10%

Source: U.S. Department of Treasury, 1995

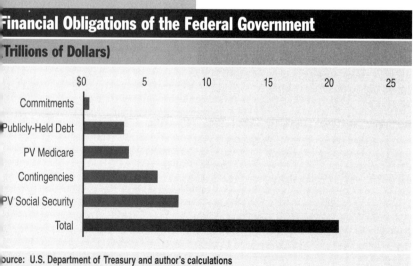

Financial Obligations of the Federal Government

(Trillions of Dollars)

$0 — 5 — 10 — 15 — 20 — 25

- Commitments
- Publicly-Held Debt
- PV Medicare
- Contingencies
- PV Social Security
- Total

Source: U.S. Department of Treasury and author's calculations

III. Focus on the Budget

Facts About the Budget

The government spends most of its money on a few major programs. In 1996, Defense, Social Security, Medicare, Medicaid and interest payments on the national debt accounted for over 70% of all federal spending.

Other controversial programs, such as Aid to Families with Dependent Children and foreign aid, accounted for much smaller portions of the budget. In 1996, these two programs together accounted for less than 3% of all federal spending.

Spending is divided into two categories—discretionary and mandatory:

- **Mandatory spending.** Mandatory spending is money the federal government spends automatically—unless the President and Congress change the laws that govern it. It accounts for 67% of all spending and includes entitlements such as Social Security and Medicare. It also includes interest on the national debt.

- **Discretionary spending.** Discretionary spending is the money the President and Congress must decide how to spend each year. It accounts for 33% of all federal spending and includes money for programs such as the F.B.I., the Coast Guard, housing, space exploration, highway construction, defense and foreign aid.

Rise in Mandatory Spending/Fall in Discretionary Spending

The percentage of the budget allocated to mandatory spending has soared in recent decades. The increase in mandatory spending is due to a rise in entitlement spending and the growing interest on the national debt. Mandatory spending is used to fund the following programs:

1. **Social Security.** Perhaps the most popular federal program ever, Social Security provides monthly benefits to over 47 million retired or disabled workers, their dependents and survivors. Since its creation in the 1930s, the program has expanded steadily; today, it accounts for 22% of all federal spending.

2. **Medicare.** Medicare provides health care coverage for over 37 million elderly Americans, providing hospital insurance as well as insurance for physicians' and other services. Since its origin in 1965, it has accounted for an ever-increasing share of spending. In 1997, it will comprise 11% of the budget.

3. **Medicaid.** Established in 1965, Medicaid provides health care services to over 36 million low-income Americans. However, the federal government shares Medicaid expenses with the individual states, which it does not do with Medicare. Funds for Medicaid make up 6% of the budget.

4. **Interest.** Net interest payments on the national debt consumed only about 7% of federal spending for most of the 1960s and 1970s. Due to the huge

> *"We went from . . . a President whose major goal was an expansion of the federal government to a President whose goal was to balance the budget in seven years."*
>
> — Newt Gingrich,
> Speaker of the House

> *"When I ran for President four years ago, no challenge loomed larger or seemed more difficult to solve than the deficit . . . The 1996 deficit has been cut to $107 billion. That's a reduction of 63% . . . the lowest deficit since 1981."*
>
> — President Bill Clinton

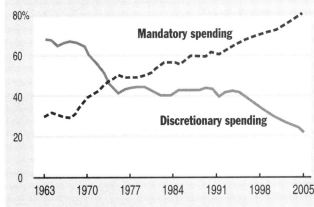

Discretionary and Mandatory Spending

By Percentage of Total Budget

As mandatory spending increases, less money is available for discretionary spending

Mandatory spending

Discretionary spending

Source: Budget of the U.S. Government, Fiscal Year 1996

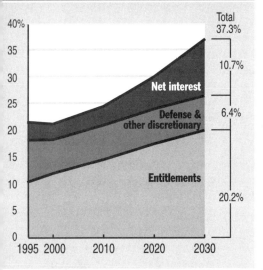

The Future?

Projected Federal Spending as a Percentage of GDP

Total
37.3%

10.7%

Net interest

Defense &
other discretionary   6.4%

Entitlements

20.2%

1995 2000 2010 2020 2030

Source: Bipartisan Commission on Entitlements, 1995

"I believe that my generation (baby boomers) must face up to our problems and balance the budget for the long haul. We must forget ourselves and sacrifice now for our children and grandchildren."

— James S. Slicker
U.S. Army, Alaska

deficits of recent years, however, that share has quickly doubled to 15% today.

5. The remaining entitlements account for 6% of the budget and consist primarily of federal retirement and insurance programs and payments to farmers.

Discretionary spending allocated to national defense totaled an estimated $259 billion in 1997, comprising 16% of the budget. Non-defense discretionary spending—which funds a wide array of programs, including education, training, science, technology, housing, transportation and foreign aid—has shrunk as a percentage of the budget, from 35% in 1966 to an estimated 17% in 1997.

"On" and "Off" Budget

From time to time, you may hear about certain programs that are "off-budget" and are therefore categorized separately from other government programs.

Specifically, the law requires that the revenues and expenses of two federal programs, Social Security and the Postal Service, be excluded from the budget totals—in other words, they are categorized as off-budget. In order to satisfy this legal requirement, the budget displays on-budget, off-budget and "unified budget" totals.

The unified budget is the most useful indicator of the government's finances and is vital in calculating how much the government must borrow. Most often the "budget deficit" is reported from the unified budget. The off-budget deficit looks larger than the on-budget deficit because Social Security is presently running a surplus.

The off-budget category is designed to give special status to certain programs. Over the years, the government has placed numerous programs off-budget and then returned them to the unified budget. But the mere listing of programs as off-budget does not, by itself, protect them from the budget process and possible cuts.

The 1997 Budget Stalemate

The law requires that by the first Monday in February, the President submit his proposed budget to Congress for the next fiscal year. The White House's Office of Management and Budget (OMB) prepares the budget proposal, after receiving direction from the President and consulting with his senior advisors and officials from Cabinet departments and other agencies.

This year, the budget encountered some obstacles. At a time when the OMB should have been preparing the 1997 budget, President Clinton and Congressional leaders of both parties were negotiating a plan to balance the budget over the next seven years.

As a result, President Clinton submitted a brief budget document on February 5 to comply with the legal requirement. The rest of the budget books, with the traditional amount of back-up details, had to be submitted later. The White House, the Republican Congressional majority and the Democrats finally came to a compromise days before the 1997 fiscal year began on October 1, 1996.

The 1997 budget passage came virtually on top of 1996 budget debates which had involved seven months of stopgap spending measures and two partial government shutdowns.

1997 Budget Highlights

Commerce

The National Institute of Standards and Technology will receive $543 million, about $77 million less than the current level but $75 million more than originally passed in the House. Most of the restored spending is for high-technology programs.

Military

A total of $244 billion will be allotted for military programs, $9.4 billion more than requested by President Clinton and $1.9 billion more than in the 1996 budget. The amount includes $44 billion for weapons procurement, to speed purchase of anti-missile systems and $800 million for two attack submarines and other major systems. It also continues financing for military operations in Bosnia and southern Iraq.

Education

There is $28.8 billion for basic educational programs, $3.6 billion more than in 1996. That money includes $7.6 billion for college student aid, a $1.3 billion increase from fiscal 1996. There is also an appropriation of $262 million (40% more than last year's $188 million) for bilingual and immigrant education programs.

Banking

The insurance fund that guarantees deposits at savings and loans will be replenished with a one-time levy on the industry, plus a hefty contribution by commercial banks to help pay off bonds floated for the thrift bailout. In return, banks got numerous small items of regulatory relief but no new powers.

Labor

Of a total of $8.7 billion, $463 million (or a 24% increase in financing over last year) has been agreed upon to finance the Community Service Employment Program of Older Americans, which provides part-time employment for underemployed, low-income people ages 55 and older.

Legal Services Corporation

The agency is to receive an additional $5 million (or a total of $283 million) to provide lawyers and legal assistance for the poor. But it maintains the restrictions on the use of agency money, prohibiting abortion litigation, representation of illegal immigrants, lobbying and bringing class-action suits.

Health and Human Services

Of $187.4 billion for the 1997 fiscal year, the National Institutes of Health received a 7% increase to $12.7 billion, and Head Start got an increase of $412 million, to $4 billion.

> *"This is the most defining moment in 30 years in this town, and the question is, is it going to be business as usual, or are we going to do the right thing for our children?"*
>
> — John A. Boehner (R, Ohio), House GOP Conference Chairman, on the 1996 government shutdown

Major Steps in the Budget Process

February – December 1995	Formulation of the President's budget for fiscal 1997.	Executive branch agencies develop requests for funds and submit them to the Office of Management and Budget. The President reviews the requests and makes the fiscal decisions on what goes in his budget.
December 1995 – February/March 1996*	Budget preparation and transmittal.	The budget documents are prepared and transmitted to the Congress.
March – September 1996	Congressional action on the budget.	The Congress reviews the President's proposed budget, develops its own budget and approves spending and revenue bills.
October 1, 1996	The 1997 fiscal year begins.	
October 1, 1996 – September 30, 1997	Agency program managers execute the budget provided in law.	
October – November 1997	Data on actual spending and receipts for the completed fiscal year become available.	

* Due to unusual circumstances, the President submitted the 1997 budget in two steps—one in February, the other in March.

Source: Office of Management and Budget

Courtesy of the Harvard Political Review

"At the moment, the stress is on balancing the budget. There should be more emphasis on growth, and jobs, and educational opportunity."

— Jack Kemp,
Republican Vice-Presidential Nominee

"We are building a huge problem for our children and our grandchildren and all future generations."

— Dennis and Nancy Stanga
Wayzata, Minnesota

Law Enforcement

The Justice Department got $16.4 billion, an increase of $1.7 billion. And $396 million would be used to build federal prisons ($100 million more than President Clinton's budget had sought). The bill also extended the Brady Bill (1994), which ensures a waiting period for handgun purchases. The Drug Enforcement Administration will receive $1 billion, more than President Clinton had sought or Congress initially had approved.

Immigration

Financing for the Immigration and Naturalization Service (INS) would rise to $3.1 billion (or $500 million more than last year). This will be used to add 1,000 agents to border patrol and $500 million will be allocated to reimburse states for the cost of incarcerating illegal aliens. At the Administration's request, the Republicans dropped parts of an immigration bill that would have reduced or denied benefits like AIDS services for legal immigrants and kept illegal immigrants out of public schools. Republicans were also unable to pass stricter regulations for legal immigrant sponsorship.

National Parks

Interior Department programs received $6.18 billion (or $22 million less than in fiscal year 1996), $421 million less than requested by President Clinton. The National Park Service would receive $1.4 billion (or $47 million more than current financing). The bill helps pay for the acquisition of the Sterling Forest and undeveloped tracts along the New York/New Jersey border.

Reduction in Bureaucracy

The budget package also calls for the elimination of about 300 minor federal programs, projects and grants, including the Office of Technology Assessment and the Interstate Commerce Commission.

Balanced Budget Amendment

The debate continues over a balanced budget amendment to the U.S. Constitution. The original measure, which was introduced in Congress last year, lost by one vote in the Senate after President Clinton lobbied against it. However, the Republicans gained two seats in the 1996 elections, and they may now have enough votes in the Senate to pass the legislation.

The President softened his opposition to a Constitutional amendment to balance the federal budget in November 1996, saying, "I don't believe that we need it, but if we have it, we ought to be able to implement it in a way that actually works and gives the country what it needs to manage a recession."

The amendment does not actually require a balanced budget; rather, it requires that permission to exceed budgetary expense limits must be approved by three-fifths of the total membership of the House and Senate (except in times of war).

Proponents of the amendment argue that we need to impose stricter rules on federal legislators to make responsible fiscal choices. Opponents argue that the amendment might limit government spending unnecessarily in times of economic crisis.

IV. Understanding Taxes

The U.S. Tax System

Our tax system relies on income taxes for the bulk of revenue. Income taxes include the individual income tax as well as taxes on capital gains. In addition, we have the corporate income tax, which is a tax on the profits of corporations, and the payroll tax, such as Social Security, which is automatically withheld from your paycheck. Many argue that the income tax is the most appropriate tax because it measures an individual's ability to pay tax.

The U.S. also maintains some consumption taxation such as the excise taxes on gasoline and cigarettes. Some argue that consumption tax is a more appropriate tax base because it measures how much of the resources available to society are claimed by an individual or household. Many European countries maintain a fairly high consumption tax called the Value Added Tax (VAT).

Makeup of Revenues

Over the past decade, there has been some change in the contribution of these taxes to our overall federal tax revenues. Three major changes in revenue proportion are:

1. An increased reliance on payroll taxes, such as Social Security, Medicare and unemployment insurance
2. A reduced reliance on the corporate income tax
3. A reduced reliance on excise taxes

Increased payroll taxes reflect changes in the Social Security system as well as the creation of Medicare. The reduction in the corporate tax revenues reflects both lower corporate income tax rates and, more important, a reduction in recent years in domestic corporate profits as a share of the economy. Over the last decade the significance of the individual income tax has ebbed and flowed without any discernible pattern.

Progressivity

A progressive tax system is one where the proportion of income paid in taxes rises with the person's income. The individual and corporate income taxes are generally judged to be the most progressive elements in the portfolio of taxes that make up the U.S. tax system. According to the Office of Tax Analysis of the Treasury Department, these elements more than offset the effects of other less progressive elements such as payroll and excise taxes. When state and local taxes are factored into the analysis, this overall progressivity is reduced but not eliminated.

The federal tax system has become somewhat less progressive over the past few decades as payroll taxes came to account for a greater proportion of overall revenues. But the tax changes made in 1990 and 1993 budget acts tend to increase progressivity both in the income tax and overall.

Subsidies and Tax Breaks

A tax system can also be used to address market failure. For instance, a tax subsidy for research activities may offset the tendency for private organizations to undertake too little research because they cannot appropriate for themselves all the benefits of that activity. In addition, taxes are used to direct consumption,

"If Americans are feeling pinched at tax time, the blame would not lie with the federal IRS. Most of the increase in the tax burden over the past decade has been at the state and local levels. The more that we shift new programs to them, the more that is going to go up."

— Lawrence Chimerine,
Chief Economist for the
Economic Strategy Institute

"Stop corporate welfare!"

— Linda Henderson
Trail, Oregon

Tax Burdens

1993 Federal, State and Local Total Tax Receipts, as a Percentage of GDP

Country	%
Sweden	49.9%
Netherlands	48.0%
Norway	45.7%
France	43.9%
Italy	43.8%
Greece	41.2%
Germany	39.0%
Canada	35.6%
Spain	35.1%
United Kingdom	33.6%
Switzerland	33.2%
United States	29.7%
Japan	29.1%
Australia	28.7%
Turkey	23.5%

Source: Organization for Economic Cooperation Development

"I know my generation will face huge tax rates—to pay back the debt other generations have created for us . . ."

— Charles Woo
Los Angeles, California

as in the case of the tax on cigarettes. A tax is placed on cigarettes to encourage people to smoke less. The government can also provide corporate subsidies and loopholes. Subsidies can take the form of direct federal payments or import quotas that limit competition with domestic goods.

Recently, many observers have called for a re-examination of these subsidies with an eye toward trimming those that lack adequate justification. An example of the corporate subsidy is that provided to the sugar producers of the U.S. The United States limits the amount of sugar that can come in from other countries so that sugar sellers in the U.S. have exclusive right to the market. Economists calculate that this subsidy costs American consumers one billion dollars a year in overpayments for sugar.

How Much Do You Pay?

In 1996, the government collected about $1.5 trillion from taxpayers. There is much debate about the overall tax rate that people face. The overall federal tax rate seeks to capture the percentage of income that we pay overall to the federal government, including not only income tax, but also our share of corporate, excise and payroll tax—and adjusting for our exemptions and deductions.

According to the Department of Treasury, the tax rate for a family earning just over $50,000 a year is about 20%. The National Taxpayers Union (NTU), a private non-profit organization, estimates a much higher overall federal tax rate of 40%. If you add in state and local taxes, they estimate the tax rate to be 51%.

Why are these two results so different? One reason is that the Department of Treasury adds health insurance costs, employer-provided fringe benefits and tax-exempt interest on tax-favored investments to overall income. This makes income look larger and thus the percentage paid to taxes less. In addition, the Department of Treasury and the NTU make fundamentally different assumptions about how to allocate corporate income tax, excise tax and other taxes to individual families.

Americans Pay Less in Taxes

Another way to measure the tax burden is as a share of gross domestic product (GDP). Federal, state and local taxes have been a fairly constant proportion of GDP for the last 30 years (between 20% and 30%), despite many changes in the federal and state tax structures. America's tax revenue as a percentage of GDP is less than in most other industrialized countries with the notable exception of Japan.

Clint Stretch, director of tax and legislative affairs for the accounting firm Deloitte and Touche, says, "the reason is that we have private sector health care and they don't." Another notable difference between the tax systems of other countries and that of the U.S. is that sales tax makes up a lower percentage of U.S. total tax revenue. Sales tax takes up 17.2% of total tax revenue in the United States, while the Organization for Economic Cooperation Development (OECD) average is 30.2%. The OECD includes the major industrialized countries.

Problems with the Tax Structure

Many argue that our taxes skew choices made about consumption and investment. The current system taxes interest on savings and capital gains, often resulting in double taxation at the corporate and individual level. Consequently, taxes create a bias against investment favoring current consumption over savings. Many also contend that our tax system is too complex, costing $40 billion in compliance costs and $3 billion in taxpayer time, according to Congressional research.

The IRS Record

The Internal Revenue Service (IRS), a bureau of the U.S. Treasury Department, is charged with the administration of the tax laws passed by Congress. The IRS functions through a central office in Washington, D.C., four regional offices, 63 district offices, and 10 service centers, with a total of 16,078 revenue agents and 2,831 tax auditors. In 1995, the IRS processed a total of 205.8 million tax forms.

A Congressional audit of the Internal Revenue Service said that the agency could not properly keep track of the $1.4 trillion that it collected in 1995. The General Accounting Office of Congress found the following persistent problems with the IRS:

- Cannot reconcile the accounting records that it keeps on individual tax payers with the revenue it collected or the refunds it paid.
- Cannot verify a significant portion of its non-payroll spending.
- Cannot accurately estimate the overdue taxes owed.

Senator Ted Stevens, a Republican from Alaska and Chairman of the Governmental Affairs Committee, raised the possibility that Congress appoint an outside control board to monitor the IRS. Members of Congress said that an outside board would be something worth considering.

The Political Debate

Taxes became a major issue in the 1996 Presidential elections with Steve Forbes calling for a flat tax, Bob Dole hailing a 15% across-the-board tax cut and President Clinton offering a variety of new tax credits to families. During the first few weeks of 1997, Speaker of the House Newt Gingrich announced that the House will lead a study of America's tax system and how it can be improved. Tax structure will certainly be a major issue in 1997.

Most Republicans are calling for a "flatter, fairer system." The flat tax gained popularity during the Presidential elections through Presidential-hopeful Steve Forbes. In general, Republican proposals of a flatter tax would eliminate many deductions and exemptions (although plans differ quite widely on which deductions stay). The tax would be "flat" (not progressive) in the sense that as income increased the percentage of that income paid in taxes would remain constant.

Plans for the flat tax generally eliminate any tax on interest or capital gains income. Proponents of the flat tax, for this reason, said it would spur investment and savings, which are discouraged by the current tax system. In addition, they argue that the flat tax would be simple and easy to administer. Opponents of the flat tax argue for some level of progressivity in the tax system, saying that the flat tax puts too much pressure on poor Americans while giving undue benefits to the rich.

The Democrats, in general, argue that we should more moderately reform the current tax system, keeping a level of progressivity but making the tax system more friendly to savings and investment.

The Clinton Administration has therefore proposed a bill of rights which contains a three-part tax package: a tax credit of $500 per child;

1996 Individual Tax Rates

Filing Status	Tax Rate	Taxable Income	
		Lower	Upper
Single	15.0%	$0	$24,000
	28.0%	24,001	58,150
	31.0%	58,151	121,300
	36.0%	121,301	263,750
	39.6%	263,751	No Limit
Head of Household	15.0%	$0	$32,150
	28.0%	32,151	83,050
	31.0%	83,051	134,500
	36.0%	134,501	263,750
	39.6%	263,751	No Limit
Joint or Widow(er)	15.0%	$0	$40,100
	28.0%	40,101	96,900
	31.0%	96,901	147,700
	36.0%	147,701	263,750
	39.6%	263,751	No Limit
Married Filing Separately	15.0%	$0	$20,050
	28.0%	20,051	48,450
	31.0%	48,451	73,850
	36.0%	73,851	131,875
	39.6%	131,876	No Limit
Estates & Trusts	15.0%	$0	$1,600
	28.0%	1,601	3,800
	31.0%	3,801	5,800
	36.0%	5,801	7,900
	39.6%	7,901	No Limit

Source: Internal Revenue Service

1996 Federal Corporate Tax Rates

Taxable Income Amount	Tax Rate
Not more than $50,000	15%
$50,001 to $75,000	25%
$75,001 to $100,000	34%
$100,001 to $335,000	39%
$335,001 to $10,000,000	34%
$10,000,001 to $15,000,000	35%
$15,000,001 to $18,333,333	38%
More than $18,333,333	35%

Source: Internal Revenue Service

"We __must__ cut back our government and its spending."

— John T. Lees
North Carolina

a tax deduction for post-secondary training and education of up to $10,000; and an expansion of IRAs to all middle class families and an easing of IRA rules.

Important Tax Terms

Adjusted Gross Income

Gross income consists of wages, unemployment compensation, tips, interest, dividends, rents, royalties and up to 85% of Social Security benefits. Items not included in gross income and thus not subject to tax are public assistance benefits and interest on securities like state and local bonds. Adjusted gross income is then determined by subtracting alimony paid, payments to an IRA and Keogh retirement plans and self-employed health insurance payments.

Deductions

A person can choose to standardize or itemize their deductions from their tax burden. The standard deduction is a flat dollar amount that is subtracted from the adjusted gross income of taxpayers. The standard deduction depends on the taxpayer's filing status and is adjusted annually for inflation.

In 1996, major itemized deductions include: mortgage interest on a taxpayer's first and second homes, interest on home equity loans, state and local income taxes, real estate taxes and personal property taxes, theft losses, professional dues, surgeries and some gambling losses. Other deductions include employee business expenses, including travel, entertainment and gifts.

Credits

Taxpayers can reduce their income tax liability by claiming the benefit of certain tax credits. Each dollar of tax credit offsets a dollar of tax liability. Some of these credits are:

- **Earned Income Credit.** Low-income workers who have dependent children and maintain a household are eligible for a refundable earned income credit. The credit is calculated on earned income such as wages and tips. The maximum credit for a household ranges from $2,000 to $3,000 for more than one child per family.

- **Child and Dependent Care Expenses.** The money used to pay for care of a child or a dependent so that the taxpayer can work can be a credit with value up to $2,400 a year for one dependent and up to $4,800 for more than one.

Individual Retirement Accounts (IRAs)

Single taxpayers who are not covered by a qualified employer retirement plan may take an IRA deduction up to the lesser of $2,000 or the amount of their earned income, regardless of their total income. Married taxpayers filing jointly may each take an IRA deduction, provided neither one is an active participant in a qualified retirement plan. Income earned from IRAs will remain tax-free until the taxpayer makes a withdrawal from the plan.

Capital Gains Tax

A capital gain is the difference between what the taxpayer sells an asset for and the purchase price. Under the current law, capital gains income is never taxed at more than 28%. Capital gains income is not taxed until the asset is sold.

Declaration of Taxpayer Rights

I. PROTECTION OF YOUR RIGHTS: IRS employees will explain and protect your rights as a taxpayer throughout your contact with them.

II. PRIVACY AND CONFIDENTIALITY: The IRS will not disclose to anyone the information you give them, except as authorized by law. You have the right to know why they are asking you for information, how they will use it, and what happens if you do not provide them with the requested information.

III. PROFESSIONAL AND COURTEOUS SERVICE: If you believe that an IRS employee has not treated you in a professional manner, you should tell that employee's supervisor. If the supervisor's response is not satisfactory, you should write to your IRS District Director or Service Center Director.

IV. REPRESENTATION: You may either represent yourself, or with proper written authorization, have someone else represent you. You may make sound recordings of any meeting with personnel, provided you tell them in writing 10 days before the meeting.

V. PAYMENT OF ONLY THE CORRECT AMOUNT: You are responsible for paying only the correct amount of the tax due under the law.

VI. THE PROBLEM RESOLUTION OFFICE: Problem resolution officers can help with unresolved tax problems and can offer you special help if you have a significant hardship as a result of a tax problem. For more information write to the Problem Resolution Office or Service Center where you have the problem, or call 1-800-829-1040.

VII. APPEALS AND JUDICIAL REVIEW: If you disagree about the amount of tax liability or certain collection actions, you have the right to ask the IRS Appeals Office to review your case. You may also ask a court to review your case.

VIII. RELIEF FROM CERTAIN PENALTIES: The IRS will waive penalties when allowed by law if you can show you acted in good faith or relied on the incorrect advice of an IRS employee.

SOURCES OF INFORMATION The IRS provides a great deal of free information. The following are sources for forms, publications and additional information: Tax Information 1-800-829-3676, Forms and Publications 1-800-829-3676, IRS fax forms from your fax machine 1-703-487-4160, Internet http://www.irs.ustreas.gov.

Source: Internal Revenue Service

V. Social State of the Nation

Medicare and Medicaid

Background

In 1997, federal spending on the Medicare and Medicaid programs will total $295.7 billion, which will account for over 18% of the entire federal budget for the year. This outlay alone costs taxpayers over $30 million every hour. Under current conditions, spending for Medicare and Medicaid is projected to double every five to seven years.

Medicare was one of the most controversial issues of the budget debates and the 1996 Presidential elections. Democrats accused Republicans of wanting drastic Medicare cuts, which they said would negatively impact the health care quality of the elderly. Conversely, the Republicans argued that the Democrats were ignoring an impending crisis. In reality, both parties have proposed reductions in the rate at which Medicare funding increases, as opposed to absolute cuts.

Although various proposals have been put forth by both the President and Congress, to date there has been no legislation passed into law to reform the Medicare/Medicaid system. As costs soar and increased demand for health care stretches resources, these two programs, which so many millions of Americans depend upon, face financial crisis.

"Your generation is giving my generation a free ride and the sooner we stop it the better. There is no way on earth to eliminate the debt without touching entitlements . . ."

— Dorothy J. Richardson
with granddaughter Christie
Lutherville, Maryland

Medicare: How It Works

Medicare provides for the medical expenses of 37 million elderly and disabled Americans. All Americans who are over 65 years of age or disabled are eligible to receive Medicare. The monthly premium is $43.80 in 1997.

Medicare covers inpatient hospital care, short-term skilled nursing facility care, home health care, doctors' services, diagnostic and lab tests, outpatient hospital services, home dialysis and ambulance services.

However, all health care costs are not covered. Medicare recipients must pay, for instance, about $700 of their hospitalization fees and for various types of surgeries and specialist treatment.

Medicare was created as a part of Social Security in 1965. The program is administered by the Department of Health and Human Services through a six-member Board of Trustees. This Board is comprised of the Secretary of the Treasury, the Secretary of Labor, the Secretary of Health and Human Services, the Commissioner of Social Security and two elected legislators.

Projected Growth of Medicare Spending
(Billions of Dollars)

Year	Spending
1995	$178
1996	$199
1997	$219
1998	$240
1999	$263
2000	$288
2001	$315
2002	$345
2003	$379
2004	$416
2005	$458

Source: Congressional Budget Office, April 1995

Medicare's Hospital Insurance Trust Fund

Medicare patients' hospital expenses are paid out of the Medicare Hospital Insurance Trust Fund, which receives monies from a payroll tax (FICA) deducted from workers' paychecks. In fiscal year 1996, the fund spent $4.2 billion more than it received in taxes and other income. In fiscal year 1995, the fund began losing money for the first time since 1972, about $35.7 million. The 1996 loss was the largest financial drop in the history of the Medicare program, with the exception of a one-time transfer from Medicare to Social Security in 1983, which Congress had ordered to keep Social Security solvent. Now, as medical expenses continue to rise, the fund is expected to run even larger deficits in the future.

The $4.2 billion deficit in 1996 was covered by a large surplus in the fund of more than $125.8 billion. Even so, administration officials project that this relatively large surplus will be exhausted by 2001 if current conditions remain unchanged. Furthermore, neither party's proposals go far enough to guarantee the solvency of Medicare for the baby boomer generation, whose members begin to reach the age of 65 in 2011.

In general, health care policy experts say that the necessary changes can be relatively small and gradual if they are implemented in the near future, but they will have to be larger and more abrupt if action is delayed. So far, however, no tax increases are scheduled under current law, and federal officials do not expect a reduction in the rate of growth of Medicare spending.

Medicaid: How It Works

Medicaid provides low-cost health care for needy Americans. Here are some statistics on Medicaid:

- Thirty-three million people rely on Medicaid for some form of health care; this translates to one out of every ten Americans.
- One out of every four American children depends on Medicaid for basic care. Children make up about 50% of those who depend on Medicaid; however, they represent only 15% of all Medicaid costs.
- One-third of all births in the U. S. are paid for by Medicaid.
- The disabled and elderly represent the majority of Medicaid costs, at 39% and 28%, respectively.

Unlike Medicare, Medicaid is paid for by state governments as well as the federal government. The federal government bears the majority of the financial burden (57%, or $92 billion in 1996), but the states are in charge of administering the Medicaid programs. The federal and local governments spent nearly $175 billion dollars in 1996.

Surprisingly, the growth of Medicaid spending slowed dramatically in 1996. Medicaid costs had grown an average of 17% a year from 1990 to 1995, and the Congressional Budget Office had been predicting a growth of 10% annually from 1996 to 2002. However, in 1996, federal Medicaid outlays rose only 3.3% to $92 billion, perhaps due to the increased use of health maintenance organizations (HMOs) and other less expensive types of managed care.

> *"We must take bipartisan action in the next Congress to extend the life of the Medicare trust fund. This should be the first thing on the agenda of the Ways and Means."*
>
> — **Representative Pete Stark**
> (D, California), on the Ways and Means Committee

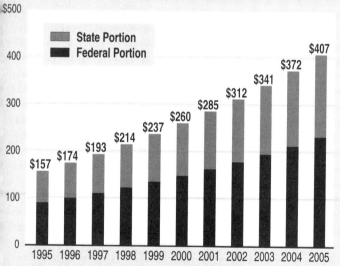

Projected Growth of Medicaid Spending
(Billions of Dollars*)

State Portion
Federal Portion

1995	1996	1997	1998	1999	2000	2001	2002	2003	2004	2005
$157	$174	$193	$214	$237	$260	$285	$312	$341	$372	$407

* State spending levels assume average state match of 43%.

Source: Congressional Budget Office, April 1995

Why the Problem Exists

Experts list three main reasons for the rising costs in Medicare and Medicaid:

- **Aging Population**. As our average life expectancy has increased and the population as a whole has aged, the number of people over 65 years of age has risen sharply. This has resulted in an increase in demand for health care, which has placed a great strain on Medicare and Medicaid resources.

- **High Health Care Costs**. Researchers and doctors are constantly endeavoring to provide more advanced health care services. This often involves the use of expensive technology, which translates into higher costs for the recipient.

- **Abuse**. Health care professionals often overcharge patients covered under Medicare and Medicaid, providing services not truly needed or charging for expensive services never rendered.

Medicare and Medicaid Reform

The President has proposed the creation of a bipartisan commission to deal with the problem, thereby taking the issue "out of politics." However, the Republicans, embittered by their portrayal as hatchet-men during the election year, are waiting for the Administration to take the first political punches.

Before the election, Congressional Republicans proposed higher premiums for most Medicare beneficiaries but Democrats fought the idea. President Clinton vetoed the bill, and the monthly Medicare premium declined in 1996 to $42.50, down from $46.10 in 1995. It rose slightly to $43.80 in 1997.

Some hope to control Medicare costs through the increased use of HMOs as well as increase revenues by requiring higher premiums for all Medicare recipients, particularly those with high incomes. With only 10% of the nation's Medicare recipients enrolled in the managed care plans, experts consider this a great opportunity to increase savings. Spending will also be reduced through lower payment to doctors and to hospitals.

Less focus has been placed on Medicaid reform; however, some proposals have been offered that decentralize the Medicaid program, giving states more control to form their own Medicaid programs.

Social Security

How It Works

Signed into law by Franklin Roosevelt in 1935, the Social Security program was created to ensure a steady income for the elderly after retirement. Since that time, Social Security has expanded to become one of the most comprehensive and expensive social programs in the industrialized world. Social Security is our most expensive federal program, absorbing 22 cents of every dollar of tax revenue. The Social Security program will cost American taxpayers $368.1 billion in 1997.

The FICA tax deducted from your paycheck is used to pay for future retirement, disability and Medicare benefits. Presently, FICA (the Federal Insurance Contributions Act, the law that authorized Social Security's payroll tax) deducts about 7.65% of workers' gross earnings from their paychecks. A matching 7.65% is paid by the employer, up to a combined value of $62,700. If you are self-

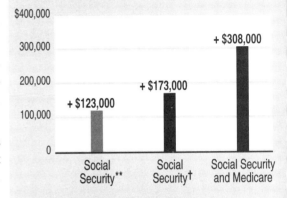

Payback in Excess of Contributions*

A typical couple retiring today will receive far more in Social Security and Medicare benefits than the value of their prior contributions plus interest

* *Contributions plus interest, in constant 1993 dollars*
** *Benefits received in excess of prior employer and employee contributions*
† *Benefits received in excess of employee contributions alone*

Source: *Retooling Social Security for the 21st Century*

"Demography delivers a message that is unambiguous and unalterable: America will soon experience an unprecedented explosion in the number of elderly."

— Peter G. Peterson
Chairman, Blackstone Group and
Director at the Federal Reserve
Bank of New York

Percent Growth in Population from 1995 to 2040

(By Age Group)

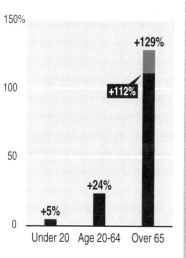

- High Cost Projection
- "Intermediate" Projection

Source: Social Security Administration, 1995; *Will America Grow Up Before It Grows Old?*

Social Security Annual Operating Budget

(Billions of Dollars)

Social Security now has a small annual cash surplus but will begin to run large annual cash deficits around 2015

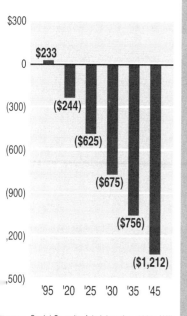

Source: Social Security Administration, 1995; *Will America Grow Up Before It Grows Old?*

employed, you must pay the full 15.3% of your income to Social Security.

In 1997, just under 47 million people will receive benefits from the Social Security program. Social Security accounts for 40% of total income of those 65 and over and keeps 38% of this group from slipping into poverty.

Social Security runs two main programs—Old Age Survivors Disability and Health Insurance (OASDI) and Supplemental Security Income (SSI). Over 40 million people receive monthly OASDI benefits. Of these, the majority (nearly 62%) are retired workers. Nine percent are disabled workers, 17% are survivors of deceased workers and 12% are the spouses and children of retired workers.

In 1996, the average monthly benefit for a male retired worker was approximately $760. The average monthly amount paid to a retired female worker was $550. People born before 1938 will be eligible for full Social Security benefits at the age of 65. Beginning in the year 2000, however, the retirement age or the age at which retirees will be able to start collecting benefits will increase from 65 to 67.

The SSI program is administered to approximately six million people. SSI beneficiaries are primarily the disabled, who comprise 75% of the recipients; the other 25% are the aged, particularly those who have very low, if any, earnings or assets.

Where Your Social Security Tax Dollar Goes

Your FICA tax goes to pay for a variety of programs: 69% goes to OASDI, 19% goes to a trust fund that pays for the health care of all Medicare beneficiaries and 12% goes to SSI.

Any money for OASDI not needed to pay the benefits of current retirees goes into the Social Security Trust Fund, which theoretically is invested in U.S. government bonds to pay the benefits of future retirees. Many argue, however, that the trust fund merely exists on paper and that the government has "borrowed" from the fund by running up huge government debts.

The Coming Crisis?

Economists claim that the Social Security program will go bankrupt by the year 2029. Part of the problem is the growing number of elderly combined with a shrinking number of younger workers to pay for their benefits. Since 1960, the number of people 65 and over has increased by 100% in comparison with a 45% growth rate for the population in general. The 85-and-over age group by itself has grown a tremendous 232%.

The Social Security system is a "pay as you go" program which means that the elderly are not supported by the payments they made, but by the current taxes on younger workers. As the huge population of baby boomers (those born between World War II and 1964) reach old age over the next two decades, the Social Security system will face a serious crisis. By the time the baby boomers become eligible to receive benefits, there will be only two workers for every senior citizen collecting Social Security, as compared to a fifteen-to-one ratio when the program first began.

The government has foreseen the impending crisis and has taken some measures to compensate. A Social Security savings account was created in 1983 by the Greenspan Commission, a bipartisan committee appointed by Congress, to cover future benefits to the baby boomers. Originally, it was believed that this fund would keep Social Security solvent for the next 75 years; however, their predictions were overly optimistic. Now, economists expect that the total erosion of the Social Security Trust Fund and the ensuing bankruptcy of the program will occur in half that time.

Reform

Three new plans were proposed this year by a Presidential advisory council on Social Security that had been reviewing the system for two years. These plans suggest investing Social Security money not only in U.S. bonds, as it does now, but also in equities, such as mutual and index funds, which could yield higher returns. Historically, Treasury securities have yielded about 4%, compared with about 7% for corporate bonds and 10% for stocks. However, some say that the riskiness of the stock market makes it a bad place to invest retirement savings.

If such a plan were adopted, it would be the biggest change in the philosophy and operation of the Social Security program since its creation in 1935 and could potentially pour as much as $150 billion of new money annually into the stock and bond markets.

Numerous other proposals have emerged, including: a reduction in benefits, an increase in the retirement age, increased payroll taxes on upper income workers, increased penalties for early retirement, reduced benefits for higher income retirees (or "means testing"), a changed benefits formula for future retirees and reduced cost of living adjustments as measured by the Consumer Price Index (CPI).

Social Security Money Owed

The Social Security Administration has identified about 700,000 people who have been underpaid since 1972 as a result of a faulty computer program, totaling $850 million in unpaid retirement benefits. The agency has already paid out more than $350 million to 400,000 of the recipients identified in the examination, but it is too late for the more than 57,000 who have already passed away and who did not have living spouses or dependents.

Three Models for Social Security

Current Law

OVERVIEW Pays benefits to retired and disabled workers and their families and to survivors of workers who die. Benefits are financed by payroll taxes of current workers.

MANDATORY SAVINGS ACCOUNT None.

TRUST FUND INVESTMENT POLICY Money in the Social Security Trust Fund can be invested only in government securities, not in private stocks or bonds.

INCOME FROM MANDATORY SAVINGS ACCOUNTS Not applicable.

Plan 1: "Maintain Benefits"

OVERVIEW Maintains current benefits structure with modest changes in benefits and revenues, and perhaps a new investment policy for the Social Security Trust Fund.

MANDATORY SAVINGS ACCOUNT None.

TRUST FUND INVESTMENT POLICY 40% of trust fund money might be invested in private market (after further federal study). Investments would be passively managed by an independent board to follow some broad index of market performance.

INCOME FROM MANDATORY SAVINGS ACCOUNTS Not applicable.

Plan 2: Personal Security Accounts

OVERVIEW Creates a two-tier system, consisting of a flat federal benefit and a mandatory personal security account to be managed by individuals. Transition to the new system would be financed with new government borrowing, taxes or both.

MANDATORY SAVINGS ACCOUNT 40% of current payroll taxes are redirected into personal security accounts. Workers can invest the money they want in a wide range of financial instruments.

TRUST FUND INVESTMENT POLICY No change from current law.

INCOME FROM MANDATORY SAVINGS ACCOUNTS Money in the account becomes eligible for Social Security retirement benefits. A worker uses it as he or she chooses. At time of death, any money in the account goes directly to the worker's estate.

Plan 3: Individual Accounts

OVERVIEW Scales back benefits to fit within current payroll tax revenues. Adds a new mandatory savings plan to be administered by the government.

MANDATORY SAVINGS ACCOUNT Workers pay an additional 1.6% of earnings into individual accounts. Workers have a limited number of investment options, perhaps five to 10 mutual funds.

TRUST FUND INVESTMENT POLICY No change from current law.

INCOME FROM MANDATORY SAVINGS ACCOUNTS Individual account is automatically converted to annuities when worker retires.

Source: Presidential Advisory Council on Social Security

How to Reach the Social Security Administration

If you have questions or concerns about your Social Security, the Administration has about 1,300 offices in various locations throughout the country. The main number is 1-800-772-1213. This is a 24-hour information service, but if you wish to speak with a representative, you must call Monday through Friday between 7 a.m. and 7 p.m.

Health Care

Rising Health Care Costs

One of the underlying causes of the large increases in Medicare and Medicaid is the rising cost of health care. The U.S. spends far more per capita on health care than any nation on earth. One dollar out of every seven spent by the government goes toward health care. Public and private health care spending represents roughly 20% of our gross domestic product.

High spending for health care is partially caused by higher prices for medical services. Increased technology and the increased life span of our people make health care more expensive. Health care costs are also driven up by fraud and the lack of incentives in our system to use health care services wisely.

The Uninsured

In late 1996, the American Hospital Association (AHA) claimed that 37 million people were uninsured and that 53% reported problems obtaining or paying for health care in the previous year. The AHA estimated that these problems had a negative impact on the physical or mental health of 17 million people.

A study by the Harvard School of Public Health similarly reported that at some time over the past year, 30% of Americans had difficulty obtaining or paying for medical care.

Young adults and the children of young adults comprise the majority of the uninsured. These individuals receive insufficient preventive care and often end up flooding emergency rooms, usually the most expensive type of health care.

High cost and an increasing lack of employer-provided coverage are the two principal reasons cited for not being insured. About 70% of the uninsured said that they had been previously employed without health insurance coverage.

The extent of employer-sponsored health insurance coverage has been steadily declining in recent years, even though many businesses were able to control health costs through employees' use of health maintenance organizations and other less expensive forms of managed care. Other businesses continue to provide health insurance but are reducing or eliminating their contributions toward the coverage of employees' family members in order to reduce labor costs.

Extending Coverage

The Clinton Administration has been developing incremental proposals to make health insurance more available to uninsured Americans. These proposals would help provide coverage for some of the nation's 10 million uninsured children and help pay premiums for workers who are in between jobs.

In August 1996, President Clinton signed a bill to expand access to health insurance. He called it "a long step toward the kind of health care our nation needs."

The new law, co-sponsored by former Senator Nancy Kassebaum (R, Kansas) and Senator Edward Kennedy (D, Massachusetts), passed the Senate unanimously and drew only two dissenting votes in the House. The bill allows workers to maintain health insurance coverage if they change or lose their jobs. In addition, it effectively bars insurance companies from denying coverage to people who have pre-existing medical conditions. The law also makes it easier for self-employed workers to afford their own insurance by increasing the portion of the cost they can deduct from their income taxes from 30% to 80%. It toughens penalties for Medicare and Medicaid fraud, reduces paperwork and offers tax breaks for those receiving long-term care.

An Average Family's* Health Care Cost

Out of Pocket Expenses	$2,280
Health Insurance Costs:	
Employer Costs	$3,650
Employee Costs	$1,280
Taxes	$2,930
Total	**$10,140**

* A family is defined as two or more persons related by birth, marriage or adoption and who live together.

Sources: Foster Higgins; Congressional Budget Office; Office of Management and Budget; National Governors Association; U.S. Census Bureau, 1992

"People believed that if the Clinton plan died, the managed care revolution would die with it and that you would be able to keep your choice of doctors."

— Bob Blendon,
Expert on public opinion and health, Harvard University

The President's efforts in 1997 to expand insurance coverage would build upon this new federal law. The Administration has not yet decided how ambitious any other new proposals will be, but it has assured citizens that it will be done in the context of a balanced budget.

Potential health care initiatives for 1997 include:

- A proposal to make it easier for small businesses to buy health insurance for their workers.
- Proposals to protect retiree health benefits, which many employers have cut or have tried to cut.
- New regulations on HMOs that limit "gag rules" and prevent certain other risky procedures like mastectomies from being performed outpatient.
- Increased efforts to insure children, a response to recent studies showing an increase in the number of uninsured children and a gradual decline in the proportion of youngsters covered by private health insurance.

HMOs

Politicians are encouraging more individuals to join health maintenance organizations (HMOs) in hopes of reducing overall health care costs. HMOs traditionally limit members to a specific group of doctors in their area and encourage people to see primary care physicians before seeking more expensive advice from specialists. Despite such restrictions, many people have joined HMOs because of their low cost.

The proportion of American workers belonging to some kind of managed care plans has grown to 74%, up from 55% in 1992 when Bill Clinton was beginning his campaign for health care reform. A study of employers of all sizes found that those offering HMOs as a health care alternative have reduced the number of alternative health plans available to their workers over the last year. Among mid-sized employers, 52% now offer their workers only one plan. The advantages of belonging to an HMO include a decrease in the paperwork involved in filing claims as well as significantly reduced costs.

But HMOs also have their drawbacks. Doctors across the country say HMOs have limited their ability to talk to patients about costly treatment options or HMO payment policies, including financial incentives for doctors to withhold care. Sixteen states have adopted laws this year to curb the use of these "gag clauses," and Congress is considering legislation to eliminate them altogether. While some HMOs have revised portions of their contracts, doctors report that gag clauses are still a serious problem. Furthermore, hospital stays were so strictly limited by some insurers that Congress recently stepped in and required that new mothers and their babies remain in the hospital for at least 48 hours.

In addition, HMOs contend they cannot legally be held accountable for the quality of care because they do not make medical decisions. The HMOs argue that they are protected against malpractice claims and lawsuits by a 1974 federal law that regulates employee benefits. Former Labor Secretary Robert Reich, whose office enforces the federal law, says that not being able to sue HMOs would compromise the right of many consumers to be compensated for injuries due to negligence.

Abortion

During his Presidency, Bill Clinton overturned some federal regulations passed during the Reagan/Bush years, making abortions easier to obtain. The Clinton Administration also created the Freedom of Access to Clinic Entrances Act, which punishes protesters for using force, threat of force or for physically

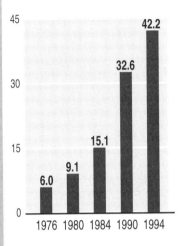

Managed Care

Enrollment in Health Maintenance Organizations (HMOs), In Millions

Year	Enrollment
1976	6.0
1980	9.1
1984	15.1
1990	32.6
1994	42.2

Source: U.S. Department of Health and Human Services

"What we are getting is managed care but without consumer protection."

— **Poll Starr**, Princeton University, worked on the 1993 Clinton plan obstructing women seeking abortions.

There are approximately 2,500 clinics throughout the U.S. where doctors perform 1.6 million abortions annually—equivalent to one-fourth of U.S. pregnancies. According to a report by the U.S. Center for Disease Control, women who obtain abortions are predominantly 24 years of age or younger, white and unmarried. A disproportionate number of black women also receive abortions.

Abortion, however, is restricted in 83% of U.S. counties, although most women who can afford an abortion are usually able to obtain one. Most abortion clinics are located in cities, so many women from rural areas must travel to obtain one. Surveys indicate that a large majority of obstetricians and gynecologists are pro-choice, yet many refuse to perform abortions because they feel the work is low-paying or against their moral convictions. Many fear harassment from pro-life protesters. The average cost of an abortion is currently about $250.

A new drug will soon arrive in the U.S. that may bring a new chapter in the abortion debate. RU-486, long available in Europe, won provisional approval from the FDA in mid-1996. RU-486 is a pill which can be taken as an outpatient and which chemically triggers the expulsion of the fetus. Anti-abortion groups, which oppose the use of the drug, have fought to prevent its sale in the U.S. RU-486 has been a rallying point for abortion rights activists, who believe that since it can be taken in the privacy of a doctor's office, it could curtail much of the violence that has plagued abortion clinics.

During the Presidential campaign, another heated debate arose over "partial-birth abortions." Partial-birth abortions, or abortions which occur in the last trimester of birth, are legal in some states. The President, despite pressure from the conservative right, refused to sign a federal law banning partial-birth abortions, arguing that the decision should be left up to the states and that the law would infringe upon women's rights, especially in cases where giving birth would endanger the life of the mother.

Disease
Cardiovascular Diseases

Cardiovascular diseases are America's number one killer. More that one in four Americans, over 70 million people, suffer from some sort of cardiovascular disease. These diseases claim approximately one million lives every year, more than 42% of all deaths during the year. Heart disease is about 70% more likely to occur in men than women. However, due to improved health care habits—decreases in smoking, fat consumption and alcohol intake—Americans have reduced their risk of cardiovascular disease.

Cancer

Cancer is the nation's second leading cause of death—approximately 500,000 people die of cancer annually. The disease is characterized as a rapid unrestrained growth of cells in the body. Overall, the rate of cancer incidence and mortality has been steadily increasing, most likely due to the increased life expectancy of our population. However, the chances of surviving cancer have steadily improved. The American Cancer Society says that the chance of survival depends on two main factors—how early the cancer is detected and where the tumor is located. More than eight million Americans are alive who have a history of cancer.

> *"If this trend continues, health coverage could be priced out of range for more and more working families . . ."*
>
> — **Jack Meyer,**
> President of the Economic and Social Research Institute

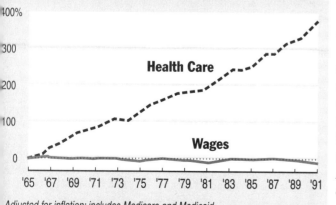

Health Care Benefits Compared to Wages

Percentage Increase From 1965 to 1991*

Adjusted for inflation; includes Medicare and Medicaid

Source: Health Care Financing Administration

AIDS

Acquired Immune Deficiency Syndrome (AIDS), first diagnosed in 1981, has claimed the lives of 250,000 Americans, nearly three times more than the Vietnam War. Anywhere from 10 to 20 million people are infected worldwide, and this number is projected to increase to 40 million by the year 2000. AIDS is caused by the human immunodeficiency virus (HIV), which is spread through contact with infected body fluids, such as blood and semen. The virus attacks white blood cells, thereby decreasing the body's ability to fight infection. Those infected with the virus may harbor it within their bodies for many years before developing symptoms. It takes an average of 10 years before a person with HIV develops AIDS. However, regardless of whether or not they display symptoms, those who carry the virus can still infect others. The Center for Disease Control (CDC) estimates that approximately one million people in the U.S. are infected with HIV.

Homosexual and bisexual males comprise approximately 54% of all adult and adolescent AIDS patients in the U.S., but the disease is spreading faster among heterosexuals and women than homosexuals. Another group commonly afflicted with AIDS is intravenous drug users, who constitute 24% of the total. Women make up 11% of all those infected, and over the next decade, 125,000 children will be orphaned because of AIDS.

The overwhelming majority of AIDS cases are concentrated in large cities and metropolitan areas. AIDS is tied for sixth place among the leading causes of premature death, but among the six it is the fastest growing, according to the CDC.

Although there is no known cure, numerous drugs are being tested, and several have been successful in temporarily suppressing the AIDS virus. The most popular of these is azidothymidine (AZT).

Welfare

The Welfare Debate

On August 22, 1996, President Clinton signed a Republican-sponsored bill that ended the 60-year-old New Deal system of welfare, sending the problem of welfare back to the states. The bill came after a long battle between Republicans and Democrats. In January of 1996, Clinton had vetoed a previous version of the bill. It was not until May of 1996 that the parties began serious negotiations again, culminating in the August legislation.

Many Democrats criticized the President for signing the Republican legislation, saying that it would hurt the most vulnerable in society—single mothers and children. Others called it merely a political move on the part of the President, who faced an electorate in 1996 who wanted welfare reform. Supporters argue that now welfare provisions will encourage recipients to join the work force.

The effect of the bill on America's poor is still far from clear. 1997 will likely bring heated debate in the state legislatures, which now must create their own welfare programs, and among federal politicians, including the President, who now say that the welfare legislation may have "gone too far."

Who Are the Poor?

The "poor" are typically defined as those whose incomes fall below the poverty line, which is defined by the federal government. Typically, a family of four that has an annual income of less than $15,569 is considered "poor." As of January 1997, 13% of all U.S. households and 22% of all children fell into this

"[Our] democratic system . . . depends on the electorate being well-informed."

— Alvin R. Tarlov
Professor, Harvard School of Public Health
Boston, Massachusetts

"I intend to speak out about welfare reform and write about it."

— Hillary Rodham Clinton

"I wish he had not signed it [the welfare bill] in its present form, but I also have great faith that he will change it . . . did you know that Hillary urged him to sign it?"

— Barbra Streisand,
Actress

Profile of the Rich and Poor (by Income)

	The Rich: More than $100,000	The Middle Class: $25,000 – $100,000	The Poor: Less than $15,569
POPULATION	6 million households 6% of households 3% of children 0.7% of elderly	52 million households 54% of households 31% of children 8% of elderly	8 million households 12% of households 22% of children 12% of elderly
FAMILY	85% married couples 3% single moms 2% single dads	70% married couples 8% single moms 3% single dads	42% married couples 52% single moms 6% single dads
EDUCATION	97% high school graduates 70% attended college 38% finished postgrad degree	87% high school graduates 29% attended college 10% finished postgrad degree	56% high school graduates 16% attended college 5% finished postgrad degree
FINANCES	92% own home $569,000 net worth 39% average tax rate 97% work full-time	78% own home $139,600 net worth 33% average tax rate 97% work full-time	45% own home $3,900 net worth 28% average tax rate 23% work full-time

Source: U.S. Census Bureau, 1995

Courtesy of the Harvard Political Review

"The connection has not been made between community solutions and the policy debate. You have the real solutions going largely unnoticed either by political leaders or by the media."

— Arianna Huffington,
Senior Fellow at the Progress
and Freedom Foundation;
commentator, columnist

poverty range, as well as 12% of all people over 65. According to these numbers, the incidence of childhood poverty is higher in the U.S. than in any other industrialized country. Households run by single mothers have a greater chance of slipping into poverty than traditional families or families headed by single fathers; in fact, they comprise 52% of all households below the poverty line.

For several decades, the relatively high rate of economic growth has caused a reduction in the poverty rate. After hitting an historic low of 11% in 1973, the poverty rate increased steadily to reach a peak of 15% in 1993. Since then, the poverty rate has decreased to 13%, where its stands today.

The majority of the poor (67%) are white, while 29% are black. Black families tend to be over-represented among the poor, based on their percentage in the overall population. In addition, the poor are less educated than the total population; only 56% finish high school, as opposed to 87% of the middle class and 97% of the wealthiest 20% of Americans.

Surprisingly, roughly one-quarter of the poor do not collect any government benefits. Fewer than half collect the cash benefits most people think of as welfare. Approximately 50% of the poor receive Food Stamps and are covered by Medicaid, and only 18% live in public or government-subsidized housing.

The Old Welfare System

Prior to the 1996 Welfare Bill, the nation's main welfare programs were Aid to Families with Dependent Children (AFDC), Food Stamps and the subsidized housing program. The largest federally funded program was AFDC, which provided cash benefits to nearly five million households. However, states report that the average AFDC check only covers 63% of what they say is needed for their poor families to survive.

In addition, the government ran programs to assist needy children, including foster care, adoption assistance, and child abuse prevention and treatment. The government also funded other welfare programs such as WIC (Women, Infants and Children), Child and Adult Care Food programs, summer food programs and nutrition programs for homeless children. All of these provide funds to low-income families for child care and nutrition.

The Welfare Bill of 1996

The 1996 Welfare Bill dismantles the entire federal welfare system and replaces it with dozens of block grants to states which will in turn craft their own welfare policies.

The grants will include money for cash welfare programs, child welfare and protection programs, child care, school meals and family nutrition programs for women and young children. The new welfare bill is projected to save the federal government $55 billion over the next six years from the previous welfare system.

States are required to inform the federal government how they intend to comply with the new law by July 1997, although the law went into effect on October 1, 1996. The first states to enter their plans were Wisconsin, Michigan, Ohio, Florida, Vermont, Massachusetts, Maryland, Oregon, Oklahoma, Tennessee and Maine. There is concern that states who had not anticipated the welfare law and were doing very little to redesign their welfare programs will encounter problems.

Cash Welfare Block Grant

This block grant, known as Temporary Assistance for Needy Families, will phase out the current federal AFDC program. The law requires states to put half of all AFDC recipients in "work activities" by the year 2002 and limits the number of months that families can receive benefits. The federal government will provide $15.4 billion each year to the states from fiscal year 1997 to fiscal year 2000. The money will be distributed in proportion to each state's share of federal funding in previous fiscal years.

Presently, fewer than 10% of those on welfare are employed. If states fail to move 20% of their welfare recipients into jobs by 1997 and 50% by 2002, they can face cutbacks in their block grants. The Clinton Administration estimates that at least a million new jobs will have to be created for welfare recipients by the year 2000 but does not want the government to provide most of the openings. It is hoped that the private sector will provide jobs.

Child Protection Block Grant

This grant will replace 23 federal child-protection programs that accounted for $3.6 billion in government spending in fiscal year 1994. These programs provide foster care, adoption assistance and child abuse services. The states can appropriate the funds in any way they deem necessary but will have to create citizen review panels to oversee protection services. The block grant will total $4.4 billion in fiscal 1997 and rise to $5.6 billion in fiscal year 2000.

Child Care and Development Block Grant

This block grant will replace nine federal child-care programs which provided for child-care services needed by low-income families. Federal health and safety regulations for child care will be repealed, and the states will be given great flexibility in spending these funds. The block grant will amount to $2.1 billion annually between fiscal years 1997 and 2000.

Family Nutrition Block Grant

This grant will replace federal nutrition programs such as WIC (Women Infants & Children), the Child and Adult Care Food Program, the Summer Food Program and the Homeless Children Nutrition Program. States will be required to use their funds to provide food to low-income pregnant women, infants and

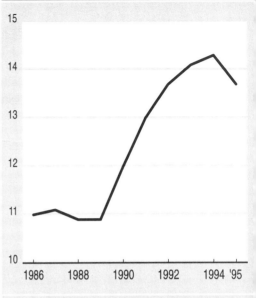

Federal Welfare Recipients

(Millions of People)

Source: Health and Human Services Department, Center on Budget and Policy Priorities

"How can you ask a welfare mom to get a job if she has to give up the medical insurance she gets on welfare, if she has no training or bus ticket to get there, if she can't find a safe place to leave her children? But I don't think anybody's listening."

— Governor Tommy Thompson
(R, Wisconsin)

Annual Food-Stamp Cuts Per Household

State	Households on Food Stamps	Avg. Cut Per Household
California	1,178,423	$530
New York	984,579	624
Florida	491,268	403
Pennsylvania	496,431	351
Illinois	466,856	344
Michigan	414,984	372
Washington	204,316	557
Utah	41,233	346
North Dakota	16,332	270

Source: U.S. Department of Health and Human Services, Center on Budget and Policy Priorities, 1996

"Simply sending women out to employers to announce they are welfare recipients bearing wage vouchers is not a good idea. To the employer it comes across as 'Hi, I'm a lemon— give me a job.'"

— Lawrence Katz,
Harvard economist and
former Clinton appointee

young children at risk for poor nutrition. Once again, states would have the latitude to decide how these services will be administered. Funding for the block grant will be $4.6 billion in fiscal 1997, rising to $5.3 billion by fiscal year 2000.

School-Based Nutrition Block Grant

This grant will replace the lunch and breakfast programs, summer food programs and special milk programs of the school systems. States will be required to fund similar types of programs and will be authorized to spend $6.7 billion in fiscal 1997, which would climb to $7.8 billion by fiscal year 2000.

In addition to awarding block grants, the new welfare system will also scale back the Food Stamp program by putting a "cap" on program funds. This means that if the number of applicants for food stamps increases, all recipients will receive proportionately less benefits.

The bill also restricts both illegal and legal immigrants from certain public benefits, such as Supplemental Security Income (SSI), cash welfare, social service block grant funds, Medicaid and food stamps. The bill also toughens eligibility requirements for SSI and the cash benefit program for the blind, disabled and elderly. Drug addiction and alcoholism, for instance, will no longer be considered disabilities under the program.

In addition, no American can receive more than five years worth of welfare in a lifetime. Single mothers on welfare who refuse to cooperate in identifying the fathers of their children could lose at least 20% of their benefits. Unmarried teen mothers are eligible for benefits only if they stay at home and in school.

Public Housing

Because much of the public housing in the U.S. is crowded and a magnet for drugs and violence, many public high-rises in cities across the U.S. are being torn down and replaced with low-rise town houses and single-family dwellings. Spurred by federal rule changes and federal money earmarked for demolition, cities are rebuilding public housing on a smaller scale. In 1992, the Federal Department of Housing and Urban Development (HUD) awarded $477 million in grants (to be used over five years) to 18 cities that target the nation's worst public housing. This money is to be used to demolish 100,000 sub-standard units by the year 2000. Those families displaced by the demolition get the first shot at new housing or vouchers to rent in the private market. The program is not without its critics, as many are concerned that low-density re-development will reduce the total number of units and exacerbate the nation's affordable housing crisis. Currently, public housing accommodates less than a quarter of those eligible (the requirement is a household income below 80% of the median income for that area). While the number of families that meet the eligibility requirements for public housing is rising, government assistance is not. This year's Congress provided for no new fundings in HUD's rent voucher program.

Education

The Public Education System

A record number of children (51.7 million) crammed into elementary and secondary schools across the U.S. this fall, stretching resources thin and causing a rush of school construction. According to the Department of Education, the surge in enrollment will continue through 2006, when three million more students will be entering the public school system.

Some of the increase in enrollment is attributable to the children of the large baby boomer generation. Other factors include a higher birth rate among African-Americans, Hispanics and other minorities. Additionally, children are entering school earlier and staying longer; pre-school enrollment is up and the dropout rate is down. Immigration in cities like Los Angeles, Miami and New York also adds to school enrollment.

The sharp increase in the number of students is causing a crisis in a public school system that is already strained. Reports to Congress by the General Accounting Office over the past two years have estimated that bringing the nation's schools up to good standards will require an investment of about $112 billion—just for building repairs and upgrades.

Five million teachers, administrators and support staff are employed by our nation's public schools. The federal, state and local governments spend nearly $400 billion annually to run our public education system. This accounts for nearly 8% of the gross domestic product and equals $6,000 in spending per student per year.

State and local governments each spend about 47% of total education expenses. The federal government picks up the other 6% of the outlays for public education.

How We Compare

Despite the fact that the U.S. spends more per pupil in grades K - 12 than any other industrialized nation, America still lags behind most other industrialized countries in the quality of high school and elementary education.

In the 1996 International Mathematics and Science Study, a comprehensive study of science and math achievements by students in 41 countries, U.S. students ranked slightly below average in math and slightly above average in science. While the results are not disastrous, we are far from achieving our declared goal of having the highest scores in the world by the year 2000. Secretary of Education Richard Riley said, "You can put the results together and say our results compared to the rest of the world are average, but . . . in this education era, average is far too low."

Another study conducted by the Department of Education and the National Assessment Governing Board reported similar findings: high-school-age students have made some gains in math and science but have made no improvement in reading and writing since the early 1970s when the groups first started testing. In addition, combined SAT scores grew by only 1% between 1983 and 1993.

According to the International Association for the Evaluation of Educational Achievement, the countries that have performed best in international comparisons tend to be ones like Singapore, where the performance of every student is closely tracked, or Japan, where teachers were found to be generally better trained and prepared than their peers in the U.S. Almost all of the top-ranked countries had

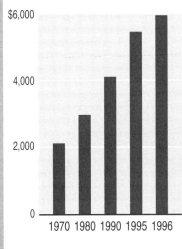

Spending in America's Public Schools

(Per Pupil)

Source: National Center for Education Statistics, U.S. Department of Education

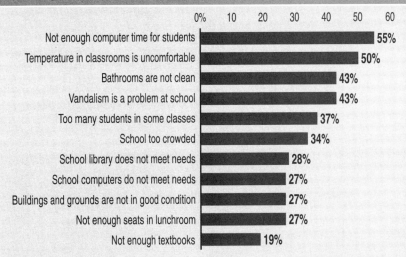

Education Problems

Percentage of Secondary School Students Who Say Each of the Following Is a Problem

Not enough computer time for students	55%
Temperature in classrooms is uncomfortable	50%
Bathrooms are not clean	43%
Vandalism is a problem at school	43%
Too many students in some classes	37%
School too crowded	34%
School library does not meet needs	28%
School computers do not meet needs	27%
Buildings and grounds are not in good condition	27%
Not enough seats in lunchroom	27%
Not enough textbooks	19%

Source: *USA Today* Poll, 1996

Ranking Math and Science Skills

A new study of student achievement in math and science ranked 41 countries. Scoring was on a scale of 200 to 800 points.

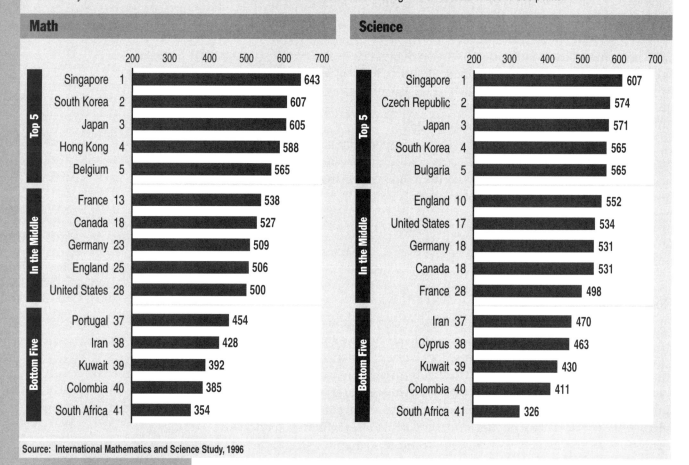

Math

		Score
Top 5	Singapore 1	643
	South Korea 2	607
	Japan 3	605
	Hong Kong 4	588
	Belgium 5	565
In the Middle	France 13	538
	Canada 18	527
	Germany 23	509
	England 25	506
	United States 28	500
Bottom Five	Portugal 37	454
	Iran 38	428
	Kuwait 39	392
	Colombia 40	385
	South Africa 41	354

Science

		Score
Top 5	Singapore 1	607
	Czech Republic 2	574
	Japan 3	571
	South Korea 4	565
	Bulgaria 5	565
In the Middle	England 10	552
	United States 17	534
	Germany 18	531
	Canada 18	531
	France 28	498
Bottom Five	Iran 37	470
	Cyprus 38	463
	Kuwait 39	430
	Colombia 40	411
	South Africa 41	326

Source: International Mathematics and Science Study, 1996

national standards that were clearly set by the federal government, unlike the U.S., which has a largely decentralized educational system.

Special Education Costs Soar

The Department of Education reports that at least one in 10 American children qualify for special education in some way. The number of special education students in the U.S. has risen 45% over the past two decades, from 3.7 million in 1976 to 5.4 million in 1994.

Along with the rise in numbers of students, the bill for combined federal, state and local special education funding has increased from about $5 billion in 1977 to almost $30 billion in 1995. In total, over $280 billion has been spent since the program first began. Nationwide, the cost of educating a special education student versus a regular student is roughly two to one. From 1967 to 1991, special education's share of total education spending skyrocketed from 4% to 17%.

Half of those who are in special education have been determined to have a specific learning disability. Of those, some 80% are there simply because they do not know how to read. The federal government's definition of a learning disability is not a physical or emotional disorder; instead, it is primarily psychological and results in an "imperfect ability to listen, think, speak, read, write, spell or do mathematical calculations." Nearly three-quarters of special education students are boys and one-quarter are black. About 70% of special education students drop out or are expelled from school.

Special Education

(Billions of Dollars)

Total special-ed spending at state, local and federal levels has soared

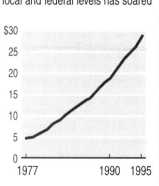

Source: U.S. Census Bureau, National Center for Health Statistics

Reform

The public school system came under attack this election year as candidates tried to address our failing school system. The Republicans favored a voucher system whereby federal funds, instead of being used to support the Department of Education (which would be dismantled) and the public school system, would be given to the states in the form of block grants. These grants would be divided into vouchers and given to parents to put toward the education of their children. Vouchers would be around $1,000 in value and would be given to all families regardless of income. Republicans said the vouchers would spur competition among schools and thus increase the quality of teaching. In addition, by dismantling the Department of Education, Republicans argued that they would eliminate costly bureaucracy.

Most Democrats opposed this proposal, contending that vouchers would only offer a minority of students greater opportunities, leaving the majority behind in an underfunded public school system. Under the voucher program, the private schools can pick who they choose to accept; thus, tougher-to-educate children would be forced to remain behind. Others say the program favors families whose children already attend private schools and tend to be the least needy. Cleveland and Milwaukee are the only school systems that currently operate on a voucher system, but 27% of the 2,000 low-income kids in the Cleveland program were already in private schools.

Some contend that we should put more money into the public school system. Opponents of increased spending point out that since 1970, funds for public education have increased by 80%, yet we have made few, if any, improvements. Others argue that we are just not spending our money wisely. According to a study by the Organization for Economic Cooperation and Development, America is alone in having an educational establishment in which more than half (58%) of the employees do not teach. A smaller share of the education dollar is currently being spent on student classroom instruction than at any time in recent history. Between 1960 and 1984, school spending on administration and other non-instructional functions grew by 107% in real terms. During the same period, money spent on teacher salaries dropped over 56%.

College Education

In general, Americans are becoming more educated. Today, 81% of students finish high school and nearly 45% get at least a partial college education. Additionally, education has become a factor in determining future levels of income. Those without a high school degree are six times more likely to end up below the poverty line. Those with a college degree are more likely to end up in the middle class or in the upper levels of income distribution.

While our high school and elementary education has proved lacking, our college-level education is considered to be the best in the world. Thousands of students from all over the world come to the U.S. each year to study at our top universities. In fact, college enrollment has risen to about 15 million in 1996.

College Costs Soar

A recent study by the College Board found that the increases in average yearly tuition for four-year colleges in 1996 – 1997 were larger than the rate of infla-

"If an unfriendly foreign power had attempted to impose on America the mediocre educational performance that exists today, we might well have viewed it as an act of war. As it stands, we have, in effect, been committing an act of unthinking, unilateral educational disarmament."

— National Commission on Excellence in Education

Performance, Spending and School Problems

School Expenditures vs. Sat Scores*

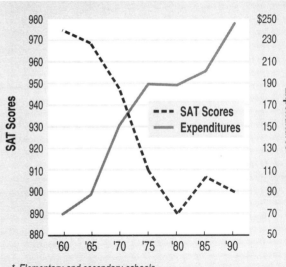

* Elementary and secondary schools
** In constant 1989 billion dollars

Source: The College Board, U.S. Department of Education

"Education must increase its productivity; we must get more education for the dollar."

— David Kearns,
Chairman of the
Xerox Corporation

College Costs Rise

College Tuition and Fees*

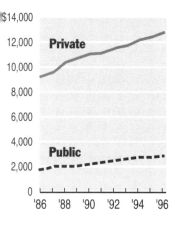

* For four-year colleges, adjusted for inflation and reflected in 1996 dollars

Source: The College Board

" . . . The schools in our area are dangerous and poor in quality, [spending] more . . . for administration than teaching."

— Thomas R. Spencer, Jr.,
Attorney
Miami, Florida

tion. Private colleges now cost an average of $12,823 annually (a 200% increase since 1980), and four-year public colleges ran approximately $6,000 per year for state residents and $11,000 for non-residents (a 214% increase since 1980). Two-year public colleges cost about $2,000 a year for state residents and $4,000 for non-residents. However, the College Board reported that more than half of all full-time undergraduates paid an annual tuition of less than $4,000, while three-quarters paid less than $8,000.

As colleges have begun to allocate a greater share of financial aid packages to loans, many students cannot avoid going into debt. The Department of Education states that student borrowing has almost doubled since 1993, from $18 billion to $33 billion in 1996.

Most of these loans are awarded under the most popular federal education aid plan, the Stafford Program, under which student loans from private institutions are guaranteed and subsidized by the government. This year, the average Stafford loan balance for students leaving four-year colleges jumped 15% to $10,146, according to the U.S. Group Loan Services, an organization that administers a $10 billion educational portfolio. Frederic Gilbert, the group's president, said, "Student debt has grown because of the rising cost of attending college, higher loan limits, expanded eligibility and the growing proportion of federal student aid offered in the form of loans rather than in grants."

Some argue that college is still a bargain. The average daily cost amounts to about $90 a day for private colleges and $35 for public institutions. In exchange for this, students generally receive instruction, room and board, three meals a day, free counseling services and job placement services. In addition, a college education generates future rewards, as college graduates usually will earn more than those without degrees.

College Cost Reform

There is $7.6 billion earmarked for college aid in the 1997 budget plan—$1.3 billion more than last year. However, most of this increase in financial aid is through loans as opposed to outright grants. President Clinton has called for an expansion of that aid.

During a commencement address at Princeton University, the President introduced a new proposal for college-bound students—a two-year, $1,500 annual tax credit for families with students attending college, along with an equivalent cash grant for those families with insufficient taxable income. Clinton said, "Our goal must be nothing less than to make the 13th and 14th years of education as universal to all Americans as the first 12 are today." In addition, the President has called for up to $10,000 in tax deductions a year for families paying college tuition.

While the President's proposal is heralded by most student groups, others argue that tax deductions, credits and loans may actually cause inflation in college costs—colleges know they can charge more, so they do. A federal commission to study the reasons for rising college costs will be appointed this year.

Immigration

Who Are Immigrants?

Today, immigration accounts for approximately 35% of U.S. population growth. With the decline in our birth rate, the U.S. may well begin to experience negative population growth in many cities by the year 2030 without continued immigration.

About 800,000 foreigners emigrate to the U.S. legally every year. In addition, the Immigration and Naturalization Service (INS) estimates another 300,000 a year enter illegally or overstay their visas, adding to the four million illegal immigrants that already live in the country. Over 70% of immigrants live in six states—California, Texas, Florida, Illinois, New York and New Jersey, and well over half are either Hispanic or Asian. The number of foreigners entering the United States has increased steadily since the early 1960s, from 1.5 million from 1960 through 1964 to 5.6 million from 1985 through 1990. About 8% of the nation's population has moved here from other countries, the highest proportion in the past four decades.

The Economic Impact of Immigration

With immigration one of the hottest political topics, Congress has passed bills to limit new entrants in response to growing sentiment that immigrants depress wages, take American jobs, soak up welfare and do not assimilate well into American culture.

Immigrants are indeed more likely to be on welfare, but many of those are political refugees. In fact, the percentage of non-refugee immigrants of working age (those between 15 and 64) is lower than that of native-born Americans. The same holds true for unemployment. Illegal immigrants, on the other hand, cannot collect either welfare benefits or unemployment—if they cannot find work, they tend to go home. They do, however, use "emergency room" health care and send their children to public schools.

According to Michael Fix, an immigration specialist at the Urban Institute (a think tank in Washington, D.C), after 10 years here, legal immigrants typically have higher than average incomes. However, another study at the University of Michigan found that among some immigrant groups, those who arrived in the U.S. after 1974 have been slower to assimilate than those who came before them. This may in part be due to the fact that family reunification has become the chief reason for entry, and thus the qualifications of new entrants have slipped. The profile of new immigrants who come to America is now less professional and educated than in the early 20th century.

There is still debate over whether immigrants depress the wages of local workers. When immigrants settle in rapidly growing areas with plenty of job opportunities, they seem to have little impact on wages. However, if immigrants settle in large numbers in poorer regions with fewer jobs, the effect on the community is more noticeable. For instance, certain concentrations of new immigrants, particularly illegal ones, in a few areas of California, New York, Texas, Florida, Illinois and New Jersey have become particularly burdensome to the local governments and economies.

Tougher Rules

After receiving much pressure from the political right, the Clinton Administration has dedicated more money and political capital to addressing immigration problems than any other administration in recent years. It has passed some of the toughest measures in decades against illegal immigrants and has doubled the budget for the INS, increasing the number of border patrol agents by 45%.

The Administration spent a good portion of the new funds on tightening the nation's borders. The border patrol grew to 5,700 agents this year, up from 3,900 in 1993, and is scheduled to nearly double by 2001. These agents are equipped with newly purchased computers, night-vision scopes, encrypted radios and ground sensors.

Immigration Policy

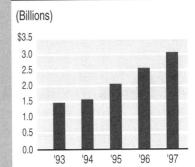

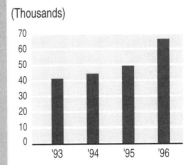

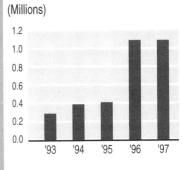

Source: Immigration and Naturalization Service

> *"The Clinton Administration has developed a comprehensive anti-illegal immigration policy that beefs up our border and workplace enforcement inspections . . ."*
>
> — Leon Panetta,
> Former White House
> Chief of Staff

> *"The 1996 welfare law may put an undue burden on legal immigrants—especially elderly immigrants."*
>
> — Aileen Josephs,
> Immigration Attorney,
> West Palm Beach, Florida

> *"The White House can be accused of backing down on critical matters of principle, like civil rights and refugee protection."*
>
> — Cecilia Munox,
> Deputy Vice President
> of the Council on La Raza, a
> civil rights group in Washington

The Administration has also streamlined the nation's political asylum process, raising requirements for asylum status and cutting the number of claims in 1995 by 55%, while more than doubling the number of cases completed. In addition, deportations of illegal immigrants in fiscal 1996 (68,790) far surpassed the total for fiscal 1995 (50,277), with criminals representing nearly half of the immigrants removed.

However, some contend the Administration's approach has been largely piecemeal. There is no senior-level official to coordinate overall policy on this cumbersome issue that spans the jurisdiction of several government agencies, including the Departments of Justice, State, Health and Human Services and Labor.

New Legislation

In late 1996, through changes in welfare legislation and immigration law, Congress has imposed new restrictions on illegal (and in some cases, legal) immigrants:

- Illegal immigrants will be ineligible for most public assistance programs financed by the federal government or the states. They cannot receive grants, federal contracts or loans, Supplemental Security Income, welfare benefits, Medicaid, housing, unemployment or financial aid.
- Medical emergencies will be covered, and children who are illegal immigrants can attend Head Start programs (federally run education programs for needy pre-schoolers).
- Pilot programs will be established in five states with high immigrant populations that will enable employers to voluntarily check the legal status of prospective workers through a Justice Department program.
- The new immigration funding will allow the INS to hire 300 more employees a year for three years. These new employees will investigate unlawful hiring of immigrants. The number of border patrol agents will be doubled to 10,000 by 2001, and 2,700 detention cells will be added. Penalties for smuggling people into the U.S. will be increased to prison terms of up to 10 years.
- Anyone trying to enter the country without the proper documentation will be subject to deportation. If someone seeking asylum is found to have no credible fear of persecution after an initial meeting with an officer, the person will be subject to removal after a hearing before an immigration judge. Hearings will take place within seven days of arrival, and there will be no additional appeals. Anyone suspected of terrorism will be immediately deported. Notices of removal proceedings will no longer be given in Spanish.
- Any former U.S. citizen who officially renounces citizenship to avoid paying taxes will not be permitted to re-enter the country. Any foreign student who violates a special non-immigrant status visa will be banned for five years.

In light of these new provisions, more than 1.1 million immigrants have applied for citizenship this year in order to maintain their benefits. Meanwhile, elderly immigrants, who as a result of the law are no longer covered by Medicaid, are certain to crowd into expensive and overburdened emergency-care facilities.

The debate over immigration will likely continue in the upcoming year. Congressional Republicans are expected to step up their attacks on the naturalization process. Conversely, President Clinton had promised that if re-elected, he would work with Congress to repeal some of the restrictions on benefits for legal immigrants.

Crime

The Good News and the Bad News

Violent crime in large cities dropped by 8% in 1995, paving the way for a 3% drop nationwide. In 1995, an F.B.I. annual crime survey of eight major cities indicated the lowest murder rate in a decade and the lowest overall rate of violent crime since 1989. The eight cities included: Chicago, Dallas, Houston, Los Angeles, New York, Philadelphia, Phoenix and San Diego.

According to other F.B.I. surveys, the number of reported crimes of all types was down 1% from a year earlier. There were 21,597 murders reported nationally in 1995, 7% fewer than in 1994 and 13% below the 1991 level. Forty-nine percent of the victims were black.

Almost 66% of all murders in the U.S. are committed with guns. Handguns alone account for more than half of all murders. About 80% of all teenage homicides are the result of a firearm injury. Fifty-five percent of murder victims were slain by strangers or unknown persons. Among the women murdered, 26% were slain by husbands or boyfriends. Wives or girlfriends killed just 3% of the men murdered. There were 97,464 forcible rapes reported, the fewest since 1989, representing a 5% drop.

Since 1990, reports of child abuse have quadrupled. Approximately 2.4 million cases of child abuse, child sexual abuse and child neglect are reported to child protective agencies each year. Furthermore, it is estimated that nearly two million children under age 18 are affected in some way by the substance abuse of their parents.

The number of prisoners in federal or state prisons in 1995 reached a record high of 1.13 million. This represents a 6.8% increase over 1994. Fifty-two percent of those are African-American.

Fighting Crime

In 1994, after much Republican opposition, Congress passed the $30.2 billion Omnibus Violent Crime Control and Prevention Act proposed by President Clinton. This legislation increased funding to hire more policemen, placed a ban on certain assault weapons, tightened the parole system and gave money to social programs aimed at reducing crime, including sports and education programs for children.

The 1996 Presidential election raised the issue of crime again. In his election speeches, the President supported a further increase in funding to hire

Courtesy of the Harvard Political Review

"All those children whom we've neglected are going to be people that we are also going to have to deal with."

— Marian Wright Edelman
Director, Children's Defense Fund

"We attribute the improvement in crime to many different causes, including our bipartisan efforts to give local law enforcement the tools they need to combat crime . . ."

— Janet Reno,
Attorney General
of the United States

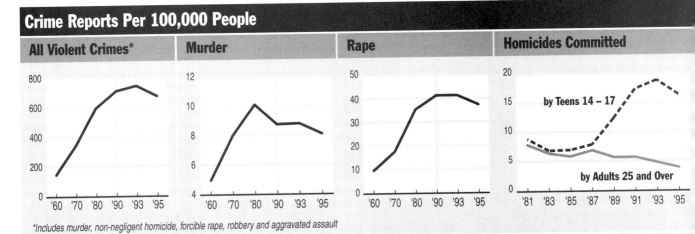

Crime Reports Per 100,000 People

All Violent Crimes*	Murder	Rape	Homicides Committed

Includes murder, non-negligent homicide, forcible rape, robbery and aggravated assault

Source: F.B.I. Uniform Crime Reports, except homicides.   Source for homicides: *"Trends in Juvenile Violence"* report to Department of Justice by James Alan Fox.

Median Prison Sentence vs. Actual Time Served

(In Years)

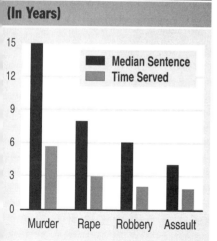

Source: F.B.I., 1992

Past Month Illicit Drug Use by Age

(Percentage of the Population)

Past month drug use between 1994 and 1995 remained flat—and less than half its 1979 peak of 14.1%

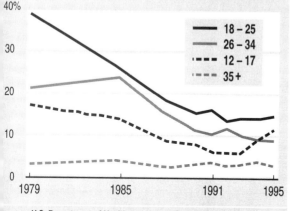

Source: U.S. Department of Health and Human Services

"Today, the anti-drug message seems to be fading away . . . "

— Nancy Reagan,
Former First Lady,
addressing Congress

---

policemen—targeting 100,000 new officers over the next two years. He also supported the prosecution of juveniles as adults for crimes involving drugs or violence, a curfew for teenagers, the construction of more prisons and capital punishment.

The Republicans seem to agree with these measures but would like to add an instant computerized background check to replace the current five-day waiting period to purchase a handgun. There has been argument about whether the Brady Bill, which imposes the five-day wait to allow for a criminal record check, puts an undue burden on states which must complete the record check and is therefore unconstitutional. A case which has been brought to the Supreme Court by a group of local sheriffs will determine the fate of the Brady Bill in 1997.

Drugs

Drug Use in America

The 1996 annual survey of the Department of Health and Human Services has reported the following statistics regarding drug use in the U.S.:

- An estimated 12.8 million Americans had used an illegal drug in the month prior to the survey; that represents no change from the previous year. The highest level of drug use was in 1979, when 25 million Americans claimed to have used illegal drugs.
  - Illegal drug use among teenagers continued to increase from 8.2% last year to 10% in 1996. The rate has doubled since 1992.
  - The number of cocaine users remained about the same, increasing slightly from 1.38 million last year to 1.45 million in 1996, but significantly lower than the peak of 5.7 million in 1985.
  - There were significant increases over the past year in marijuana, cocaine and hallucinogen use—from 6% to 8.2% for marijuana, from 0.3% to 0.8% for cocaine and from 1.1% to 1.7% for hallucinogens.
  - About 61 million Americans identify themselves as smokers, and 20% of the nation's 4.5 million 12 to 17-year-olds smoke. This statistic is virtually unchanged from the previous year.

A Columbia University survey of parent/teen attitudes on illicit drug use furthers concern about teenage drug use, showing that 46% of parents expect their kids to use illegal drugs. Twenty-two percent of teens said they expect to use drugs in the future (a mere 11% said so last year).

It is estimated that 70% of the drug trade comes to this country by way of Mexico, 20% through Puerto Rico and the Virgin Islands and the remaining 10% through the other Caribbean islands.

Combating Illegal Drugs

The increased use of illegal drugs was a big issue in the 1996 Presidential election. The Republican nominee, Bob Dole, accused President Clinton of abandoning the war on drugs, citing that drug use among teenagers more than doubled during his Administration.

In 1993, President Clinton reduced the Office of National Drug Control Policy from nearly 150 staff members to just 25, and once remarked on MTV that he would inhale marijuana "if I could." In 1996, after complaints that he was not doing enough to combat drug use, President Clinton appointed Barry McCaffrey as "drug czar." McCaffrey is a four-star general who fought during the Gulf War and has also served as Commander-in-Chief of the Army's Southern Command, which endeavors to block illegal drug trade.

The President signed an order in 1993 that focused more effort on curtailing drug production in South America and less on using the military to counter international drug trafficking. After the influx of drugs increased from Mexico, he ordered "Operation Hard Line," an effort led by law enforcement agencies to halt drugs at the southwestern border.

President Clinton did propose more new funding for drug treatment but failed to win significant spending increases. He also supported the Safe and Drug-Free Schools program, through which police educate students about the dangers of drugs. His last two budgets have restored much funding for the "drug war," bringing the proposed total for 1997 to an all-time high of $15 billion.

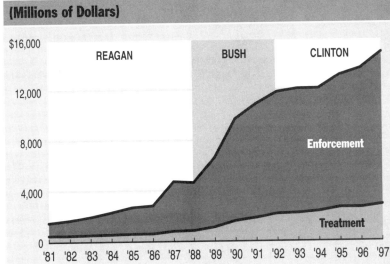

Federal Spending on the Drug War

(Millions of Dollars)

REAGAN   BUSH   CLINTON

Enforcement

Treatment

Source: White House National Drug Control Strategy, 1996

Discouraging Smoking

President Clinton announced this year new federal regulations cracking down on the marketing and sales of cigarettes to teenagers. The new regulations would give the Food and Drug Administration significant new powers and pose the biggest government challenge to cigarette manufacturers since the 1964 Surgeon General's report that linked smoking to lung cancer.

He proposed sweeping regulations to require purchasers of cigarettes and chewing tobacco to show proof that they are at least 18 years old, to ban the sale of cigarettes in packs of fewer than 20, to outlaw brand-name tobacco advertising at sporting events and on items unrelated to tobacco, like T-shirts, and barring all tobacco advertising within 1,000 feet of schools and playgrounds. The legislation would ban the sales of cigarettes in vending machines and restrict cigarette advertising in youth-oriented magazines to black and white text without photographs or drawings.

Legalization of Marijuana?

A heated political debate has sprung up over California's Proposition 215, which removes limits on the amount of marijuana an individual can grow or smoke and requires only permission from a doctor to obtain the narcotic. Proponents of the bill argued that marijuana provides precious relief from chronic illness and the pain of chemotherapy and AIDS. Therefore, it is worth the risk that people will abuse the law.

There are those who believe that Proposition 215 will become a national model. Several states have already passed non-binding resolutions supporting the medical use of marijuana. Federal drug laws still make marijuana illegal, regardless of state statutes; however, the Drug Enforcement Administration does not have the resources to effectively police small-scale abusers. Barry McCaffrey, the drug czar, condemned the passing of the proposition, saying it would have negative consequences on America's ability to fight illegal drugs.

"All of us in positions of responsibility are somewhat responsible . . ."

— President Clinton,
on the rise in teenage drug use during his Administration

"There's a relationship between kids thinking marijuana is not harmful and their use of marijuana."

— Donna Shalala,
U.S. Secretary of Health and Human Services

Courtesy of the Harvard Political Review

"Will we be able to talk about race in such a way that we can get beyond the finger-pointing and name-calling . . . so we can be empowered and enabled instead of paralyzed and debilitated?"

— Cornel West,
Professor of African-American Studies,
Harvard University

"Black people don't know enough about their own history in America. Most don't know that blacks were instrumental in founding this country. Until I learned that on my own, I didn't know it either."

— Kareem Abdul-Jabbar

Race Relations

Growing Equality?

For the first time since the Census Bureau began recording statistics in 1959, the poverty rate for African-Americans is below 30%, and median income has risen by 3.6%—more than the growth rate for white families (2.2%). Black Americans are the only demographic group whose real median income has improved since 1989. In addition, the proportion of young black adults who have completed high school has now caught up with that of young white adults.

The black teen-age birth rate fell by 9% in 1995—down 17% from 1991. There was also a slight drop in the percentage of children born out of wedlock, the first drop since 1969.

The Future of Affirmative Action

In November 1996, voters across the nation approved state measures to bar government affirmative action programs. California's approval of Proposition 187, which eliminates racial and sex preferences in public hiring, contracting and education is likely to have a broad impact. The proposition, the California Civil Rights Initiative, would amend the state constitution to prohibit state agencies and local governments from using race or gender as a basis for hiring, for educational policies and for contracting. Clinton had hoped to ease the controversy last year when he promised to rework federal affirmative action programs and used the motto "Mend It, Don't End It," but it appeared that California had voted by a 55 to 45 margin essentially to "End It."

Civil rights groups filed suit after the election to prevent the measure from becoming law and vowed to organize politically to defend their programs. Considering California's position as a bellwether of political change, the results are bound to influence politics everywhere. One conservative activist, Grover Norquist, predicts that measures similar to the one in California will reach the ballot in as many as ten states by 1998.

Discrimination in Corporate America?

The equal opportunity system at Texaco Corporation, the nation's 14th largest corporation, has come under scrutiny after the disclosure in November 1996 that senior company executives had plotted to destroy documents

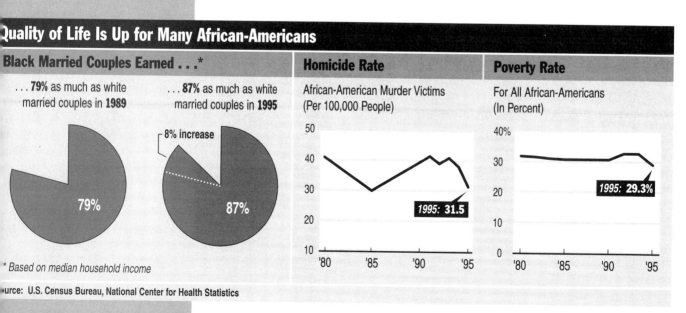

demanded in a 1994 employment discrimination suit and had used racial epithets in discussing black employees. The tapes were made public by Richard Lundwall, a former Texaco executive.

Black English?

On December 18, 1996 the Oakland Unified School District unanimously approved a resolution that effectively declared its 28,000 black students to be bilingual, speaking both standard English and black English, or "Ebonics," which some linguists consider a distinct language, not just dialect.

The vote immediately cast the school system at the center of a national debate about race and education. District officials said they were not sure how the Ebonics designation would manifest itself in schools but suggested that programs might include classes to educate teachers in the rudiments of Ebonics, workshops on West African culture and increased funding for bilingual teaching.

Black Churches and Politics

Spurred by the growing influence of the Christian Coalition and a rash of black church burnings in 1995 and 1996, black churches attempted to rouse their members to become active politically in the 1996 elections. The Congress of National Black Churches Inc., a coalition of the eight major, historically-black denominations representing about 65,000 churches and more than 19 million people, oversaw the political resurgence. The Congress worked on black voter registration and on campaigns in districts with black populations of 20% or more.

O.J. Simpson Highlights Division

In 1996, O.J. Simpson, the famed football star and commentator, was found not guilty of the murder of his former wife, Nicole Brown Simpson, and her friend Ronald Goldman. This verdict highlighted a division between blacks and whites. Whites argued that the predominantly black jury voted on the basis of race, while blacks argued that the Simpson case was a triumph for the black people who have been repeatedly discriminated against in the U.S. Justice system. The civil trial in the Simpson case began in mid-1996 in Santa Monica, California. The all-white jury produced a verdict of guilty in the death of Brown and Goldman, awarding $8.5 million to the Goldman family.

The Environment

Our Biggest Threats
Global Warming and the Depletion of the Ozone Layer

Global warming reportedly occurs when sunlight is trapped inside the earth's atmosphere by carbon dioxide and other gases that are released from factories, cars and certain man-made products. This phenomenon is more commonly known as the "greenhouse effect."

Greenhouse gases include chlorofluorocarbons (CFCs), methane and nitrous oxide. The most dangerous gases are the CFCs because they also destroy the ozone layer, which protects the earth from the sun's harmful ultraviolet rays. CFCs have traditionally been used in air-conditioning, cleaning, insulation and as aerosol propellants.

Scientists believe that at the current rate, the earth is likely to warm by as much as 3°F to 5°F over the next 50 years. This increase in temperature could set off a chain of events, beginning with the melting of the polar ice caps, which would result in a rise in sea level. This would in turn cause widespread flooding

"If the politicians harp on the need for black self-help, I am in 1,000% agreement with them. Government should create the opportunity, create the atmosphere, but then the burden falls on us and I think in the past, we relied too much on government."

— Louis Farrakhan,
Nation of Islam leader who hosted the
World Day of Atonement Rally at the
U.N.—a year after his historic Million
Man March on Washington D.C.

"Our political agenda should include action to invest in our children—because it is the right thing to do."

— Tamara M. Wilso
Pelham, New Hampshi

Environmental Risks

High Risk	Habitat Destruction
	Global Warming
	Ozone Layer Depletion
	Species Extinction
	Biological Diversity
Medium Risk	Pesticides
	Surface Water Pollution
	Air Pollution
Low Risk	Oil Spills
	Radioactive Materials
	Ground Water Pollution

Source: Environmental Protection Agency

"This is one of the most important decisions I will make to protect the public health and this country."

— Carol M. Browner,
EPA Administrator,
on recommending higher standards

and the eventual destruction of most coastal land.

In 1995, the United Nations World Meteorological Organization claimed to have discovered a hole in the ozone over Antarctica which covered 3.86 million square miles, an area about the size of Europe. The organization also says that this large ozone hole could move positions over time, perhaps eventually exposing the southern tip of South America. Measurements taken by the organization in August of 1996 indicate that ozone levels in the southern hemisphere have declined 10% from last year's levels. Scientists say that any sustained increase in the level of ultraviolet radiation that reaches earth will lead to an increase of cancer in humans and animals as well as a reduction in crop yields.

In Europe and North America, ozone has declined by 10% since the late 1950's, which means that 15% more radiation will reach the earth's surface. These latest findings support the idea that despite actions by governments to reduce dangerous emissions, the situation of ozone depletion continues to get worse.

Deforestation and Loss of Biodiversity

The majority of deforestation occurs in the tropical rain forests located in Central and South America, equatorial Africa, Southeast Asia and northeastern Australia. It is estimated that the world may be losing more than 49 million acres of tropical rain forest each year due to logging, farming and new building.

With the loss of the forest comes the loss of biodiversity. In a four-mile radius, a typical patch of rain forest contains 750 species of trees, 750 species of plants, 125 species of mammals, 400 species of birds, 100 species of reptiles and 60 species of amphibians. The destruction of this rich ecosystem could have dire consequences for the human race. For example, of the 3,000 plant species that help fight cancer, 70% are located in the rain forest.

Destruction of Wetlands

Wetlands are areas which regulate water flow by storing water and buffering the effects of storms. They also purify and filter water, providing a habitat for a wide variety of plants and animals.

Over the past several decades, though, America's wetlands have been drained, cleared, exploited and built on. It is estimated that America has destroyed over half of its original wetlands. This loss has resulted in the pollution of fresh water, species extinction and the erosion of land.

Recent Legislation and the Future of Environmental Protection
The Everglades Bill

In October 1996, President Clinton signed a $3.8 billion federal water projects bill authorizing up to $75 million to help preserve the Florida Everglades. The bill calls for the completion by July 1, 1999, of a plan to preserve, restore and protect the Everglades and the rest of South Florida's ecosystem.

The measure was part of a broader bill outlining Army Corps of Engineers projects. About $890 million (approximately 25% of the bill) will finance environmental work. In addition to the Everglades project, the Administration has also taken steps to protect tracts of wilderness in Utah and to block the construction of a gold mine on the border of Ulster National Park in Montana. As he announced the initiative, President Clinton explained, "The bill will create or improve almost 120 national parks, trails, rivers or historical sites in 41 of our states."

EPA Recommends Higher Standards

The EPA is recommending tighter national standards for chemical emissions and particles that form smog and soot. This new definition of "clean air" may prove to be one of the biggest environmental fights of 1997, embroiling the Oval Office, Capitol Hill and the federal courts.

Under the proposal, hundreds of communities that comply with the Clean Air Act under its current rules would fall out of compliance, roughly tripling the number of counties where state and local officials need to take further steps to clean up the air. At least 100 million people live in these areas.

Strategies suggested by the EPA for localities to reach compliance include mass transit projects, incentives for companies to limit emissions, newer require-ments for pollution controls on factory smokestacks and improved programs for vehicle inspections. The EPA will seek a standard of around 80 parts per billion of ozone in the air, compared with 120 parts per billion tolerated under current regulations. Other regulations include limitations on the duration and frequen-cy of violations, the precision of their measurement and much more.

In Congress, Republican leaders have already signaled that they will chal-lenge the EPA's proposed rules, saying that the regulations are too strict and that they overburden localities and businesses.

Environment and the 1996 Elections

A concerted campaign effort by leading environmental groups to influence the elections met with mixed results. Some of their candidates won, but some of their ballot initiatives lost in the face of strong industry opposition.

One intensive campaign was thwarted in Florida, where an advertising bar-rage by the sugar industry persuaded voters to reject a proposed one-cent tax per pound of sugar. The money would have been used for the environmental restoration of the Everglades, a sensitive ecosystem, which has been damaged for decades by the run-off from sugar farms.

The biggest disappointments for environmentalists came from close Senate elections that went against them. Despite such setbacks, environmental groups prevailed in other important races, including two contests in the House, where environmentalists helped Democrats successfully defeat Republican freshmen: Representative Andrea Seastrand of California was defeated by Walter Holden Caps, while Representative Dick Chrysler of Michigan lost to Debbie Stabenow, a state legislator.

The Cost of Environmental Protection

It is important to consider the costs of environmental policies as well as their benefits. The total of public and private expenditures associated with the regulations of the Environmental Protection Agency (EPA) have been estimated at between 1.6% to 1.8% of GDP since the mid 1970s—a small but significant share of total economic activity. In absolute terms, current dollar expenditures for environmental protection in 1996 were slightly over $100 billion. These esti-mates include direct costs associated with environmental regulations and other regulations to restrict natural resource use.

Science and the Government

Life on Mars?

A NASA team announced in August 1996 that it had discovered microscopic chemical evidence of minute forms of microbial life in a meteorite believed to have been cast off from Mars by a massive impact 16 million years ago. The rock had landed in the Antarctic 13,000 years ago and was found in 1984. Dr. David McKay and Dr. Everett Gibson of the Johnson Space Center were the leaders of the team.

These findings have stimulated greater investment in Mars research. Prior spacecraft observations of the planet strongly suggest that Mars was once a warmer and wetter world which could have supported at least some form of life. A series of survey missions are underway in order to learn more about the planet. The Mars Global Surveyor and Mars Pathfinder were launched in November 1996 to conduct a mapping mission. The two missions were the beginning of a planned 10-year effort to explore Mars, particularly to seek evidence that life might have once existed on the planet.

Privatized Space Shuttle

In 1996, NASA contracted out its space shuttle program to a private contractor, the United Space Alliance (a joint venture between the Lockheed-Martin Corporation and Rockwell Aerospace Company). The signing of the six-year, $7 billion contract, which goes into effect at the beginning of fiscal year 1997, was intended to reduce government control of the nation's space shuttles. The contract consolidates 12 earlier individual contracts involving several companies, transferring greater responsibility to the U.S. Alliance.

The new arrangement is part of the first stage in gradually removing NASA from standard shuttle operations. If the contract is successful, NASA has said it would consider bundling together another 16 contracts that cover more critical operations. Privatization is a necessity in light of NASA's shrinking budget, says NASA Administrator, Daniel Goldin, who remains optimistic: "People in the past measured the vitality of NASA by how much money went in. The agency is now more interested in output, and it is meeting its demand to do more with less. We have downsized to 10,000 people and started 25 new programs."

Proponents of privatization claim that it would lower costs and keep the U.S. competitive in the space race. Aerospace companies are expected to rapidly take over the shuttling of astronauts and payloads into space, with an eye toward reaping profits from satellite communications, space labs, exploration and eventually tourism.

Funding for Academic Research

Federal funding for academic research increased just 0.4% in 1996, a far cry from the annual increases of 4.2% averaged in the 1980s. Industry, however, has stepped in to fill the gap in funds. Corporations paid for about 7% of university research in 1995, up from just 4% in 1980. This new money comes with strings attached, however; corporations not only direct the type of research but often have control over when and to whom the research is released. Schools are also trying to boost their budgets by aggressively patenting their employees' work.

Research and Development Spending

The American Association for the Advancement of Science estimates that the budget for non-military R&D funds, currently $34 billion a year, will drop to a staggering inflation-adjusted 20% by 2002.

The worst hit will likely be Democratic-backed applied work in academics and industry, while basic research supported by the Republicans may fare better. The R&D lobby has warned that such reductions will imperil the future of the nation. Mary L. Good, Under Secretary for Technology at the Commerce Department, has stated that "to cut the R&D budget below present levels is suicide." However, in the 1997 budget package, the National Institutes of Health received a 7% increase in funding to $12.7 billion.

VI. Economic State of the Nation

Understanding the Debt

How Big is the Debt?

In January 1997, the national debt was $5.3 trillion. The debt can be defined as the accumulation of our annual deficits. In other words, it is the total amount that we have borrowed over the years from our citizens and foreign lenders to finance government "over-spending."

Just how large is the national debt? Steven Moore, author of *Government: America's #1 Growth Industry*, provides the following illustrations:

- If Congress paid down the deficit a dollar every second, it would take 130,000 years, or roughly the amount of time that has passed since the Ice Age, to pay down the present debt.

- If you laid the debt out in dollars from end to end, it would reach out into space four times the distance between the earth and the sun.

The Origin and Growth of the Debt

The deficits that have arisen throughout the 1980s and 1990s exist due to the inability of tax revenue to cover a dramatic rise in federal spending.

The federal government has grown faster than any other segment of the U.S. economy since 1960. The government now represents about 25% of the gross domestic product of the U.S. If current spending levels persist, this percentage will climb above 30% by the year 2010.

The tax cuts of the early 1980s exacerbated the rise in the deficit as federal tax receipts fell and defense spending increased. While our deficit has decreased in the last four years, because of increased tax revenue and decreased discretionary spending, we still must face trillions of dollars in debt and large interest payments. Over 80% of this debt was accumulated in the 1980s and 1990s.

The Cost of Living With Debt
Low Growth and Low Savings

For the past two decades, our economic growth rate has hovered around 2.5%, a sharp decline from the 3.5% to 4.0% average during the post-World War II era. If the economy had grown at such a rate over the past 20 years, the average American household would earn an income at least $12,000 higher than today.

If the United States were to maintain a 2.5% economic growth rate, the average per capita personal income would be approximately $40,000 by 2020 and $65,000 by 2040. However, a growth rate of 4% would result instead in an average income of $60,000 in 2020 and $130,000 in 2040. A couple of points in the economic growth rate can make a huge difference over the long run.

"A refreshing break from number-free journalism."

— Kathryn Brookin
with daughters **Laura** and **Juli**
Roxbury, Massachuset

Drawbacks of Living with Deficits and Debt

- **Higher Interest Rates**
- **Lower Investment**
- **Lower Growth Rate**
- **Lost Revenue to Pay Interest on Debt**
- **Being a Debtor to Foreign Countries**
- **Large Burdens on Future Generations**
- **Long-Term Decrease in the Standard of Living**

Low Investment

Net Business Investment as Share of GDP (%)

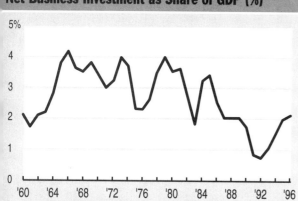

Source: U.S. Department of Commerce

Many economists believe that a major cause of our low growth rate is that we, as a people, save very little. This means that there is less money available for U.S. investment. The government dissaves by spending more money than is received in taxes, which results in deficits. Also, the government must finance these deficits by encouraging people to buy U.S. bonds. This draws money away from the private sector and into public sector bonds, reducing the funds available for private investment and growth.

Lost Money on Interest

Another drawback of living with debt is paying the interest. Interest on the national debt is now the third largest expense for the government. In 1996, that amount was $241 billion, over four times the amount spent by the federal government on education.

Generational Inequity

By increasing our debt, we are borrowing from future generations. Eventually, someone will have to pay the debt we have accumulated as well as suffer the resultant low growth rates. The Congressional Budget Office projects that children born today may face tax rates as high as 82% if we continue to spend at today's rate.

Economist Allen Auerbach, from the University of California at Berkeley, calculated that a man who is 70 years old in 1990 would have received $46,000 in benefits from the government during his lifetime. In contrast, a man who is 25 years old that same year can expect to make net payments (taxes paid less benefits received) of $226,000 over his lifetime.

This example demonstrates that huge transfers from future generations are being made to the present generation—leaving future generations with higher taxes, fewer benefits and lower growth rates.

The U.S. is not the only nation transferring debt to future generations. Germany, Italy and Sweden are other nations that are creating large future obligations. Japan, with its aging population and large state pension liabilities, will also face crisis. Estimates indicate that Japan's net-debt-to-GDP ratio will jump from an estimated 13% this year to more than 300% in 2030. In contrast, America's is forecast to rise from 38% to 100% over the same period.

Financing the Debt

According to some experts, the U.S. does not finance its debt optimally. Joseph Fichera, a former managing director at Bear Stearns and an executive fel-

Indexed Bonds: A New Security

The Treasury Department is planning to offer a new type of security in 1997. The security will be a bond which is indexed to inflation to stimulate long-term saving. They will be issued in sizes small enough for consumers to save for college tuition or retirement. Other features of the bonds remain to be determined, but it is likely that they will have a maturity somewhere between 10 and 30 years and be available in increments as small as $100. Such bond issues could potentially become very popular through 401(k)s and other retirement plans, which let workers make their own investment decisions.

low at Princeton's Woodrow Wilson School of Public and International Affairs, contends, "The government ignores the long-term market and bond structure that can give stability and flexibility to its budgets."

The government sells only straight debt. In order to minimize the long-term costs, however, some economists and business leaders say it should offer more innovative and flexible types of securities.

For instance, when the U.S. Treasury issued $12.7 billion of 30-year debt in February 1985 at 11.4%, it did so with no call option (the ability to recall the debt and thus refinance at lower rates). As a result, 10 years later, government (and therefore the taxpayers) continued to pay an exorbitant interest rate, although the 30-year rate had fallen to 7.5%. If the government had implemented a standard 10-year call option and refinanced the bonds, taxpayers could have saved $450 million a year for the remaining 20 years until maturity.

Economists point out that restructuring the debt may give the government a strong incentive to control inflation. This would in turn keep interest rates low, so the government could then refinance at a substantial savings. Presently, however, inflation helps to reduce the national debt by making the dollars owed worth less.

Vital Signs

GDP Growth

During 1996, average gross domestic product (GDP) growth was 2.2%, reaching a high of 4.7% in the second quarter of 1996. The annual gross domestic product measures the dollar value of all the goods and services produced in the U.S. during a given year. GDP growth is the most commonly used measure of economic growth.

The Clinton Administration has forecast that the real GDP growth rate over the next seven years will average 2.3%, which reflects a projected 1.2% productivity growth and a 1.1% average growth rate of the labor force.

Real GDP is projected to grow at an average rate of 2.2% during the remainder of 1997, as lower interest rates cause an increase in investment in both housing and the business sector and as consumption is supported by recent gains in the stock market.

Inflation Stable

Perhaps the best economic news of 1996 is that inflation remained low and stable during the year, despite an unemployment rate that had previously been associated with rising inflation.

The Consumer Price Index (CPI), the most widely used measure of inflation, tracks the change in price of a typical 'consumer market basket of goods.' Average inflation, as measured by the CPI, increased to 3.1% in 1996, up moderately from 2.5% in 1995. This resulted as food and energy prices, which had held down the overall rate of price increase in 1995, rose in 1996.

The CPI is expected to drop slightly as revised procedures gradually remove some of the upward biases in current CPI inflation figures. CPI inflation is likely to slow by 0.2% in 1997, when the Bureau of Labor Statistics (BLS) will implement procedures to correct problems associated with bringing new stores into the survey sample. In 1998, the CPI is expected to drop by another 0.1% when the BLS updates the CPI market basket to reflect more recent data on expenditure patterns. These adjustments are expected to bring CPI inflation to 2.8% in 1998.

"We are receiving more than we earn, so America either has to make more, spend less, or become more efficient."

— Joel Spore
Student, Stonehill College
N. Easton, Massachusetts

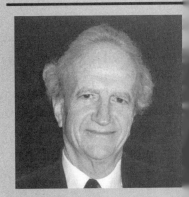

"Human capital is as much a part the wealth of nations as are facto ries, housing, machinery and othe physical capital."

— Gary S. Becke
University of Chicag
Fellow of the Hoover Institu
Nobel Prize for Economic Scienc
Chicago, Illin

Consumer Prices

Year-Over-Year Change in CPI by Month (Not Adjusted for Seasonal Variations)

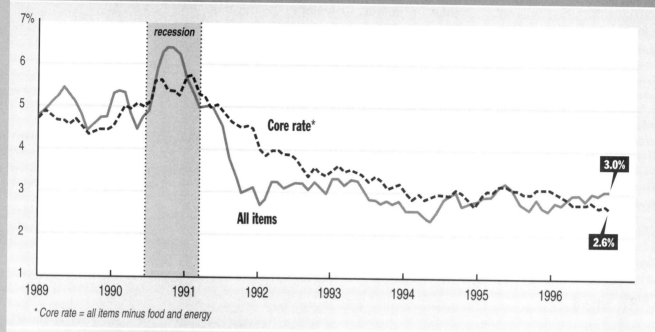

* Core rate = all items minus food and energy

Sources: Datastream International; U.S. Department of Labor, 1996

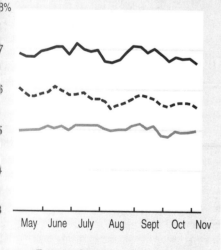

Interest Rates

1996, In Percent

— Treasury Bonds
- - - Municipal Bonds
— Three-Month Treasury Bills

Source: *The New York Times*, November 4, 1996

An Overheated Economy?

As overall unemployment levels dropped in 1996 to a low of 5.1%, some experts worried that the economy was overheating and that would cause a rise in inflation. In general, however, even economists who expect the strong economy to continue are not worried about inflation. William Dudley of Goldman, Sachs and Company claims that it will take at least a year for the exceptionally low unemployment levels and higher wages to touch off higher inflation. He believes that the unemployment rate in today's economy would have to slip to 4.5% to cause a half-percentage point increase a year later. Unlike the 1970s and 1980s, when higher wages touched off higher inflation, many liken the current situation to the mid-1960s, when inflation remained low despite tight labor markets.

Savings Rates Low

Despite the growth of tax-deferred savings plans and growing doubts about the availability of future retirement income, the U.S. personal savings rate has fallen from 8% of disposable income two decades ago to about 4% today. Total net savings, including the public and private sectors, is less than 5% of the nation's output, down from an average of 11% during the 1960s.

This low savings rate translates into less funds available for investment domestically. Despite the growing integration of global markets, domestic investment still depends, for the most part, on domestic savings. "Maybe one-third of the world's capital is in the global pool—the rest stays home," says Stanford University economist Paul R. Krugman.

There are several possible reasons for our low savings rate. Four of the more popular theories are: (1) our tax system discourages savings, (2) our large national debt and deficits drain public savings, (3) entitlement programs like Social Security discourage Americans from saving for retirement, and (4) culturally, we are predisposed to high levels of consumption.

There are alternative hypotheses as well. In a study released by the *New England Economic Review*, Lynn Elaine Browne and Joshua Gleason of the Federal Reserve Bank of Boston contend that a main cause of decreased savings is America's desire for more and better health care. Medical services currently consume 5.8% of personal income. Employer contributions for health insurance have grown dramatically as well, from 2% of wages and salaries in the mid-1960s to about 8% today.

Some argue that because we save less, the cost of capital (the interest rate we pay to borrow money) is much higher than it was in the 1960s. Then, triple-A rated corporations could issue long-term bonds at 5% (a real rate of 2.5%) and still outpace the rate of inflation. In the 1990s, overall inflation has averaged 3.3%, but corporate inflation rates have averaged 8.2%, a real rate of almost 5%.

Business Climate

Economists and businessmen are generally predicting flat to negative growth in the stock markets over the course of 1997; however, expectations appear to vary according to economic sector. Dun & Bradstreet's survey of business expectations found that large companies are expecting higher sales and profits for 1997, while small businesses are predicting slower growth.

Joseph Duncan, chief economist at D&B, commented that small business owners tend to feel shifts in the economy before anyone else and that "their new pessimism may be an early sign that conditions will soften in the first half of 1997." In line with such expectations, other surveys suggest that manufacturers are keeping stockpiles low in order to deal with expected weak demand in 1997.

The National Federation of Independent Businesses, an industry group comprised of 600,000 small businesses, said that most companies expect hiring rates either to fall slightly or remain steady in 1997. An exception is the service sector, which expects an increase in employment levels over the next year.

The Stock Market Soars

As 1996 ended, the stock market soared, with the Dow Jones Industrial Average above 6600, up 19% from last year and dramatically recovered from the 1987 stock market crash when the Dow bottomed out at 2002. The Dow has now risen six years in a row, from 1991 to 1996.

Investors are saying that the bull market is being led by a handful of premier companies like General Electric, Gillette, DuPont and Microsoft rather than smaller, lesser-known companies. The Dow Jones Industrial Average is composed almost entirely of large stocks and has performed better than all other major market averages. Other reasons cited for the bull market include continued low U.S. inflation rates and increased U.S. corporate productivity (a 15% annual rate from 1992 to 1995).

With about 40% of Americans invested in the stock market, either directly or through 401(k)s and company pension plans, most people continue to feel good about the stock market, with projected corporate earnings slowing but still at 10% for the rest of 1997.

Other investors say that profit growth will slow to the 5% to 7% range in 1997 and that the growth in big companies that led

> *"The central economic fact of the past quarter century is that the very forces of technological change, flexible production and globalization, that have enriched America's most educated and powerful have hurt nearly 45% of its population."*
>
> — Benjamin Schwarz,
> Senior Fellow at
> the World Policy Institute

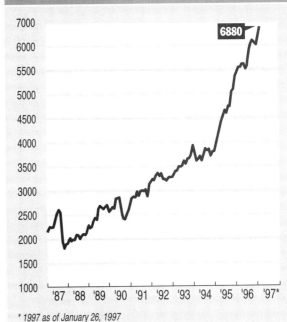

Dow Flying High

Performance of the Dow Jones Industrial Average

6880

* 1997 as of January 26, 1997

Source: New York Stock Exchange

For Social Security, Potential Erosion

The average monthly Social Security benefit paid to those retired by December 31, 1984*

Average benefits vary by retirement date.

Source: Social Security Administration, 1996 and *The New York Times*

the bull market is slowing. In late 1996, Federal Reserve Chairman Alan Greenspan remarked that there might be an "irrational exuberance" in the market, indicating that stock prices may be inflated beyond their true value.

Miscalculated Statistics?

The figures the government produces have an enormous impact on our personal finances. Each of the three times the Dow Jones Industrial Average lost 100 points or more in 1996, it was a reaction to economic reports released by the government. In January 1997, the monthly Social Security checks sent to 47 million Americans jumped an average of $21 based on the belief that inflation was growing at 2.9%. The interest rates we pay when we buy a car or a home, or receive when we invest in bonds, are all indirectly based on what government statisticians say.

There has been much debate this year over how these figures are calculated, and questions have arisen regarding their accuracy. In 1995, a commission was appointed by the federal government to study the CPI. The CPI, as a measure of inflation, is used to index benefits like Social Security, veterans' benefits, and federal pensions, as well as to index tax rates. About 30% of federal spending is indexed to the CPI.

When the commission released its findings in late 1996, it claimed that the CPI overstates inflation by about 1.1%. The commission reported that the way the Bureau of Labor Statistics (BLS) calculated the CPI did not capture benefits from technological change nor the consumer's inclination to purchase cheaper "substitute" goods when other goods became more expensive (e.g., buy rice instead of pasta if the price of pasta rises). While the BLS said they will attempt to fine-tune their measurements, they claimed that no radical changes would be made to the CPI before 1998.

Politicians hope that adjustments to the CPI can help control the rate of growth of some of America's most troublesome entitlement programs, such as Social Security (which faces bankruptcy in 2029 with the aging of the baby boomers), as well as assist in efforts to balance the budget over the next seven years.

Some experts say the findings on the CPI are just the tip of the iceberg. The consulting firm DRI/McGraw-Hill estimates that productivity growth is being understated by three-quarters of a percentage point. *USA Today* also reports that GDP growth is understated, claiming that the government underestimates output. These miscalculations can have major consequences. For instance, if

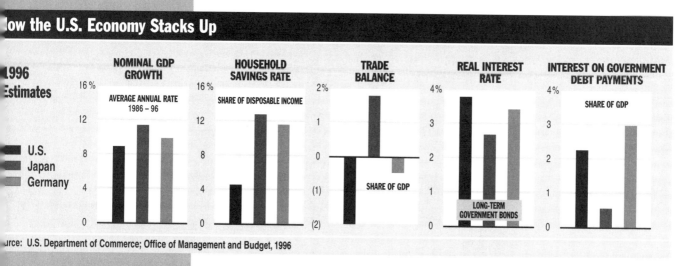

ow the U.S. Economy Stacks Up

urce: U.S. Department of Commerce; Office of Management and Budget, 1996

long-term, inflation-adjusted GDP is understated by just one-half of a percentage point, it adds $200 billion to federal budget deficit estimates.

Senator Patrick Moynihan (D, New York) and Senator John Kerrey (D, Nebraska) have proposed a three-year, $10 million study geared toward improving our statistical system. They claim that Canada and Great Britain spend five times more per dollar of GDP than the U.S. does on collecting and analyzing economic data. *The Economist* has consistently ranked America sixth or lower in statistical quality compared to other industrialized nations.

Consumer Price Index

Affects annual cost-of-living adjustments for:

- 47 million Social Security recipients
- 27 million food stamp recipients
- 4 million military and civil service retirees
- 26 million children who get aid for school lunches
- 2 million private workers covered by union wage contracts
- 119 million federal income taxpayer brackets and personal exemptions

Source: U.S. Bureau of Labor Statistics; *USA Today*, December 3, 1996

Labor Markets

Income

The Census Bureau's latest data (1994) showed real median household income at $32,264, 0.3% less in real terms than it was in 1992 and 5.2% below the 1989 peak. Median family income grew only slightly during the 1980s and fell every year between 1989 and 1993. Moreover, real per capita disposable personal income has grown just 2% per year from 1993 to 1995, with 1995 per capita income at $22,788.

Income Distribution

Economists measure income differentials by dividing the population into five income groups of equal size. By comparing the percentage of total U.S. income earned by each group over time, economists can keep track of the disparity in wages.

Presently, we are experiencing the widest gap between the rich and poor since the U.S. Census Bureau began keeping track of such statistics in 1947. The top one-fifth of all families currently brings home 44.6% of the total income of the U.S., compared to 4.4% earned by the bottom fifth. From 1979 to 1994, the top 5% of American earners saw their incomes grow by 45%, compared to the lowest 20% of earners, who saw their incomes drop by 13.5% in real terms. Those in the middle of the income distribution also received proportionately less of the nation's income. The middle 60% of households received only 53% of the aggregate household income in 1968. By 1994, that figure had declined to 48%.

While wage inequality between income groups is on the rise, inequality among races and sexes has decreased. Black households showed a significant increase in median income for the past two years. In addition, incomes for men and women are growing closer together. Presently, a woman makes about 72¢ on the male dollar.

The Education Factor

The increase in wage inequality is thought to be caused partially by the growing premium that is being placed on education. Currently, there is less demand for blue-collar workers than in the past. Cheaper labor has transferred many blue-collar jobs abroad and technology has eliminated the need for many of these workers. *Business Week* observed, "The well-paying blue-collar jobs that gave U.S. workers rising living standards for most of this century are vanishing. Today, you can all but forget about joining the middle class unless you go to college."

Households in which both the husband and wife had at least a partial education beyond high school level were the highest wage earners. In fact, 44% of

Courtesy of the Harvard Political Review

"The kind of investment that the government can do is primarily investment in people. It's skills a education. It's also technology."

— Alice Rivl
Vice-Chairmar
the Federal Rese

Big Gap in Income Growth

Changes in Average Family Income

Income Group	1979	1994		Percent Change
Lowest 20%	$12,008	$10,387	▼	13.5%
Second 20%	$25,962	$24,575	▼	5%
Middle 20%	$39,153	$38,808	▼	1%
Fourth 20%	$53,904	$57,366	▲	6.4%
Fifth 20%	$92,456	$115,608	▲	25%
Top 5%	$136,856	$198,336	▲	45%

All incomes in 1994 Dollars.

Source: U.S. Census Bureau

"The emergence of large numbers of female-headed families can be directly connected with poverty trends in the U.S."

— Nicholas Eberstadt,
Economist with the
American Enterprise Institute
in Washington, D.C.

Where to Apply

Selected Occupations in the U.S., Forecast Percent Change 1994 – 2005

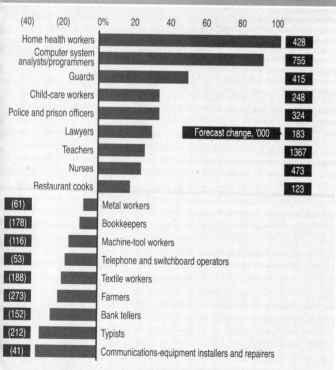

Source: U.S. Bureau of Labor Statistics, 1996; *The Economist*, September 28, 1996

such households were in the top income quintile.

In 1979, male workers with college degrees earned 49% more than men who had only finished high school. By 1993, the differential was 89%. Of those men who turned 21 years old after 1980, only 32% with a high school diploma or less reached the middle income standard by the time they were 30. For those that had turned 21 before 1980, almost half achieved the standard.

The Makeup of Households

The rise of double-income households, a result of the increasing number of women joining the work force, has emerged as one of the central causes of the growing income inequality. These households are more likely than ever to enter the upper class. The average earnings for a two-income household increased 44% between 1969 and 1994 to $42,000 (due to increased wages and labor-force participation of women). The U.S. Labor Department reports that 30% of all double-income households were in the top fifth of America's income distribution in 1993, compared with 14% of single-income households.

While two-income households continue to outperform the rest of American families, the rise in female-headed households continues to bring down the average. According to the U.S. Census Bureau, a full 13% of U.S. households were headed by unmarried females in 1993, compared with just 11% in 1980. Many of these women were jobless, forcing the family to live on welfare. Households headed by unemployed women experienced the steepest drop in average income during 1996, as earnings fell 11% to under $10,000.

Wealthiest Americans Lose Some Ground

Despite reports of growing income inequality, a study conducted by the U.S. Federal Reserve and the IRS showed that the wealthiest 0.5% of Americans took dramatic losses in the 1990s. This category, which includes about 500,000 households, represents multi-millionaires who controlled nearly 29% of all U.S. private wealth in 1989. Three years and a recession later, the study found that the group had lost billions in stocks and bonds and controlled only 22.8% of all wealth.

Overall, private wealth increased to $21 trillion between 1989 and 1992, a modest after-inflation increase of about 4%. Interestingly, those gains were made primarily by the bottom 90% of households. These new findings startled economists and added to the already lively dispute over income equality.

Income Mobility

Some argue that a better measure of wage equality in the U.S. is income mobility, or the ability to move up the income ladder. Economists at Syracuse University claim that within five years, almost half of the people between ages 25 and 55 will have moved up or down at least one income group.

Mobility seems to be highest among middle-income Americans, but the poor frequently jump income groups as well. According to the Census Bureau, less than 50% of people who were below the poverty line in the 1980s remained there over a year. In addition, virtually all of the poor who were employed full-time had managed to rise above the poverty level.

However, there is evidence that income mobility may be slowing. One study at the University of Michigan found that before 1980, more than a third of low-income families moved up to the middle class over a five-year period. After 1980, only a quarter did.

Minimum Wage

In 1996, America raised the minimum wage from $4.25 an hour to $4.75. A second increase to $5.15 is planned for September 1997. While many members of Congress heralded the increase as a boon to American workers, most wage earners will be unaffected. The number of employees who received an immediate raise was small, just 4.2 million. The percentage of workers earning minimum wage has fallen from 8.9% in 1990 to 3.3% today. The minimum wage (when adjusted for inflation) had fallen over the past decade and with it the income of all those who earn it.

Former Secretary of Labor Robert Reich defended the latest increase, saying, "It is easy for commentators to 'poo-poo' the significance of the $1,800-a-year raise, but when you are earning $8,500, that raise is far from insignificant." However, it is argued that such a small increase in minimum wage is not significant enough to lift families above the poverty line. The minimum wage would have to jump to $7.80 an hour, which translates to a $15,600 annual income.

Unemployment Rate Low

Since President Clinton took office in 1993, the economy has spun off 10.1 million new jobs at a rate of 245,000 a month, even faster than under the Reagan Administration. With unemployment at 5.3% at the end of 1996, labor has been in tight supply during Clinton's time in office. However, two-thirds of the jobs created under President Clinton have been service and retail positions, which tend to be lower-paying jobs. New manufacturing jobs have accounted for less than 2% of employment growth in 1996. In fact, since March 1995, manufacturing employment has actually dropped by approximately 300,000 jobs. Government employment has grown by 700,000 jobs since January 1993. This growth has occurred primarily at the state and local level, while the number of federal jobs has fallen slightly.

Wages and Labor Costs

Despite the strongest labor market in at least seven years, the growth of American workers' wages and benefits slowed in the third and fourth quarters of 1996. The slowdown partly undercut earlier indications that workers were

Who Owns Corporate America?

Although the percentage of the American population that owns stock (directly or through pensions or mutual funds) has almost quintupled since 1952, the vast majority of total stock assets are still owned by the country's richest citizens.

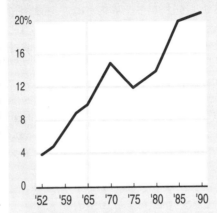

Percentage of Population that Owns Stock

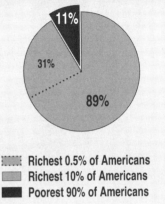

Percentage of Total U.S. Stock Owned by Income Level

11%
31%
89%

░░░ Richest 0.5% of Americans
▓▓▓ Richest 10% of Americans
■■■ Poorest 90% of Americans

Source: Economic Policy Institute; *Harper's Magazine*, May 1996

"Never giving up is the American Way."

— Carol Allego
Single mother who educa
herself and her daught
Hypoluxo, Flor

CEO Compensation

Ratio of the pay of a typical worker to that of a typical CEO

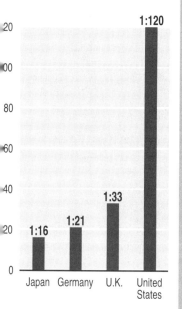

Source: *Harper's Magazine*, May 1996

beginning to enjoy increases in pay that outpaced the rise in the cost of living. The employment costs index, probably the most accurate compensation gauge, climbed just six-tenths of a percent in the third quarter, the lowest reading in a year. One reason for this, said Roseanne Cane, an economist at CS First Boston, "...was the minimal wage pressure. Labor is poorly organized to take advantage of their scarcity."

Average hourly labor costs (that is, the cost of labor faced by employers) in the U.S. and in France are roughly equal at $17.50 according to research done by the Swedish Employers Confederation. In the U.S., as opposed to France, most of the $17.50 goes toward wages for time worked. In France, $5.00 goes to Social Security and other taxes, and $3.00 goes for holiday time. In the U.S., $3.50 goes to taxes and only $1.00 to holiday time. Germany, however, has the highest hourly wages, more than $27.00. However, a greater percentage of their income goes toward taxes. Japan's holiday bonus pay tops the list at almost $6.00 an hour, or 27% of the hourly rate of $22.00.

The cost for employee benefits in the U.S. has risen since the 1980s. A survey done by the U.S. Chamber of Commerce showed that benefits, including Social Security and other payroll taxes, holidays and vacations, now account for about 42% of payroll costs. Employers spend an average of $14,800 on non-wage benefits per employee.

Worker's benefits have been increasing for a number of reasons. First, because of a lot of corporate restructuring, there have been increases in benefit costs as well as increases in permanent layoffs and early retirement buyouts. In addition, expensive health care insurance has contributed to the rising cost of benefits. In 1996, employee benefits showed some signs of slowing down, growing just 1.8%, which is less than wage growth.

Downsizing

Throughout the 1980s and 1990s, there has been a growing concern about job security—due to record numbers of corporate layoffs. The rate of job loss hit a peak of 3.4 million in 1992 and has remained nearly that high ever since, despite a growing economy and a booming stock market. According to the Bureau of Labor Statistics, during most of the 1980s, one in 25 workers lost a job in any two-year period. In the 1990s, it has risen to one in 20. According to a *New York Times* poll, nearly three-quarters of all households experienced a close encounter with a lay-off since 1980, and one-third actually lost their jobs.

Job dislocation is spreading to include nearly every sector of the economy. Blue-collar workers still make up the majority of layoffs, but in the 1990s layoffs are being felt more and more by white-collar workers, professionals and administrators. A University of Michigan study found that layoffs of college-educated workers over the age of 50 doubled from the 1980s to the 1990s.

Downsizing

Company	Date	# of Layoffs
T&T	Jan. 1996	40,000
oeing	Feb. 1993	28,000
hemical/Chase Manhattan	Aug. 1995	12,000
elta Air Lines	Apr. 1994	15,000
igital Equipment	May 1994	20,000
eneral Motors	Dec. 1991	74,000
TE Corp.	Jan. 1994	17,000
M	July 1993	60,000
cDonnell Douglas	July 1990	17,000
YNEX	Jan. 1994	16,800
hilip Morris	Nov. 1993	14,000
ears, Roebuck & Co.	Jan. 1993	50,000
cott Paper	N/A	11,000

Source: *Newsweek*, February 26, 1996

VII. International State of the Nation

Defining a New Strategy

The International Relations Debate

Since the end of the cold war in the late 1980s, America has been struggling to redefine its foreign policy. The old world order, which polarized loyalties to either the U.S. or the Soviet Union, and which had kept nationalistic tensions in check for so many years, no longer exists. The globe is torn by war and civil unrest in Bosnia, Somalia, Rwanda, the Middle East and throughout the former Soviet Republics. As 1996 came to a close, there were over three dozen hot spots around the world—either in open conflict or ready to erupt at the slightest provocation.

Amidst the turmoil, America debates how to react. Should America remain the protector of democracy and human rights around the world? If so, which groups should we support in civil wars? Should we merely send troops to keep the peace as we did in Rwanda, or should we allow our forces to attack, as we did in the Gulf War? If we do engage in combat, will the American people be willing to give up valuable resources that could be used domestically, in addition to the lives of our soldiers?

Questions to Consider

However we decide to act in the future, we will have to consider certain trends that are shaping the international scene:

1. It will become more difficult to separate our domestic and foreign policies. As the U.S. grows increasingly dependent upon other nations for goods, services and export profits, we must realize our foreign policy will often affect our standard of living at home.

2. We must realize that our international economic policy and our international security policy are closely related. Traditionally, America's presence abroad has been secured by a military relationship with countries throughout Europe and Asia. In order to pursue our economic agenda, we must also consider our military involvement in these areas. Conversely, in order to make decisions about our military involvement in these regions, we must also consider the economic ramifications.

3. The United States must balance its resources among various regions. In 1996, the Chinese complained that former Secretary of State Warren Christopher had visited China only once, whereas he visited Israel over 20 times. As regional conflicts arise throughout the world and nations clamor for American attention, foreign policy officials must perform a delicate balancing act.

4. The United States must choose to act either unilaterally or multilaterally in international conflicts. The U.S. must re-evaluate its role in the United Nations and in the North Atlantic Treaty Organization (NATO).

5. The U.S. must be prepared to deal with new powers like Russia and

"While the world as a whole increasingly accepts the new habits of global civilization, another contradictory process is taking place; ancient traditions are reviving, different religions and cultures are awakening to new waves of being . . ."

— Vaclav Havel, President, Czech Republic

"Those who say America has to dominate the world and that you have to either control everything or go home don't understand the way power is projected at the end of the century."

— Madeleine Albright, U.S. Secretary of State

China. Both are in the midst of volatile political transitions, and their influence must be respected by virtue of their large populations, growth rates and technological advances. Russia and China are both nuclear powers with separate agendas. Neither are democracies and relationships with them may prove challenging.

American Security

Defense Strategy

In order to adapt to a new world order, America has had to redirect its military to confront the outbreak of ethnic and civil wars. Since the end of the cold war, the U.S. military has attempted to transform itself from an entity capable of conducting an all-out nuclear war against the Communist world to one able to launch small, fast, conventional units to keep peace in distant lands.

The Department of Defense (DOD) highlights the following national security objectives for the future:

- Readiness for regional conflicts involving national, ethnic, religious and economic tension
- Preparedness for new types of threats through the proliferation of technology
- The non-proliferation of nuclear weapons
- U.S. leadership and support of a complex array of formal alliances, bilateral treaties and temporary coalitions
- Peace efforts as well as other operations to promote national security and humanitarian or disaster relief which place demands on U.S. forces
- Maintaining the global economy as a national priority

The DOD further states, "The national security strategy now emphasizes promoting democracy and economic advancement worldwide. The military component of this strategy supports creating and maintaining the stability required to allow democracy and economic growth to flourish and staying ready to protect our interests.

"While our view of the future does not envision another nation's achieving military capabilities equal to those of the United States during the next 20 years, that possibility must be considered. A growing number of nations may have the economic means needed to achieve substantial military power singly or in combination."

Defense Budget

Amidst a need to trim government spending, the military has experienced significant budget cuts. In real terms, the defense budget has been cut approximately 35% since its 1985 high under President Reagan. The number of personnel in uniform has dropped over 25% since 1990. The Army has trimmed down to 12 active divisions from 18; the Air Force has cut its 24 tactical wings down to 13; and the Navy currently has 373 battleships, compared to 546 in 1990.

Although defense spending has decreased dramatically over the past 10 years, the Pentagon spent over $1 trillion during the first term of the Clinton Presidency (about $30 million an hour, more than the rest of the world's top ten armies combined).

For fiscal year 1997, President Clinton approved a $256.6 billion armed services spending bill ($11.2 billion more than

> *"No democracy likes to spend on the military . . . the real worry, though, is that if you don't spend money on the military, you won't be a democracy very much longer."*
>
> — Caspar Weinberger,
> Former U.S. Secretary of Defense

Military Personnel

(In Thousands)

	1989 (cold war)	1997 Projected	2001 Target
Active	2,130	1,457	1,418
Guard & Reserves	1,171	901	893

Source: Budget of the U.S. Government, Fiscal Year 1997

originally requested by the DOD) in order to "restructure" and "reinvent" air military operations.

However, defense spending is still lower than it was in the 1980s during the Reagan defense build-up. In 1986, the United States spent a high of 6.3% of its GDP on the military. In 1997, it will spend only 3.6%, the lowest since before World War II.

Both the Democrats and Republicans are in favor of continuing to reduce defense spending in order to balance the budget by 2002. In the past decade, defense cuts have accounted for virtually all of the net reductions in federal spending. The Republican plan would cut defense a total of 13%, while the President's plan would cut defense by 10% from 1997 levels.

Nuclear Proliferation

In September of 1996, President Clinton signed a treaty that would ban all nuclear weapons testing, calling on world leaders to take further steps to limit weapons of mass destruction. The comprehensive accord is intended to thwart the development of new types of weapons by banning all nuclear explosions.

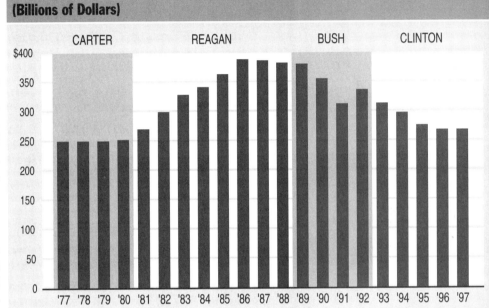

Tracking Military Spending*

(Billions of Dollars)

CARTER   REAGAN   BUSH   CLINTON

* Adjusted for inflation in 1996 dollars, for the fiscal years ending September 30

Source: Office of Management and Budget

An overwhelming majority of countries, including the five declared nuclear weapons powers—the U.S., Britain, China, France and Russia—have agreed to the treaty. But India, which set off a nuclear explosion in 1974 and is believed to have a clandestine nuclear weapons program, has said that it will not sign because the treaty does not set a date for the total elimination of such weapons. Pakistan, also thought to possess a covert nuclear weapons program, has indicated that it will boycott the pact if India does.

During Clinton's Administration, the U.S. has joined 14 of the former Communist states in a kind of "neo-NATO," which is working to dismantle more than $2 billion of nuclear weapons. Meanwhile, President Clinton is continuing research on a ballistic missile system which could be used as an alternative to a nuclear defense.

While the effort to constrain nuclear proliferation has made significant headway, many experts are still worried that the unstable economic order in the former Soviet Republics could lead to the sale of weaponry to terrorist groups. The Russians currently possess 25,000 fully ready and 75,000 semi-ready nuclear missiles capable of reaching American soil that President Clinton claims "are no longer targeted at the U.S." Unfortunately, it would take fewer than 60 seconds to retarget them.

President Clinton has outlined six priority goals to further decrease the threat of nuclear and other weaponry:

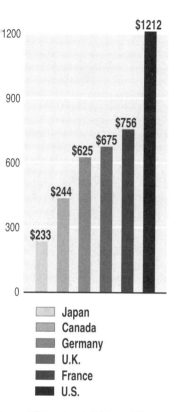

Footing the Bill for Military Spending

Per Capita Defense Spending

- Japan
- Canada
- Germany
- U.K.
- France
- U.S.

Source: U.S. Department of Defense, 1995

1. Reduce the risk that an outlaw state or organization could build a nuclear device by negotiating a treaty to freeze the production of fusion materials used in such weapons.
2. Continue to reduce our own nuclear arsenals.
3. Reinforce our efforts against the spread of nuclear weapons by supporting the nuclear non-proliferation treaty. Also, give the International Atomic Energy Agency more power and better tools for conducting worldwide inspections.
4. Protect the American people from chemical attack by bringing a Chemical Weapons Convention into existence as soon as possible. Such an organization would make it harder for terrorists to use poison gases through investigation and limited trade in certain chemicals.
5. Protect the U.S. from biological warfare by giving the Biological Weapons Convention the means to strengthen compliance, including the authority to conduct on-site investigations when such weapons are believed to have been used or when suspicious outbreaks of disease occur.
6. End the carnage caused by landmines, which murder and maim more than 25,000 people a year.

The Threat of Information Warfare

Our nation's growing reliance on computer networks and telecommunications is making our military war rooms, power plants, telephone networks, air traffic control centers and banks increasingly vulnerable to cyber-attacks.

In July 1996, President Clinton created the Commission on Critical Infrastructure Protection to craft a coordinated policy to deal with such threats. The CIA recently created an information warfare center, and the National Security Agency intends to set up a similar unit with both offensive and defensive capabilities, staffed by as many as 1,000 people as well as a 24-hour response team.

John Deutch, Director of Central Intelligence, said the CIA had determined that cyber-attacks "are now. . . [with]in the capabilities of a number of terrorist groups," including the Hezbollah in the Middle East. Barry Horton, the Principal Deputy Assistant Secretary of Defense, who oversees the Pentagon's information warfare operations, points out, "Even a third-tier country has access to first-class programmers and to state-of-the-art computer software and expertise."

The weapons used in information warfare consist primarily of computer software, like destructive logic bombs, or advanced electronic hardware, such as high-energy radio frequency devices and viruses. In theory, these weapons could cripple the information highways of our nation. Our computer systems control everything from banks to electric utilities to battlefield tanks.

The DOD has highlighted the following technology issues:

- Rapid changes in technology may work in America's favor by advancing the DOD's capabilities, but adversaries may benefit as well, either by developing new capabilities before they are available to the DOD or by achieving technical advances that nullify U.S. technology.
- The DOD will have to build stronger ties to civilian research institutions and innovative businesses to ensure its access to emerging technologies, many of which will be developed outside its traditional sphere of influence.
- Advances in technology that can revolutionize military affairs must be adapted and coupled with equally revolutionary adjustments to concept and doctrine.

Arms Trade

Russia was the leading supplier of arms to the Third World during 1995, with $6 billion in sales. However, roughly two-thirds of this amount is represented by one large deal with China for Russian fighter aircraft and related equipment. The U.S., however, remains the world leader in arms trade overall. Over the past four years, the U.S. has conducted roughly half of all arms sales worldwide, more than all other major suppliers combined. However, the Third World market for arms sales may be shrinking. In 1995, U.S. arms exports to the developing world dropped to $15 billion, down roughly 25% from their peak in 1988.

Gulf War Ailments

In November of 1996, the Presidential Advisory Committee on the Gulf War Veterans' Illnesses condemned the Pentagon's "superficial" investigation into the exposure of American troops to Iraqi chemical weapons during the 1991 Persian Gulf War and called for an independent inquiry into more than 15 incidents in which nerve gas and other chemical agents were detected by American troops.

While the panel has not issued a definitive statement on the cause of the illnesses affecting tens of thousands of Gulf War veterans, panel members say that an "overwhelming" amount of evidence indicates that the culprits might include chemical weapons and nerve gas released when American troops blew up a massive Iraqi ammunition depot shortly after the war. Thousands of U.S. troops were deployed in the area of the explosion.

Terrorism

Over the past several years, America has suffered a growing list of casualties arising from terrorist attacks, including the World Trade Center bombing, the Oklahoma City bombing, the Una-Bomber attacks, the pipe-bomb at the Atlanta Olympics and potentially TWA Flight 800.

In September 1996, President Clinton's Administration unveiled a $1.1 billion plan to fight terrorism worldwide, including $429 million to improve security at U.S. airports. The plan includes provisions to increase the number of federal anti-terrorist agents, to equip the nation's airports with high-tech bomb detection devices and to track passengers with suspicious travel patterns.

The plan was based on recommendations by Vice President Al Gore's Commission on Aviation Safety and Security. Mr. Clinton also ordered immediate criminal background checks on airline workers with access to secured areas and promised to provide bomb-sniffing dogs for security at key airports.

U.S. Involvement Abroad

Operations Abroad

The United States military maintains a presence in over 30 countries around the world. As part of the United Nations (U.N.), the North Atlantic Treaty Organization (NATO), as well as other multinational organizations, U.S. forces seek to stabilize various political environments around the globe.

One of the Clinton Administration's main foreign policy objectives has been to effect a peaceful resolution of several of the world's ongoing civil conflicts. Specifically, the Clinton foreign policy team is actively engaged in efforts to resolve the Bosnian, Irish, Israeli and Palestinian crises. Experts predict that these conflicts—highly lethal, localized civil wars between rival factions—will become more prevalent in the coming years.

Arms Transfers to the Third World

The U.S. has been the major supplier of arms to the Third World, followed by Western Europe. Together they provide over three-fourths of all arms transfers to the Third World.

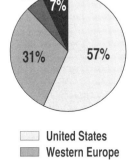

5%
7%
31%
57%

☐ United States
☐ Western Europe
☐ Russia
■ All Others

Source: U.S. Department of Commerce, 1994

"The United States can in fact be threatened via unconventional means, such as terrorism and weapons of mass destruction, by nations whose conventional military capabilities cannot come close to matching ours."

— W. Bruce Weinrod,
Former Deputy Assistant
Secretary of Defense,
International Security Policy

The United Nations

For the 51st consecutive year, the United States will be the largest contributor to the U.N., both monetarily and in terms of peacekeeping troops. The U.S. pays for 25% of the U.N. budget. Presently, the U.S. owes $1.3 billion for fees and for peacekeeping expenses. President Clinton and the State Department, although committed to paying off our accumulated obligations within the U.N., have used the debt as a carrot to exact concessions from the organization, such as the removal of former U.N. Secretary General Boutros Boutros-Ghali.

The Bosnian crisis has rekindled a longstanding debate in the United States over the American role in the U.N. The Clinton Administration argues that the U.S. cannot afford to assume the role of global policeman and must act in concert with other powers as it did in the Gulf War or Bosnia in order to maintain peace.

Even some of the U.N.'s harshest critics have contended that the international body is being blamed unfairly for the failure to bring peace to Bosnia. "In some ways, the strongest supporters of the United Nations have been the organization's worst enemy," remarks Ted Gallon Carpenter, Director of Foreign Policy Studies at the CATO Institute, a conservative think tank in Washington. "They've tried to have it do too much; they've tried to have the organization perform functions for which it was never designed." Experts agree that for the U.N. to work effectively, it must undergo reforms to strengthen its methods of influence, given post-cold-war politics.

The cold war had provided an international stability by dividing the world into two spheres of power that overshadowed any ethnic or civil dispute. Now that the cold war is over, nationalistic conflicts are erupting all over the globe—stretching the U.N.'s resources thin. "For the first 45 years of its existence, the U.N.'s operational responsibility was very much limited by the confrontation of the two super-powers," says Dick Thornburgh, former Under Secretary General of the U.N. in the Department of Administration and Management. "Then almost overnight, it was asked to become operational in a wide variety of situations around the world, becoming a kind of worldwide 911 emergency number, and it was simply not geared up for that kind of activity."

Amidst this need for redefinition, politics within the organization has been anything but smooth sailing. The U.S. had particular problems with the former Secretary General of the United Nations, Boutros Boutros-Ghali. The Administration accused Mr. Boutros-Ghali of not pressing for organizational reform with sufficient vigor. In addition, Boutros-Ghali frequently did not support U.S. initiatives in the U.N.

Kofi Annan of the West African country of Ghana was appointed the new Secretary General in late 1996. Annan said that he hoped to work with the Clinton Administration to persuade Congress to begin paying the $1.3 billion in debt the U.S. owes to the United Nations—debt which he claims has driven the U.N. to the brink of financial ruin.

NATO and Russian Relations

In 1996, President Clinton called for NATO to extend full membership to a group of former Soviet-block nations by the spring of 1999, the 50th anniversary of the traditionally-Western military alliance. Formed in response to the cold-war threat, this alliance between the U.S., Canada and 10 Western European nations has become a major peacekeeping force in the world, most notably in Bosnia. The Clinton Administration is known to favor Hungary, Poland and the Czech Republic as prospective NATO members but is also evaluating Rumania and Slovenia.

President Clinton commented that a gray zone of insecurity must not

"In pursuit of security, Russia has produced insecurity for all of its neighbors. Russia has generally excluded Eastern Europe, the Balkans and Central Asia from the operation of the balance of power—insisting on dealing with them unilaterally, and often by force."

— Henry Kissinger,
Former U.S. Secretary of State

"You have to understand that a lot of money and effort during the past 50 years was invested to create the image of NATO in Russia as an 'evil empire.' An evil empire which is preparing for the final stroke against Russia."

— Yegor Gaidar,
Former Prime Minister of Russia

Courtesy of the Harvard Political Review

U.S. TROOPS ABROAD

A Look at American Military Forces Around the Globe, Highlighting the 12 Largest Contingents

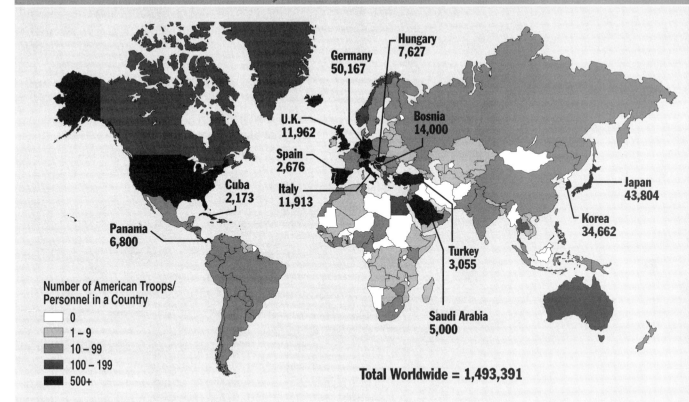

Germany
50,167

Hungary
7,627

U.K.
11,962

Bosnia
14,000

Spain
2,676

Italy
11,913

Cuba
2,173

Panama
6,800

Japan
43,804

Korea
34,662

Turkey
3,055

Saudi Arabia
5,000

**Number of American Troops/
Personnel in a Country**
- ☐ 0
- ☐ 1 – 9
- ☐ 10 – 99
- ☐ 100 – 199
- ■ 500+

Total Worldwide = 1,493,391

Source: U.S. Department of Defense, as of March 31, 1996

emerge in Europe. He encouraged Russia to view the expansion of NATO to include former Warsaw Pact countries as an arrangement that would "advance the security of everyone." Russia is wary of such an alliance with nations that were once Soviet satellites during the cold war, but Mr. Clinton has promised that "no new NATO members would have a veto" as current members do. He urged the Russians to stop viewing the organization through a cold-war prism.

Many experts fear that a mishandled NATO expansion could bolster Russian nationalists, who could feel suddenly isolated. Andrei Korunov of Moscow's Russian Research Center said that the U.S. must show that "Russia is more important to NATO than some of the small countries that might join." To assuage Russia, the U.S. plans to negotiate a charter which would give Moscow the right to consult on a wide range of NATO operations. Former Secretary of State Warren Christopher advised that the accord should include joint training and a crisis-management mechanism.

The price tag for restructuring NATO could be anywhere from $60 to $125 billion through 2010; however, the Administration argues that up to 90% of the cost will be born by European nations.

Operations in Bosnia

America first became heavily involved in the Bosnian peace process when Richard Holbrook, Assistant Secretary of State for European Affairs and chief U.S. negotiator in Bosnia, helped push through the Dayton Accord, under which the warring parties of the Serbs and Croats gave NATO the authority to force a peace. Under the agreement, Bosnia and Herzegovina were split roughly in half

"The bedrock of our common security remains NATO. That's why the United States has taken the lead in a three-part effort to build a new NATO for a new era. First, by adapting NATO with new capabilities for new missions. Second, by opening its doors to Europe's emerging democracies. Third, by building a strong and cooperative relationship between NATO and Russia."

— President Bill Clinton

"I think that the American President is a unique leader because constructive organization for peace does not happen in the world without American leadership. This calls for a President who is a hands-on manager."

— Richard Lugar,
Senator (R, Indiana)

Courtesy of the Harvard Political Review

"There are times when only America can make the difference between war and peace, between freedom and repression, and between hope and fear."

— President Bill Clinton

to form a Serb republic and a Muslim-Croat federation, presided over by a weak central government.

In 1994, President Clinton sent 16,900 American troops to the Balkan nation as part of a 50,000-member NATO peace-keeping force. Originally, he had promised the troops that they would serve there only a year. But with the peace in Bosnia fragile at best and the delay of the Bosnian 1996 municipal elections, NATO has now suggested keeping troops there well into 1997.

NATO has proposed a new American-led force of 31,000, one-third U.S. troops and the rest from Russia and 23 other countries. These personnel would replace those sent to oversee Bosnia's compliance with the peace accords negotiated over a year ago. The force would most likely be comprised of both air and ground troops, and their mission would be "to prevent an upstart of new fighting and to provide freedom of movement for Bosnians," according to President Clinton.

Former Defense Secretary William J. Perry has said that this operation would cost $2 billion: $1.2 billion for the forces in Bosnia, $500 million for the support troops outside the country and $300 million for fighters to enforce NATO's ban on military flights over Bosnia.

Refugees in Zaire

Another chapter in the historic turmoil of West Africa opened in 1996 as the tribes of the Hutu and the Tutsi battled along the border between eastern Zaire and Tutsi-controlled Rwanda.

The current feud was sparked when Zairian officials announced a plan to expel 300,000 people of the Tutsi tribe into Southern Kivu, the southernmost province of the nation. The announcement was the culmination of a long-running feud between the Tutsi, who have prospered economically, and several poor local tribes led by the Babembe tribe. This set off a Tutsi rebellion against the Zairian government of President Mobutu Sese Seko.

Hundreds of thousands of Hutu citizens from the neighboring countries of Rwanda and Burundi, who had been living in refugee camps in Zaire, flocked northward to escape the fighting. The Hutu first fled their native Rwanda in 1994, fearing vengeance from an advancing Tutsi army for a previous Hutu militia-led massacre of Tutsis. More than a million of the Rwandans had settled in the refugee camps in Zaire and remained there until they were driven out by the current fighting.

In December 1996, the United Nations debated the need to deploy thousands of soldiers to provide humanitarian aid to hundreds of thousands of Rwandan refugees in Zaire as part of a Canadian-led mission. President Clinton had announced that the U.S. was prepared to contribute as many as 4,000 troops, but with many refugees now returning to their homeland due to conciliatory efforts by the Zairian government, the need for a full-scale relief mission seems to be waning.

Friends and Foes in the Middle East

The issue of "land for peace" continues to be a major source of controversy, not only between the Israelis and the Palestinians but also among factions within Israel.

The idea of land for peace emerged out of the historic Oslo agreement between Israel and the Palestine Liberation Organization in September of 1993. In the peace accord, the PLO recognized Israel's right to exist, and Israel recognized the PLO as the representative of the Palestinians. The two sides agreed to limited Palestinian self-rule in Gaza and in the West Bank, beginning with the city of Jericho. In July 1994, Jordan and Israel declared an end to their 46-year state of war. In September 1995, Palestinians and Israelis furthered the process, signing an agreement which required further Israeli withdrawal and greater Palestinian rule in the West Bank.

The Middle East peace accords starkly defined the division between the religious and secular Israelis and between the political left and right. It highlighted the differences between the religious nationalists intent on stopping the handover of territory they consider part of their biblical land and liberal Israelis willing to trade land for peace.

The peace agreements were signed under the leadership of Prime Minister Yitzhak Rabin and the Labor Party. Rabin, a strong voice for the peace movement in the Middle East, was assassinated on November 4, 1995, by Yigal Amir, a nationalistic Jew who was opposed to the Prime Minister's peace accord with the Palestinians. In May of 1996, the Likud Party under Prime Minister Benjamin Netanyahu was voted into office. The election of Netanyahu, a politician who openly opposed the land-for-peace basis of the agreements, has slowed the completion of the accords.

Particularly, the Palestinians accused the Israelis of seeking to make major changes in the agreement on their withdrawal from Hebron on the West Bank, which was to take place by March 1996. Israel refused, after a series of Palestinian suicide attacks against Israelis, to evacuate its 500 military nationalistic Jewish settlers living in the center of Hebron, a city of 160,000 Palestinians. Much fighting and terrorist activity has erupted over this dispute. In April 1996, Israel retaliated for the suicide bombings against the Hezbollah, one of the most active Islamic militant groups, bombing their bases in southern Lebanon. Israel also caused a stir near a sacred Muslim site in Jerusalem, setting off days of violence between Israeli soldiers, Palestinians and police.

While Israeli withdrawal from Hebron was completed in late January 1997, Yassar Arafat, leader of the Palestinian state, said that he was concerned the conservative Likud government could stall on carrying out the other portions of the agreement, which call for further Israeli withdrawal from the West Bank. Conservative Israelis feel the West Bank is part of the "biblical land" of Israel.

Continued Discord with Iraq

In the five and a half years since the Persian Gulf War (a U.S.-led coalition which countered the Iraqi attack on Kuwait in 1991), Saddam Hussein, still the leader of Iraq, has repeatedly tested the limits of U.S. resolve. In the aftermath of the Persian Gulf, Iraq drove Kurdish insurgents and civilians to the Iranian and Turkish borders, causing a refugee crisis. The Kurds have been the longtime political enemy of Saddam Hussein. Saddam's government had launched bloody attacks on the Kurdish minority in the 1970s and 1980s, when the Kurds supported Iran in the Iran-Iraq War.

In addition, since the war, the Iraqi military has played cat and mouse with U.N. inspectors looking for chemical and biological weapons facilities within Iraq. In 1993, the U.S. launched a missile attack aimed at Iraq's intelligence headquarters in Baghdad, saying that the attack was retribution for sponsoring a plot to kill former President George Bush during his visit to Kuwait in April 1993. In August 1995, two of Saddam Hussein's sons-in-law, who held high positions in the Iraqi military, defected to Jordan. Both were killed after returning to Iraq in February of 1996.

More recently, in September of 1996, in what U.S. officials said was one of the largest Iraqi military buildups since 1991, Saddam amassed 30,000 to 40,000

"The Clinton Administration failed to appreciate adequately the determination and willingness of certain Israelis and Palestinians to use violence to destroy the 1994 Israel/PLO Peace Agreements."

— Ernest Evans,
Professor of Political Science,
U.S. Army Command

troops along the de facto demarcation line that protects Iraq's Kurdish minority. The troops were there to settle fighting between two Kurdish factions—one allied with Iraq, the other with Iran. The Clinton Administration responded by warning Saddam that the U.S. "would consider any aggressive action to be a matter of grave concern." Clinton ordered reinforcements of 30 Air Force planes and two Navy carriers—positioned within striking distance of Baghdad. The U.S. launched missile strikes against air defense sites within Iraq and renewed sanctions against Iraq. Saddam withdrew most of his forces from the region.

U.S. Policy on Cuba

Prior to 1996, President Clinton had been pursuing a delicate policy, encouraging democratic change inside Cuba while maintaining the decades-old U.S. trade embargo on Fidel Castro's regime. However, in 1996, he shifted sharply to the right when he agreed to support the "Cuban Liberty Bill" sponsored by Senator Jesse Helms and Representative Robert Burton.

The bill authorizes Americans to sue foreign firms that do business in Cuba over property confiscated by the Castro government. It would deny U.S. visas to executives of such companies and their families and it further encourages the President to promote the downfall of Castro's government through additional economic pressures.

The President supported the bill after two Cessnas flown by anti-Castro pilots were shot down by Cuban MIGs in 1996. Mr. Clinton called the attack "an appalling reminder of the nature of the Cuban regime." In addition, he won a GOP compromise that permits him to delay implementation of the bill for up to six months if he deems it necessary for the national interest.

The United Nations condemned the Helms-Burton Act and overwhelmingly passed a resolution urging the U.S. to lift its embargo. The resolution called on all countries to refrain from enacting laws that unilaterally apply "economic and trade measures by one state against another which affect the free flow of international traffic." The resolution specifically cited the Helms-Burton Act, saying that it "affects the sovereignty of other states . . . and the freedom of trade and navigation."

Foreign Aid

Amidst budget cuts, in June 1996, the House passed legislation that would trim the nation's foreign aid commitments.

The bill would cut funding for every overseas relief project with the exception of aid to Egypt and Israel. It would also abolish three international agencies—the Agency for International Development, the Arms Control and Disarmament Agency and the U.S. Information Agency—incorporating their functions into the State Department. President Clinton has threatened to veto the bill if it passes the Senate in its present form.

In fiscal year 1996, America spent $18.6 billion on its foreign aid programs. This represented a decrease of $2.6 billion from 1993, or 12.3%. In 1997, the President proposed spending of $19.2 billion.

Foreign aid is given to accomplish three basic goals:
1. To provide humanitarian aid where needed
2. To help poor countries' economies grow
3. To improve U.S. security interests abroad

Although less than 1% of our entire budget, foreign assistance is a hot topic politically. Many argue that our funds usually provide little relief. In fact, many

'There is a trend for the U.N. to use more non-government organizations rather than U.S. troops."

— Nicole Williams,
Georgetown University
Washington, D.C.

of the nations that we give foreign assistance continue to have oppressive governments which, many argue, are likely to waste our money. One study by the Heritage Foundation showed that our top 10 aid recipients have serious barriers to trade. Furthermore, of the 21 worst-rated countries for human rights and free trade, all but six received U.S. foreign aid in 1995.

In defense of our foreign assistance program, it can be argued that some of the nations which we have aided have succeeded. For example, South Korea once received U.S. foreign aid and now sends some $100 million to poor countries. The State Department points out that the $14.8 billion in U.S. exports to South Korea in 1993 amounted to more than all of the U.S. aid sent there during the 1960s and 1970s.

Aid to Poor Countries

In September 1996, seven of the world's major industrial powers agreed to forgive up to 80% of debts owed to them by the world's poorest nations if those countries agreed to economic reforms. The reforms would require these nations, which are located primarily in Africa and Southeast Asia, to lower trade barriers, prioritize state industries and be more open to foreign investment. Treasury Secretary Robert Rubin said that this agreement, reached by the finance ministers of the nations, would be formally enforced by the World Bank and the International Monetary Fund.

For decades, the world's largest countries have insisted that indigent nations repay all of their loans, fearing that a forgiveness program would discourage such countries from enacting economic reforms. However, this policy made it virtually impossible to attract private investment from abroad, as virtually all foreign exchange entering the countries was used to pay debts. In 1995, the United States was the fourth largest contributor of aid to poor countries ($7.3 billion), behind Japan ($14.5 billion), France ($8.4 billion) and Germany ($7.5 billion).

International Trade

Growing Interdependence

The United States has become increasingly dependent on foreign trade. Between 1965 and 1995, U.S. export production grew by more than 500%, while world export production rose approximately 150% in comparison. Over a third of America's economic growth is due to this increase in exports.

During the past several years, various trade organizations have grown in importance, including the World Trade Organization (WTO, formerly GATT— General Agreements on Trade and Tariffs). In addition, over the past decade there has been a growing emergence of free trade zones among nations, such as in the European Union (Europe), NAFTA (North America), Mercosur and the Andean Pact (South and Central America) and APEC (Asia).

As the U.S. realized through the heated political debate surrounding NAFTA, the creation of free trade zones is not always an easy adjustment for the countries involved. As a result, nations often lose entire industries to other countries and must rebuild their economic structures. Nations in free trade zones also tie their currencies together. Thus, while free trade can be beneficial by creating specialization and greater efficiency, it also causes nations to become more interdependent—to suffer and to prosper together.

> *"The presence of U.S. forces is important not only for peace and security on the peninsula but also to keep the balance in Northeast Asia. They are the most important deterrent to the possibility of war in this region."*
>
> — Kim Young Sam,
> President of South Korea

Freeing Up Technology Trade

Last year, at a WTO meeting in Singapore, the U.S. and the European Union resolved a host of differences on a proposal to eliminate tariffs on computers, software and other technology products within three years. The agreement will pave the way for over 35 other countries to liberalize trade in the constantly growing information technology market.

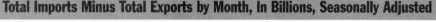
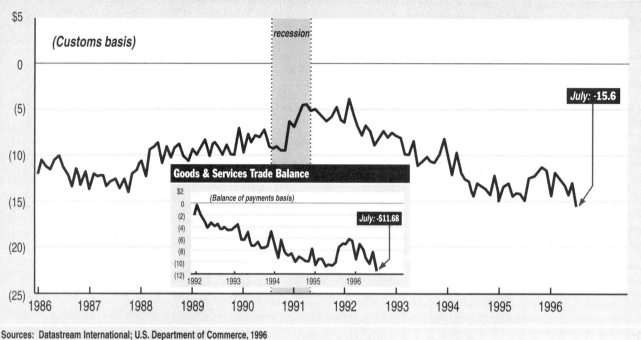

Sources: Datastream International; U.S. Department of Commerce, 1996

The Trade Deficit

The overall 1996 U.S. trade deficit (the difference between what the U.S. exports to other countries and what our citizens consume in foreign imports) is projected to be close to $165 billion, one of the highest in U.S. history and the deficit's fifth consecutive annual increase. Economists remain concerned about the persistent U.S. trade imbalance with Japan (although it is down 24% from 1995) and the lack of further progress in opening China's vast markets to American goods.

U.S. exports were slightly hindered in 1996 by a strengthening dollar, which made U.S. goods more expensive in foreign markets, as well as by some sluggishness in the Japanese and European economies. The biggest declines in our exports occurred in autos and auto parts.

America's growing trade imbalances with Canada and Mexico, a slowdown in Europe's economy and high prices for imported oil could keep the country's trade deficit from dropping significantly in 1997. The trade deficit is a problem, according to most economists, because it is a signal that the U.S. is consuming (in imports) more than it is producing (in exports) and thus has to finance the difference through debt to foreigners. This explains the high level of foreign investment in the U.S. In other words, the U.S. is financing consumption through selling U.S. assets like real estate, stock and U.S. bonds.

Foreign Direct Investment

Foreign direct investment is defined as the amount of money that foreigners invest in a particular country, either by moving corporations and industries there or by buying real estate and other permanent resources. In 1995, the U.S. was the single largest destination of foreign direct investment, attracting a total of $41 billion.

Although the U.S. was in first place, investment funds are being drawn increasingly toward the emerging markets. Cross-border direct investment in developing countries comprised $80 billion in 1995, 40% of the estimated $205 billion total. This number has been rising steadily throughout the 1990s. Nations receiving the highest amount of direct investment are China, which received $30 billion; India, which received $4 billion; and Mexico, which received $8 billion. Other nations receiving large quantities of foreign investment include South Korea, Kenya and Singapore.

The U.S. Dollar

There is much debate over the virtue of maintaining a strong dollar against foreign currencies. Generally, a strong currency favors American consumers over American exporters. When the U.S. dollar soared against other currencies in the 1980s, Americans could buy foreign products much more cheaply; however, U.S. exports were priced much too high for foreign markets and sales suffered, causing the U.S. to lose world market share.

The dollar has appreciated by roughly 40% against the Japanese yen since 1995, and experts claimed at the end of 1996 that the dollar had reached its peak against the yen. Ron Leven, Global Securities Strategist at J.P. Morgan, believes that the dollar will likely depreciate relative to the yen because "we are still running trade deficits and Japan is still running surpluses." Leven cites the depreciation of currency in countries with trade deficits over the last 10 to 15 years.

Overall, however, the dollar has remained relatively steady over the course of 1996, trading almost on par with the German mark. Richard E. Witten, a partner at Goldman, Sachs, and Company, remarked, "If the dollar doesn't [move] . . . it will be the narrowest range . . . since 1972." Other analysts predict that the global currency market, which has been extremely lethargic in general for much of 1996, could begin to revive, causing an increase in the volatility of the dollar.

American Export Strategies

The Commerce Department is largely responsible for crafting the trade policy of the U.S. Ron Brown, the former Secretary of Commerce who died in a plane crash in 1996, implemented a national export strategy which actively seeks to win export contracts for American companies.

Under Ron Brown, the Commerce Department also launched the Advanced Technology Program (ATP), a government joint venture with private companies which funds what the Commerce Department calls "pre-competitive technologies." These efforts will be the basis of entire industries in the future, thus providing strong export growth, but are now deemed too risky for private capital. Spending on these pre-competitive technologies has shot up from $68 million in 1993 to $431 million in 1995 and is projected to reach almost $750 million by 1997. While some argue whether financing such projects is a wise idea, many argue that ATP is high-tech pork.

The Clinton Administration has made a commitment to liberalize what it has identified as the 12 big emerging markets, or BEMs, over the next decade. By the year 2000, the Commerce Department estimates that the U.S. will export over $200 billion to the BEMs, which include China, India, Indonesia and Brazil—almost as much as current U.S. exports to Europe and Japan combined. The Administration hopes to break down trade barriers in BEMs early in order to avoid increasing the trade deficit.

U.S. Trade with China

United States trade policy toward China has been a topic of much debate because of China's human rights abuses, its piracy of American movies and com-

Courtesy of the Harvard Political Review

"You have to know that the basic problem is that the Chinese are using trade to frighten American companies and the American government . . . It seems Americans need Chinese badly. That is not true; Chinese need Americans badly. Why? You are looking at the whole economic system in China. The production system—the so-called state-run enterprise system—never worked. It lost money. The central government [has] a big budget [and] the money from trade and foreign investment to pay for these losses, these state-run enterprises. The money comes from the West. If you cut off the money, the whole system is upside down . . . This is the fuel that is driving the Chinese communist vehicle."

— Harry Wu
China human rights activist

Value of Imports and Exports

(Billions of Dollars)

From a standstill in 1978, China has now become the world's 11th-ranking trader.

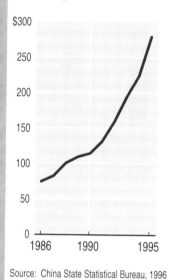

Source: China State Statistical Bureau, 1996

puter software and its treatment of political dissidents, such as the imprisonment of former Tiananmen Square student leaders.

The U.S.-China trade deficit has grown dramatically over the last few years and is now approximately $40 billion, up roughly 17% from 1995. This is due in part to China's free-market reforms, which have attracted $150 billion in foreign investment, much of which is used to produce exports bought in the U.S.

While the high Chinese import tariffs have decreased, all imports still require a permit and little improvement is expected in the foreseeable future. Charlene Barshefsky, the acting U.S. Trade Representative, said that nothing China has put on the table would give U.S. manufacturers or service companies free access to China's markets.

In 1997, China will seek membership in the 124-nation WTO, which would confirm its status as a major trading power and win China the most favorable trading status from member nations. Perhaps more important, by locking in the most favorable U.S. tariff rates, it would tie Congress's hands in using trade policy as a carrot to improve human rights in China.

Beijing also cares deeply about the U.S. Presidential visits scheduled for 1997 and 1998, as they are looking for a permanent renewal of their most favored nation trading status, which allows China the lowest tariff rates to sell their products in the U.S. market.

Beijing has historically been unhappy with U.S. diplomacy. Former Secretary of State Warren Christopher has paid 20 visits to the Middle East but only one to China. Another subject of dissent is Taiwan. In the spring of 1995, after China launched missiles to warn the Taiwanese against declaring independence, Washington responded by sending the U.S. Navy into the Taiwan Strait.

However, despite historically tense relations, both sides seem willing to sit down at the bargaining table. Indeed, there is much to gain financially from an agreement. In July 1997, the international trading port and financial powerhouse of Hong Kong will revert back to Chinese control. The event may foreshadow how China will approach free trade in the future.

Trade with the United States

(Millions of Dollars)

Country	Trade Imbalance		Exports to		Imports from	
Japan	#1	($59,136.5)	#2	$64,342.6	#2	$123,479.1
China	#2	($33,789.6)	#13	$11,753.6	#4	$45,543.2
Canada	#3	($18,122.7)	#1	$127,226.1	#1	$145,348.7
Mexico	#4	($15,392.5)	#3	$46,292.1	#3	$61,684.6
Germany	#5	($14,449.8)	#6	$22,394.3	#5	$36,844.0
Taiwan	#6	($9,682.2)	#7	$19,289.6	#6	$28,971.8
Malaysia	#7	($8,636.6)	#17	$8,816.1	#10	$17,452.8
Italy	#8	($7,486.7)	#16	$8,861.6	#12	$16,348.3
Venezuela	#9	($5,080.4)	#24	$4,640.4	#15	$9,720.8
Thailand	#10	($4,683.1)	#18	$6,665.0	#13	$11,348.1
TOTALS*		($158,703.0)		$584,742.0		$743,445.0

Includes trade with all nations—not just for those listed.

Source: U.S. Department of Commerce, 1995

U.S. Trade with Japan

During the first 10 months of 1996, the U.S. trade deficit with Japan dropped 24%. The decline resulted as American exports to Japan increased and overall U.S. consumption of Japanese imports dropped. Since 1993, exports to Japan have grown 34%. Total exports in 1995 to Japan were $64 billion.

Half of the improvement in the deficit is attributed to the auto sector. U.S. auto exports to Japan increased by 37%, while imports of Japanese cars fell for the first time in a decade.

New trade negotiations with Japan are expected over the course of 1997. Along with talks on autos, there will likely be discussion of the construction industry, as the U.S. has accused Japan of shutting American firms out of the bidding process for Japanese projects.

VIII. Politics and Election 1996

The 1996 Presidential Election

On November 5, 1996, William Jefferson Clinton was re-elected President of the United States without the majority of the popular vote, just as he was in 1992. President Clinton and Vice President Al Gore carried 31 states and the District of Columbia to win re-election with 379 electoral votes (109 more than needed), while capturing 49% of the popular vote overall.

Former Senate Majority Leader Bob Dole—who had retired from his post to concentrate on his campaign—and Republican Vice-Presidential candidate Jack Kemp never overcame Clinton's lead in the polls. They ended with 150 electoral votes and 41% of the popular vote.

Ross Perot, the Reform Party candidate, won 8% of the popular vote, down from the 19% he had captured in the 1992 election. The other 2% was spread among the remaining candidates.

Campaign Statistics

Percentage of Americans who believe politicians don't grant special favors to large campaign contributors:	5
Change since 1980 in the number of people who check the Presidential campaign donation box on their taxes:	-10,000,000
Number of times speakers at the Republican National Convention mentioned Ronald Reagan:	60
Number of times speakers at the Democratic National Convention mentioned Newt Gingrich:	114

Source: *Harper's Magazine* Index

1996 Congressional Elections

Despite Clinton's victory, Republicans retained control of both houses of Congress in 1996. There had been concern that the GOP might lose the hard-won advantage that it gained during the 1994 "Republican Revolution," when the Republicans won a majority in the House of Representatives for the first time in 40 years. This year, all 435 seats were at stake; the GOP managed to hold onto 227 of them, while the Democrats claimed 207. Although the total number of Republican seats slipped slightly (down from 235), they won more than the 218 seats needed to maintain control.

In the Senate, where 34 of the 100 seats were being filled, the Republicans garnered a net gain of two seats for a total of 55. With many outspoken liberal incumbents retiring, the new Senate looked more conservative than the last. The Democrats lost open seats in Alabama, Colorado and Arkansas, but managed to unseat one incumbent, Republican Larry Pressler of South Dakota. Several other Senate incumbents survived strong challenges, including the "Dean of the Senate," Strom Thurmond (R, South Carolina), who was re-elected at the age of 93. Jesse Helms (R, North Carolina), perhaps the Senate's most outspoken conservative, defeated Harvey Gantt (D), who had hoped to become the South's first black Senator since Reconstruction. As for the Democrats, incumbent Paul Wellstone (Minnesota), one of the most outspokenly liberal Senators, survived a rematch with former Senator Rudy Boschwitz (R).

In a high-profile race, Democrat John Kerry of Massachusetts defeated the state's popular Republican governor, William Weld. In New Jersey, Robert Torricelli (D) prevailed over Dick Zimmer (R) for the seat held by retiring Senator Bill Bradley. This hard-fought campaign was highly criticized for "negative advertising" by both sides.

"We need to elect a legislature tha. puts the welfare of America ahead of partisan politics."

— Irvin and Eileen Nol
Key West, Flori.

HOW THE PARTIES FARED

The Race for the Presidency: The Electoral and Popular Votes

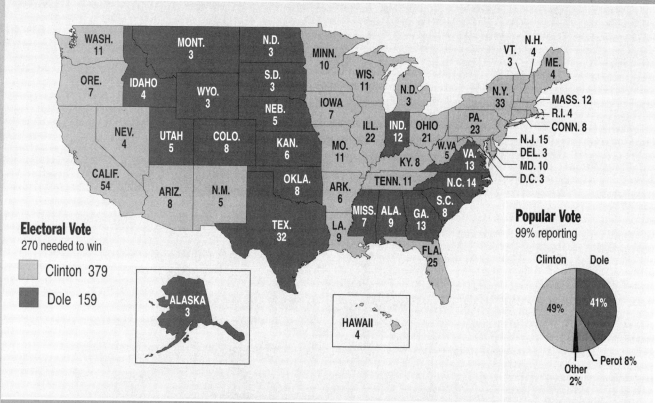

Electoral Vote

270 needed to win

Clinton 379

Dole 159

Popular Vote

99% reporting

Clinton 49%
Dole 41%
Perot 8%
Other 2%

Control of Congress

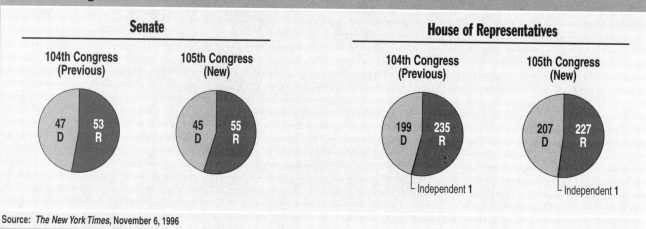

Senate

104th Congress (Previous)
47 D   53 R

105th Congress (New)
45 D   55 R

House of Representatives

104th Congress (Previous)
199 D   235 R
Independent 1

105th Congress (New)
207 D   227 R
Independent 1

Source: *The New York Times*, November 6, 1996

1996: The Issues

Once again, Clinton and his advisors focused on the economy. Clinton boasted that 10 million jobs had been created during his first four years in office and that the unemployment and inflation rates were at impressive lows while the stock market was at a record high.

Dole and the Republicans countered with figures indicating that economic growth was sluggish compared to historical rates and that most of the jobs created were in the low-paying service sector. Republicans blamed the Clinton tax hikes, which affected middle to high-income families, and his reluctance to balance the budget for these ills.

Dole and Kemp endorsed an across-the-board tax cut of 15%. In his campaign speeches, Dole said that the reduction would encourage consumer spending, thereby stimulating the economy and creating jobs. This stance, long endorsed by supply-siders like running mate Jack Kemp, was not received well by voters, who were concerned that the cut would increase the deficit.

Medicare was another hot topic. Democrats accused Republicans of wanting to cut Medicare spending, which would hurt senior citizens. The Republicans contended that they only wanted to reduce the rate at which Medicare spending was increasing rather than make absolute cuts. Clinton himself supported such a cut, though of lesser magnitude.

The Republicans were hurt by some social issues. The issue of abortion divided the party. In addition, Clinton stole some of the "family-value" thunder of the Republicans during his term with many pro-family initiatives such as the Family and Medical Leave Act, student loan increases, a raise in the minimum wage and the Crime Bill of 1994, which Clinton claimed helped lower the crime rate nationwide.

The issue of drugs hurt both parties. The Republicans attributed the increased rate of drug use among teenagers to White House ambivalence and a President who proclaimed on MTV that he would have inhaled marijuana if he could have. Meanwhile, Dole was labeled a puppet of the tobacco lobby when he said that cigarettes had not been proven to be addictive.

Then, late in the campaign, Dole sought to make character a main focus. Clinton had been embarrassed by a steady stream of scandals involving the White House, his tenure as Arkansas governor, as well as his personal life. Reform Party candidate Ross Perot warned voters to expect a "second Watergate" if Clinton were re-elected. Both Perot and Dole cited reports that the Democrats had accepted large amounts of questionable foreign donations.

"I voted, although I know most in my generation didn't. I don't think it's from lethargy, but more so a general distrust of Washington."

— Amy Gwiazda
Screenwrite
New York, New Yor

Voter Apathy

Despite successful initiatives like the Motor Voter law, which registered 15 million new voters in 1995 as they applied for driver's licenses, and the natural-ization of over a million immigrants during the 12 months prior to the November election, voter turnout was still remarkably low. In fact, most Americans had found the campaign boring. According to initial reports, less than 50% of eligible voters participated in the election.

Reasons cited for the disinterest in the 1996 campaign, according to the Pew Research Center for the People and the Press, include a strong economy, the press, excessive polling, negative advertising and bland issues. A total of 65% said that there was less focus on the issues this year than in previous elections. However, 75% of voters felt informed enough to choose among the candidates and believed that the candidates generally slung less mud than in 1992.

Voter Demographics

President Clinton won the majority of votes among female, black and younger voters. Clinton also garnered a high percentage of votes from swing groups (i.e., independents and suburbanites). Clinton's strongest showings were in the West, East and

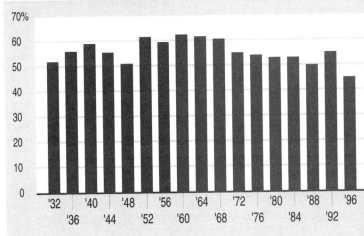

Voter Turnout

Turnout for Presidential Elections, as a Percentage of the Voting-Age Population

Source: Nationwide telephone surveys conducted by *The New York Times* and CBS News

ETHICAL ISSUES FACING THE WHITE HOUSE

	Political Fund-Raising	Independent Counsels	Whitewater	Whitewater Pardons
ISSUE	• Whether the White House condoned or aided the solicitation of legally questionable political contributions by John Huang, a longtime Clinton friend and ally of Indonesian interests who was a top fund-raiser for the Democratic National Committee. • Whether the White House has traded political influence for large campaign contributions.	Four independent counsels, a record number, are examining: • The Clinton's role in Whitewater and other matters. • Efforts to influence former Agriculture Secretary Mike Espy. • The truthfulness of Housing Secretary Henry G. Cisneros. • Business ties of former Commerce Secretary Ronald H. Brown.	• Whether the Clinton's varied dealings with James B. McDougal, owner of a failing Arkansas savings and loan, broke any laws. • Whether Mr. Clinton, as governor, traded influence for promise of financial gain. • Whether the White House illegally obstructed federal inquiries into the matter after Mr. Clinton became President.	• Whether Mr. Clinton should renounce his power to pardon convicted Whitewater felons who might be potential witnesses against him in some future court case.
STATUS	• Mr. Clinton campaigned on a promise to reform political fund-raising. It dropped from his agenda after Congressional Democrats resisted. He has since become the biggest collector of large political donations in Presidential history, watchdog groups say. • The Democratic National Committee returned a questionable $250,000 donation solicited by Mr. Huang. The Justice Department has begun a preliminary inquiry into the matter.	• Whitewater and Espy inquiries are still producing indictments, convictions and some exonerations. Espy resigned. • The Cisneros inquiry continues. • The Brown investigation was effectively closed after his death.	• The Whitewater independent prosecutor says the inquiry is at a "very important" stage. Nine guilty pleas and three convictions have come so far, but none touch on the Clintons. Two others were acquitted of hiding Clinton campaign donations from the I.R.S. • Mr. Clinton calls the inquiry a "clear" political vendetta without "a single solitary shred" of incriminating evidence.	• Mr. Clinton says he will give no "special treatment" to anyone and will obey the law, but he has not ruled out pardons. Bob Dole and Ross Perot accused him of sidestepping a clear conflict of interest.

Source: *The New York Times*, November 1996

"What Clinton does is what any good sailor does: he tacks. The wind is blowing this way, so . . . he shifts his sails and he goes that way. He's still working his way toward the exit sign, but he's not being an idiot about it."

— **Dick Morris**,
former political advisor
to President Clinton

Midwest. Dole, however, performed well in the South, the wheat belt and the mountain states. His strongest advocates were Republicans, conservatives and white Protestants.

Other notable trends affected the voting demographics this year:

• **The Gender Gap.** The gender gap is the difference between a candidate's number of votes from men and women. The term was first coined in 1980, when men were 8% more likely to support Ronald Reagan than women were. Since then, the gender gap had ranged from four to seven points in magnitude until 1996, when there was an 11 point gap between Clinton's voters—with women more likely to vote for Clinton. The gap was observed in all age groups—from 17 points between men and women under 30, to eight points for those in the 45 – 59 age group. A gender gap also exists among black voters, although both black men and women voted overwhelmingly for Clinton.

ETHICAL ISSUES FACING THE WHITE HOUSE (continued)

Missing Billing Records	F.B.I. Files	Travel Office	Withholding Documents	
■ Whether the White House illegally hid from investigators subpoenaed records of Mrs. Clinton's legal work on land deals for McDougal's savings and loan.	■ Why low-level White House aides improperly obtained F.B.I. background files on more than 900 people, including officials of past Republican Administrations. ■ Whether the confidential reports were used for political purposes, an inquiry that has been complicated by a six-month gap in the log book recording access to the files.	■ Whether the 1993 dismissal of the White House travel office staff was part of a plan to shift travel business to Clinton friends. ■ Whether the White House later lied or covered up evidence of wrongdoing. ■ Whether it used the F.B.I. for political gain when it ordered a criminal investigation of the former staff members, who were later cleared.	■ Whether the White House has misused the legal concept of executive privilege to deny Congress potentially embarrassing documents on the travel office firings and its handling of the anti-drug efforts.	**ISSUE**
■ Mrs. Clinton denies any coverup of documents, which show some work on a land swap later ruled fraudulent. ■ The White House gave the records to prosecutors in January, two years after they had been subpoenaed. A secretary had found the documents on a table in the Clintons' private residence five months earlier. ■ Mrs. Clinton testified on the matter before a Whitewater grand jury last January.	■ Mr. Clinton apologized; an aide says the "completely honest bureaucratic snafu" occurred when an outdated personnel roster was used for employee background checks in 1993. Republicans charge a coverup. ■ The Whitewater independent counsel is inquiring, making "substantial progress" toward answers.	■ Mr. Clinton apologized but denied any "discrepancies" in handling the affair. Mrs. Clinton says she was uninvolved. ■ Republicans say White House documents show she ordered the firings. ■ The Whitewater independent counsel's inquiry is making "substantial progress."	■ The White House turned over 2,000 pages of travel office documents last summer after a long battle with Republicans in the House, who charged a systematic coverup. The White House calls the Republican complaints "rumor and innuendo." ■ The White House was still in sole possession of anti-drug campaign documents when Congress adjourned in September.	**STATUS**

Source: *The New York Times*, November 1996

- **Party Loyalty**. In the 1996 election, Clinton was successful at retaining the votes of self-proclaimed Democrats. Even Democrats who described themselves as conservative threw their weight behind the Democratic ticket, but Republicans who characterized their political ideology as liberal were closely divided between Clinton and Dole. Independent voters had split their votes evenly among the three candidates in 1992, but this year Clinton's share of the independent vote increased to 43%, while only 17% supported Perot.

- **Hispanic voters**. Hispanic voters account for an average of 5% of the voting population of the U.S. That figure rises to more than 10% in states like Arizona, Texas and California. Until 1996, Hispanic voters lagged well behind most of the American population in election participation; eligible Hispanics were only about 80% as likely as other Americans to register to vote. However, a sharp increase in voter registration occurred in 1996,

Courtesy of the Harvard Political Review

"Next, I think that campaign finance reform is not going to happen on the inside but will happen when pressure is generated from the outside. It makes it clear why it's important to take money out of politics. Those are the reasons why I'm leaving."

— Bill Bradley,
former Senator (New Jersey)

when Democrats held voter drives to register Hispanics, and from a deep concern among the Hispanic community that Republicans were intent on constraining Hispanic immigration and reducing welfare benefits for immigrants. Not surprisingly, Clinton won three out of four Hispanic votes.

Political Action Committees (PACs)

The most politically active special interest groups during the 1996 election were the Christian Coalition, which handed out 45 million voter guides the Sunday before election day and put tremendous political pressure on Republican candidates to stay "right" on the issues, and the AFL-CIO, which used its hefty $35 million political budget to influence the most contested Senatorial and Congressional elections. In addition, the National Rifle Association bought billboards, newspaper ads and radio spots in support of conservative candidates in about 30 closely contested Congressional races. The National Federation of Independent Businesses, the National Education Association, the National Restaurant Association and the National Association of Realtors also had strong lobbies. Most voters had a negative view of the influence of PACs in the 1996 election and were angry over the amount of money the committees were allowed to contribute to candidates.

Campaign Spending at Record Levels

The issue of campaign finance reform surfaced once again in 1996, amidst allegations that both Democrats and Republicans had raised funds illegally and over the large amounts of questionable funds that were donated to the candidates through their political parties. By law, individuals are allowed to contribute up to $2,000 per candidate, while political action committees are limited to $5,000 per candidate. These rules were established in 1974 and have not been readjusted for inflation.

In order to avoid the constraints of these laws, the majority of money donated to the 1996 campaigns came through what is called the "soft money loophole." Soft money is defined as funds contributed to a political party instead of to a specific candidate. By law, it should be spent by the party on "party-building activities" and not on campaigns. In reality, however, large amounts of soft money are used to finance campaigns and to gain access to powerful politicians. This type of donation poured into campaign coffers in 1996, as there are no limits whatsoever on the size of soft money contributions.

The Federal Election Commission's records indicate that in the first 21 months of the Presidential race, both parties took in nearly $470 million in "soft dollars." Republicans raised $274 million in soft money, significantly more than the Democrats, who raised only $195 million. These 21-month totals amount to more than double what was raised in the entire two years of the 1992 Presidential race.

To put things in perspective, 99.97% of Americans do not make political contributions over $200. In other words, .03% of the population has the strongest political influence.

Who's Giving

Top 10 Overall Campaign Contributors (1996)

Rank	Contributor	Total*	Democrat	Republican
1.	Philip Morris	$2,741,659	$608,704	$2,131,955
2.	AT&T	2,130,045	858,462	1,270,583
3.	Assoc. of Trial Lawyers of America	2,106,325	1,747,725	353,600
4.	Teamsters Union	2,097,410	2,005,250	87,160
5.	Laborers Union	1,938,250	1,778,750	153,500
6.	Int'l. Brotherhood of Electrical Workers	1,821,710	1,785,260	31,950
7.	RJR Nabisco	1,765,306	341,406	1,423,900
8.	National Education Assoc.	1,661,960	1,618,110	38,850
9.	American Medical Assoc.	1,633,530	321,114	1,309,166
10.	American Federation of State/County/ Municipal Employees	1,616,125	1,578,700	32,425

* Includes soft money to the national parties, PAC money to candidates, PAC and individual contributions to the Clinton and Dole campaigns and individual campaign contributions to all federal candidates.

Source: *The New York Times,* November 1996

These issues are being raised as federal financing for the Presidential election is at an all time high. Both Clinton and Dole each received $74 million from the federal government, in theory to release them from having to raise additional money for their campaigns.

The Center for Responsive Politics, a non-profit group that studies campaign finance, estimates that the entire 1996 Presidential race cost about $800 million (three times as much as the 1992 campaign) and that another $800 million was spent on Congressional races. In addition, their reports state that businesses raised $242.4 million for campaigns in 1996, most of which was donated to Republicans. Organized labor, on the other hand, raised $35 million, mostly for Democrats. The top business donor and soft dollar contributor was Wall Street, which gave nearly $60 million, mostly to Republicans.

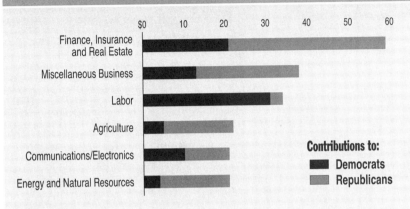

Business Is Top Campaign Spender

Top Six Sectors of Business and Labor in Campaign Contributions, 1/1/95 to 6/30/96, In Millions of Dollars

Finance, Insurance and Real Estate
Miscellaneous Business
Labor
Agriculture
Communications/Electronics
Energy and Natural Resources

Contributions to:
■ Democrats
■ Republicans

* Includes soft money to national parties, PAC money to candidates and PAC and individual contributions to the Clinton and Dole campaigns.

Source: Center for Responsive Politics

Campaign Finance Reform

Many of the campaign finance loopholes arose from the 1976 Supreme Court decision *Buckley vs. Valleo*, which ruled that restrictions on campaign spending were also restrictions on free speech. The court case focused particularly on instances in which individuals could help finance their own campaigns.

In June of 1996, the Supreme Court upheld a decision allowing political parties to spend unlimited funds on candidates' advertisements, and nearly a dozen lower courts upheld the rights of corporations, political action committees and individuals to contribute money to campaigns.

In light of such strong judicial support for unlimited campaign spending, it would be difficult for Congress to draft effective legislation. However, in response to citizens' anger over extravagant campaign spending, President Clinton pledged his support, along with that of other Congressional leaders, to the McCain-Feingold bill, sponsored by Senator John McCain (R, Arizona) and Senator Russ Feingold (D, Wisconsin). This bill would limit personal and corporate spending, restrict out-of-state contributions, eliminate soft money contributed to parties after existing limits on contributions to individual candidates had been reached and ban contributions by corporations and labor unions to parties. In addition, Senators McCain and Feingold said they will amend the bill to bar contributions by non-citizens.

Asian Scandal

In the final days of his campaign, allegations arose that Clinton and the Democratic National Committee had illegally solicited donations from the Lippo Group, a powerful Indonesian banking family, through an executive at the Commerce Department, John Huang. The relationship between wealthy former Lippo Group executive James Riady and Bill Clinton goes back to the President's days as the governor of Arkansas, where Riady was involved in banking.

More than 24 members of Congress (mostly Democrats) have received cash from individuals associated with the Lippo Group. John Huang was suspended from his fund-raising duties after questions were raised about an event he staged

"Congress is now the captive of spe cial interest lobbies, and their ow personal interests ... at the fault the American people. The people must take control of their government once again."

— Charles E. Sac
former U.S. Mari
Vero Beach, Flori

"During my lifetime I have witnessed a marked decline in ethical standards, that of individuals in our society as well as those of our public figures. Dishonesty is not new—but it has become so pervasive in our society . . . "

— Robert Bierig
Hopkington, Massachusetts

last spring at a Buddhist temple in Los Angeles. The fund-raiser involved Vice President Gore and allegedly gathered $140,000 from Buddhist nuns and monks who had supposedly taken vows of poverty.

Nearly a third of the $1 million donated from Riady's associates was donated by an Indonesian couple, Arief and Soraya Wiriandinata, who were relatives of the wealthy former Lippo executive. The couple were resident aliens with green cards who had lived for a time in the Virginia suburbs of Washington. They gave $425,000 to the Democratic party while in the U.S. and another $320,000 after they had returned to Indonesia. Some experts believe that such offshore donations, even by aliens with green cards, violate campaign laws.

Ethics Questions for the Speaker

The Speaker of the House, Newt Gingrich (R, Georgia), faced allegations that his use of tax-exempt foundations—which filtered money into his college course—violated tax law and questions about whether Mr. Gingrich provided 'accurate, reliable and complete' information to a panel of investigators. After more than a year of deliberations, the House subcommittee on ethics recommended Gingrich be charged over $300,000 in punitive damages for the violations, and the Congress overwhelmingly voted in favor of these recommendations. Despite these questions, Mr. Gingrich was re-elected to his position as Speaker.

"The Washington Phrase Book"

Lewis H. Lapham, Editor of *Harper's Magazine*, Spoofs Politics . . .

Maybe politicians thought that the language spoken in Washington was so heavily encrusted with euphemism that it defied translation into the vulgar dialects spoken elsewhere in the country. I had worked out the meanings of a few of the principal words and phrases:

The Deficit:	The dogma or slogan that serves as Washington's replacement for the Cold War. Not one politician in fifty can explain the theory of deficit reduction, but then neither could one politician in fifty explain the mystery of supply-side economics or the mechanics of the hydrogen bomb.
Congressional Debate:	Ritual performances meant to sustain the belief in democracy. Like the church, the government derives its income from the tithes imposed on the faithful and require the proofs of principled disagreement and plain argument. All present on Capitol Hill share the same urgent need for money, but in order to obtain it they must make a successful show of their differences of opinion, belaboring one another with the props and catchphrases of political truism.
The American People:	Admired and excessively praised as an abstraction but distrusted when encountered in person. Too many of them cling to the superstition that their money is their own.
Gridlock:	A comfort presented as an affliction. When speaking for the record, even a first-year Congressman can be counted upon to nominate the condition as the chief obstacle to the just reforms that otherwise would take place no later than next Wednesday afternoon. Speaking privately, all present welcome the condition as the best of the available excuses for the failure to act. Inaction is always preferable to action because actions of even the smallest and most hesitant kind (subtracting the subsidy from the suppliers of mohair or closing down an ancient submarine base) imply friction, and friction is un-American because friction translates into resentment, and resentment loses votes.

Courtesy of Lewis H. Lapham, editor of *Harper's Magazine*

IX. Financial Review

PART I: NOTES FROM THE AUTHOR

Understanding the Financial Review

Just like all public corporations, the federal government is required to produce a set of Consolidated Financial Statements (CFS). These financial statements include a Balance Sheet, which totals all of the assets and liabilities and then gives a "net asset value" for the entity, and the Statement of Operations (or Income Statement), which provides a snapshot of all of the revenues and expenses that the entity had for a given year. (A Cash Flow Statement, which tracks the flows of cash in and out of the entity for a given year, is not provided by the government.)

Of course, accounting for the finances of the federal government can be tricky. It requires different rules and methods than accounting for a corporation. For instance, it is difficult for the government to measure the value of a space shuttle, a federal highway or the education it helps provide in America's public schools.

Specifically, there is much debate about how the government should account for its assets and liabilities. Should the government include Social Security as a liability owed to future generations? Should we count educated citizens as an asset to the federal government? If so, how do we put a dollar figure on that?

The Treasury Department is responsible for compiling the financial statements which are reprinted in this financial review. The Treasury follows rules created by the Federal Accounting Standards Advisory Board. For a complete understanding of their method of accounting, please read "Notes to the Financial Statements," which follow the CFS. The most recent accounting by the Treasury is for fiscal year 1995.

Problems with Federal Accounting

Arthur Andersen and Company, one of the "Big Six" accounting firms, was commissioned in 1993 as consultant to the Treasury Department on the production of the CFS. Arthur Andersen cited the following problems with the way the Treasury presented information:

- **Accuracy and Completeness**. Treasury does not maintain or control the accounting information from which the CFS is prepared. Treasury has established a process to compile the accounting information submitted by federal entities; however, the reliability of the underlying information used to prepare the CFS rests with the individual federal entities. Much of this information is currently either not subject to audit or is considered unreliable as a result of audit. Additionally, because the CFS is prepared primarily from information submitted by the entities prior to audit, the CFS does not reflect certain changes arising from such audits. Treasury's process for identifying and recording changes resulting from audits of federal entities' financial statements is not adequate to detect material misstatements or omissions in the CFS.

"We in the business world are trying to cut costs and balance our budgets. All that we ask is that the government follow in line."

— W. S. McGinn
Bellota Ranc
Tucson, Arizor

- **Accounting and Reporting.** A comprehensive set of accounting standards and reporting criteria do not currently exist for federal entity financial statements. The Federal Accounting Standards Advisory Board is in the process of developing such standards and criteria. For example, the extent to which actual and budget data are reported and reconciled, whether long-lived assets should be capitalized and depreciated, the accounting and reporting for public domain assets, and how social security, pension plans, contingencies and unfunded liabilities should be recorded must be resolved.

- **Consolidation and Analysis Process.** As a result of incomplete or inaccurate reporting by federal entities, it is necessary for Treasury to make adjustments to the submitted information. However, Treasury's accumulation and analysis process, while detecting many errors, is not sufficiently comprehensive to ensure that all significant errors or omissions would be identified.

  The development of a comprehensive approach for preparing the CFS is required, including matters such as (1) communication and disposition of changes resulting from audits, (2) reconciliation and elimination of intra- and inter-entity amounts, (3) adaptation of the consolidation process to respond to evolving accounting standards and reporting requirements, including a discussion of the government's performance, and (4) identification and resolution of CFS reporting entity issues, such as coordination of legal matters and contingencies with entity management and general counsel, and with the Department of Justice.

The good news is that the Government Management Reform Act of 1994 increased the amount of financial information subject to audit by requiring the 24 major executive agencies to undergo agency-wide audits beginning with fiscal year 1996 and requiring that the CFS be audited beginning with fiscal year 1997. Effective implementation of this legislation, combined with a strong commitment on the part of federal entity Chief Financial Officers and Inspectors General, as well as GAO, OMB and Treasury, to address these challenges, is essential to improve the reliability and meaningfulness of the government's financial information.

The discussion, analysis and financial tables in Part II of this Financial Review are reproduced from the Department of Treasury's Certified Financial Statements (CFS) for the U.S. federal government.

PART II: 1995 DEPARTMENT OF THE TREASURY'S CONSOLIDATED FINANCIAL STATEMENTS

Discussion and Analysis

After rapid acceleration in fiscal 1994, economic growth slowed in fiscal 1995 to a rate more in line with steady, long-term trends consistent with low inflation. Despite the slower pace, job growth continued through the fiscal year, with over 2.5 million new jobs added. The unemployment rate remained within a very low 5.4% to 5.7% band. Inflation was well contained, with the underlying rate of inflation dropping below 3% over the fiscal year for the first time in 23 years. The federal budget deficit continued to fall, declining by $39 billion in fiscal 1995, for a total drop of $127 billion over the past three fiscal years.

The Economy in Fiscal 1995

Real gross domestic product (GDP) grew by 2.0% across the four quarters of fiscal 1995, which encompasses the fourth quarter of calendar 1994 through the third quarter of calendar 1995. This was much slower than growth over the four quarters of fiscal 1994, when GDP expanded by 3.9%. That rate of growth had led to increased concerns about a possible speed-up in the rate of inflation, prompting the Federal Reserve Board to tighten monetary policy during the course of fiscal 1994 and on into fiscal 1995. The rate of economic growth dropped from 3.0% at an annual rate in the first quarter of fiscal 1995 to an average of just 0.6% in the next two quarters. Growth accelerated to a 3.8% pace by the final quarter of the fiscal year.

All sectors of the economy slowed in fiscal 1995, but the deceleration was most dramatic in housing. Residential construction (in real terms) had surged by 11.6% over the four quarters of the prior fiscal year after mortgage interest rates dropped to a 25-year low. As rates moved up and growth in jobs and income settled down, expansion of residential housing eased, and by the end of fiscal 1995, residential construction spending was 3.0% lower than at the end of fiscal 1994.

Consumer spending moderated in fiscal 1995 to a 2.4% increase from 3.0% in fiscal 1994, with most of the softness occurring in the second quarter of the fiscal year. Business investment spending also slowed over the fiscal year, especially in the second half. Growth in business fixed investment averaged 13.7% at an annual rate in the first two quarters of the fiscal year but just 4.2% in the final two quarters.

Employment gains also moderated in fiscal 1995, but the economy still added more than 2.5 million new jobs. Most of those jobs were in the private service-producing sector, with especially strong growth in business services. Employment in manufacturing remained essentially flat over the fiscal year after growing by 330,000 in fiscal 1994. The unemployment rate stayed within a very narrow range of 5.4% to 5.7% over the course of fiscal 1995, the lowest rates of unemployment in five years. Broad measures of inflation remained very subdued in fiscal 1995. Consumer prices increased just 2.5% over the year, below the 3.0% rate of increase in fiscal 1994. Declining energy prices contributed to the lower rate, but underlying inflation was also well-behaved. Excluding food and energy, the "core" rate of inflation dipped to 2.9% in fiscal 1995, the first time it has been below 3.0% since 1972.

Growth in the first three quarters of fiscal 1996 started out weak but then

Elizabeth, 83, retired three times and still working in the Juvenile Courts Clerk's Office, would like to have a detailed accounting of the "cost of the government."

— Elizabeth "Jo" Lanteig
Miami, Flori

picked up speed. The economy slowed to a 0.3% rate of growth in the first quarter of the 1996 fiscal year but then accelerated rapidly over the next two quarters. Inflation in fiscal 1996 remains under control—higher energy prices at the beginning of the fiscal year have since receded. Over the next several quarters, the economy is projected to resume a moderate growth rate consistent with its long-term potential.

Budget Results

The federal budget deficit narrowed significantly in fiscal 1995, declining by $39 billion to $163.9 billion, the lowest in six years. After reaching an all-time high of $290.4 billion in fiscal 1992, the deficit has dropped by a total of $126.5 billion over the past three years. As a share of GDP, the deficit fell from 4.7% in fiscal 1992 to 2.3% in fiscal 1995, the lowest share since fiscal 1979.

The large improvement over the last three years resulted partly from passage of the President's Economic Plan in 1993 (the Omnibus Budget Reconciliation Act) and partly from the speed-up in economic growth since 1992. The 1993 Budget Act provided for $505 billion in total deficit reduction across the five years ending in fiscal 1998 from what otherwise would have occurred. That figure was about evenly split between revenue increases and curbs on growth of spending.

In fiscal 1995, growth of outlays was held to $58 billion, or 4.0%. That figure was held down a bit by a timing quirk in the calendar, which artificially boosted outlays in fiscal 1994, and by large asset sales in the deposit insurance account, which are counted as negative outlays. Excluding the timing differences and the outlays of the deposit insurance agencies, growth of outlays in fiscal 1995 was closer to 5.0%.

Outlays for defense continued to decline in fiscal 1995, down by $9.5 billion, or 3.4%. Along with lower defense spending, budget balance was also assisted by declines in farm support payments, resulting from strong farm prices, and in unemployment insurance benefits, reflecting lower unemployment. Net interest payments, in contrast, jumped by $29.2 billion, or 14.4%, in fiscal 1995 due to higher interest rates.

Receipts increased by 7.8% in the fiscal year, which was more than three percentage points faster than the rise in economic activity over the fiscal year, as measured by the nominal value of GDP. Growth of receipts in 1995 was led by an 11.8% advance in corporate income tax receipts, reflecting a strong gain in profits.

The deficit is on track to decline further in fiscal 1996. The fiscal 1996 deficit is expected to fall to $116.8 billion, $47 billion below the fiscal 1995 level. If realized, this would be the smallest deficit in 15 years. It would represent less than a 1.6% share of GDP, the lowest since fiscal 1974.

Revenues and Expenses

The graphs on this page show the amounts of the U.S. government revenues and expenses for fiscal 1995 and 1994. The charts below show categories of revenues by source and a breakdown of the government's expenses by agency. Charts are in billions of dollars. All revenues levied under the government's sovereign power are reported on the cash basis. Revenues earned through government business-type operations and the data supporting the graph of expenses by agency are reported on the accrual basis.

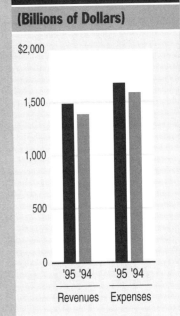

Revenues and Expenses

(Billions of Dollars)

Source: U.S. Department of Treasury

Sources of Revenues

(Billions of Dollars)

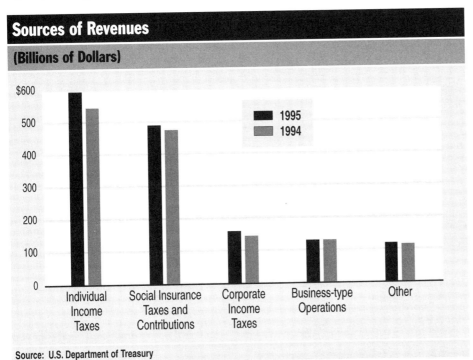

Source: U.S. Department of Treasury

Categories of Expenses

(Billions of Dollars)

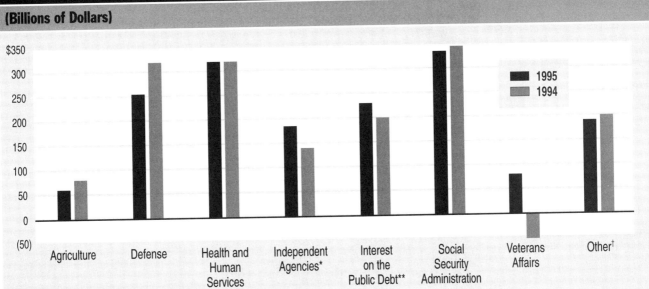

* Includes EPA, GSA, NASA, OPM, SBA and other independent agencies.
** Does not include interest on investments held by government agencies.
† Departmental agencies with expenses less than $50 billion.

Source: U.S. Department of Treasury

Total Assets

(Billions of Dollars)

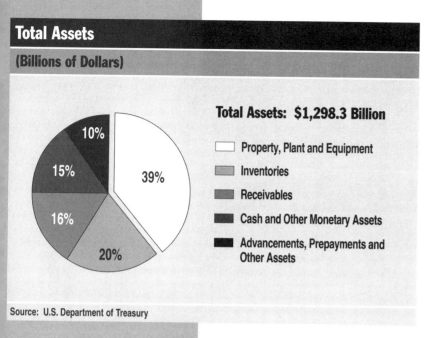

Total Assets: $1,298.3 Billion

☐ Property, Plant and Equipment

▨ Inventories

▨ Receivables

■ Cash and Other Monetary Assets

■ Advancements, Prepayments and Other Assets

Source: U.S. Department of Treasury

Major Categories of Assets as of September 30, 1995

Assets are resources owned by or owed to the federal government that are available to pay liabilities or to provide future public services. The chart depicts the major categories of assets as of September 30, 1995, as a percentage of total assets. The components for each of these categories are contained in Notes to Financial Statements.

Assets, Liabilities, and Accumulated Position as of September 30, 1994 – 1995

The chart below depicts assets, liabilities, and accumulated position reported in the Statement of Financial Position, as of September 30, 1994 – 1995.

Assets, Liabilities and Accumulated Position

(Billions of Dollars)

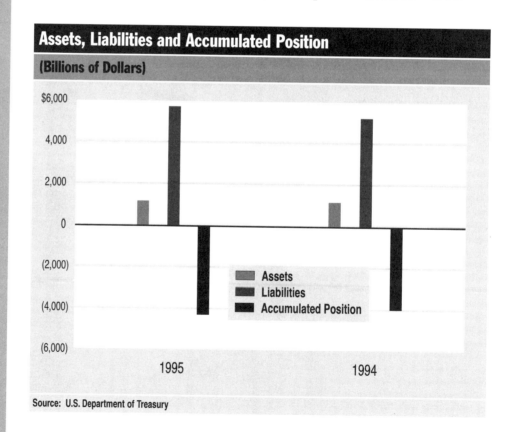

Source: U.S. Department of Treasury

Gross Accounts and Loans Receivable as of September 30, 1995

The amounts in these graphs were derived from the agencies' adjusted trial balances (ATB) as reported on the Federal Agencies' Centralized Trial-Balance System (FACTS). These gross amounts, less allowances, are $79.4 billion and $68.8 billion for accounts receivable and loans receivable, respectively.

Accounts Receivable

(Billions of Dollars)

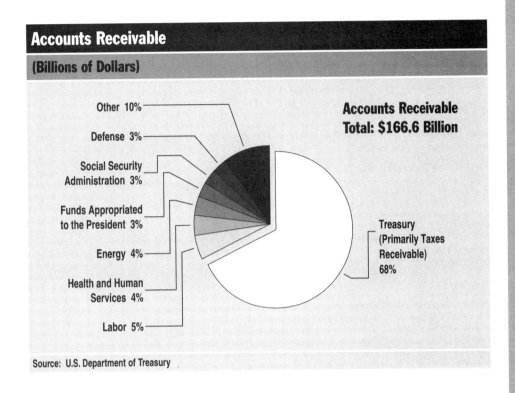

Other 10%
Defense 3%
Social Security Administration 3%
Funds Appropriated to the President 3%
Energy 4%
Health and Human Services 4%
Labor 5%

Accounts Receivable
Total: $166.6 Billion

Treasury (Primarily Taxes Receivable) 68%

Source: U.S. Department of Treasury

Loans Receivable

(Billions of Dollars)

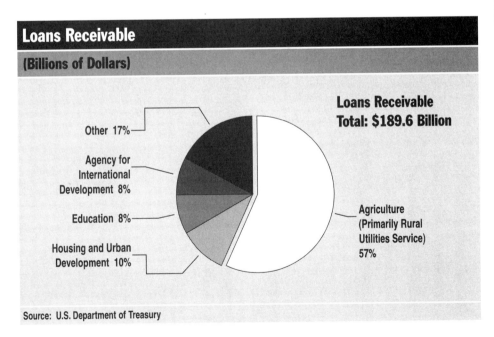

Other 17%
Agency for International Development 8%
Education 8%
Housing and Urban Development 10%

Loans Receivable
Total: $189.6 Billion

Agriculture (Primarily Rural Utilities Service) 57%

Source: U.S. Department of Treasury

Commitments and Contingencies

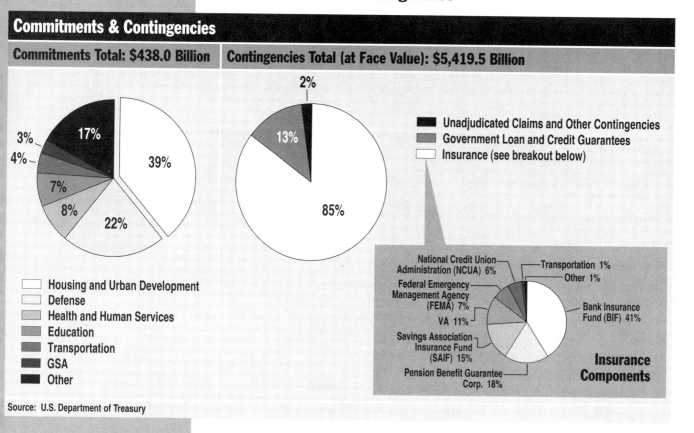

Commitments & Contingencies

Commitments Total: $438.0 Billion

Contingencies Total (at Face Value): $5,419.5 Billion

- Unadjudicated Claims and Other Contingencies
- Government Loan and Credit Guarantees
- Insurance (see breakout below)

- ☐ Housing and Urban Development
- ☐ Defense
- ☐ Health and Human Services
- ☐ Education
- ☐ Transportation
- ☐ GSA
- ☐ Other

National Credit Union Administration (NCUA) 6%
Federal Emergency Management Agency (FEMA) 7%
VA 11%
Savings Association Insurance Fund (SAIF) 15%
Pension Benefit Guarantee Corp. 18%
Transportation 1%
Other 1%
Bank Insurance Fund (BIF) 41%

Insurance Components

Source: U.S. Department of Treasury

Federal Debt

The following charts represent different facets of the net federal debt, excluding intragovernmental investments.

Federal Debt (Billions of Dollars)

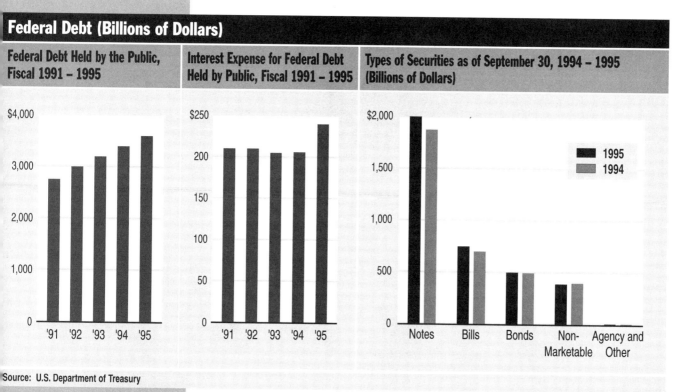

Federal Debt Held by the Public, Fiscal 1991 – 1995

Interest Expense for Federal Debt Held by Public, Fiscal 1991 – 1995

Types of Securities as of September 30, 1994 – 1995 (Billions of Dollars)

■ 1995
■ 1994

Notes | Bills | Bonds | Non-Marketable | Agency and Other

Source: U.S. Department of Treasury

Consolidated Financial Statements

U.S. Government Consolidated Statement of Financial Position (Unaudited)

(Billions of Dollars)	As of September 30, 1995	
	1995	1994*
ASSETS		
Cash	$66.8	$56.3
Other monetary assets (Note 3)	126.7	126.2
Accounts receivable, net of allowances (Note 4)	87.2	76.6
Inventories and related properties	259.1	222.9
Loans receivable, net of allowances (Note 4)	120.8	118.8
Advances and prepayments	24.2	22.8
Property, plant and equipment, net of accumulated depreciation	503.4	576.2
Other assets	109.4	151.1
Total assets	$1,297.6	$1,350.9
LIABILITIES		
Accounts payable	$51.2	$48.4
Interest payable	51.3	45.1
Accrued payroll and benefits	17.3	17.2
Unearned revenue (Note 8)	33.8	36.0
Federal debt held by the public (Note 9)	3,603.3	3,432.3
Pensions and other actuarial liabilities (Note 10)	1,628.2	1,526.2
Other liabilities	425.5	251.9
Total liabilities	$5,810.6	$5,357.1
ACCUMULATED POSITION	$(4,513.0)	$(4,006.2)

The accompanying notes are an integral part of this statement.

* Amounts are restated due to Defense audit adjustments.

Source: U.S. Department of Treasury

U.S. Government Consolidated Statement of Operations (Unaudited)

(Billions of Dollars)	Year Ended September 30, 1995	
	1995	1994*
REVENUES		
Levied under the government's sovereign power:		
Individual income taxes	$590.2	$543.1
Corporate income taxes	157.0	140.4
Social insurance taxes and contributions	484.5	461.5
Excise taxes	57.5	55.2
Estate and gift taxes	14.8	15.2
Customs duties	19.3	20.1
Miscellaneous	27.3	22.0
Earned through government business-type operations:		
Sale of goods and services	$83.0	$82.1
Interest	11.4	10.6
Other	36.0	35.9
Total revenues	$1,481.0	$1,386.1
EXPENSES BY AGENCY		
Legislative branch	$2.9	$2.5
Judicial branch	3.2	2.6
Executive branch:		
Funds appropriated to the President*	$1.8	$1.2
Departments:		
Agriculture	$60.1	$73.6
Commerce	4.7	3.2
Defense (military)**	248.6	274.1
Defense (civil)	30.2	26.5
Education	34.6	29.0
Energy	7.7	26.2
Health and Human Services	342.5	301.2
Housing and Urban Development	34.6	29.0
Interior	9.7	6.7
Justice	9.2	6.9
Labor	39.6	34.3
State	6.2	6.9
Transportation	40.2	37.6
Treasury:		
Interest on debt held by the public	$234.2	$207.7
Other	33.5	26.2
Veterans Affairs	86.5	21.1
Independent:		
Social Security Administration	$362.7	$330.6
Other†	198.3	134.2
Total	$1,791.0	$1,581.3
Veterans Affairs adjustment for actuarial liability change	--	(65.6)
Total expenses	$1,791.0	$1,515.7
EXPENSES IN EXCESS OF REVENUES	$310.0	$129.6

The accompanying notes are an integral part of this statement.

* Includes Executive Office of the President.
** Fiscal 1994 amount includes Defense audit adjustments.
† Includes EPA, GSA, NASA, OPM, SBA, and other independent agencies.

Source: U.S. Department of Treasury

Notes to Financial Statements

1. Summary of Significant Accounting Policies

Principles of Consolidation

The "Consolidated Financial Statements of the United States government, Prototype 1995" (CFS) were prepared using federal agencies' financial data. Agencies submit their pre-closing adjusted trial balances under the Federal Agencies' Centralized Trial Balance System (FACTS) to the Financial Management Service electronically, via the Government On-Line Accounting Link System (GOALS).

The Consolidated Financial Statements report on the financial activity of the legislative, judicial and executive branches of the federal government and those government corporations that are part of the federal government; the Federal Reserve System and the government-sponsored enterprises are excluded. The legislative branch provides limited reports voluntarily. The judicial branch does not provide financial reports to Treasury. Therefore, the financial information on the judicial branch presented in the CFS is an estimate based on the "Final Monthly Treasury Statement."

All significant intragovernmental transactions were eliminated in consolidation.

Basis of Accounting

The Secretary of the Treasury, the Director of the Office of Management and Budget (OMB) and the Comptroller General of the United States, principals of the Joint Financial Management Improvement Program (JFMIP), established the Federal Accounting Standards Advisory Board (FASAB) in October 1990. FASAB recommends accounting standards to the JFMIP principals for approval. Upon approval, they become effective on the date specified in the standards published by OMB and GAO.

In March 1991, the JFMIP principals approved the FASAB's recommendations governing interim accounting standards used in preparing financial statements for audit. Until a sufficient set of comprehensive "generally accepted accounting principles" have been published by JFMIP principals, the revised guidance recommends a hierarchy of "other comprehensive basis of accounting" to be used for preparing federal agency financial statements. The hierarchy is as follows:

Carl Zimmerman points out that the federal government needs to do a great deal more work in creating and explaining an understandable balance sheet for the American people.

— Carl Zimmerma
Augusta, Wiscons

1. Individual standards agreed to and published by the JFMIP principals.
2. Form and content requirements included in OMB Bulletin 93-02, dated October 22, 1992, and subsequent issuance, OMB Bulletin 94-01.
3. Accounting standards contained in an agency accounting policy, procedures manuals and/or related guidance as of March 29, 1991, so long as they are prevalent practices.
4. Accounting principles published by authoritative standard-setting bodies and other sources (1) in the absence of other guidance in the first three parts of this hierarchy, and (2) if the use of such accounting standards improves the meaningfulness of the financial statements.

To date, FASAB has recommended eight accounting standards. However, the majority were not yet effective for fiscal 1995.

Principal Financial Statements

The principal statements are unaudited and consist of the statements of Financial Position and Operations. They use the accrual basis of accounting in their presentation. However, revenues levied under the government's sovereign power are reported on the cash basis.

Other Monetary Assets

As of September 30, In Billions of Dollars

Monetary Asset	1995	1994
Gold*	$100.5	$103.4
U.S. reserve position in the IMF**	14.7	12.0
Special drawing rights	11.0	10.0
Non-purchased foreign currencies	0.3	0.3
Other	0.2	0.5
Total other monetary assets	$126.7	$126.2

* At market value of $385.00 per troy ounce for 1995 and $394.85 for 1994.
** International Monetary Fund

Source: U.S. Department of Treasury

Accounts and Loans Receivable

As of September 30, In Billions of Dollars

	Accounts		Loans	
Receivables	1995	1994	1995	1994
Gross receivables	$166.6	$144.5	$189.6	$181.4
Allowances for losses*	(79.4)	(67.9)	(61.6)	(57.4)
Allowance for subsidy**	--	--	(7.2)	(5.2)
Net receivables	$87.2	$76.6	$120.8	$118.8

* Allowance for losses represents estimated amount of uncollectable receivables.
* Allowance for subsidy represents unamortized credit reform subsidy for direct loans and for defaulted guaranteed loans assumed for collection by the federal government.

Source: U.S. Department of Treasury

Inventories and Related Properties

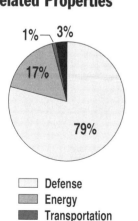

- ☐ Defense
- ☐ Energy
- ☐ Transportation
- ■ Other

Source: U.S. Department of Treasury

Fiscal Year

The fiscal year of the U.S. government ends September 30.

2. Cash

The cash reported in the financial statements represents balances from tax collections, customs duties, other revenues, public debt receipts, foreign currencies and various other receipts maintained in accounts at the Federal Reserve banks and the U.S. Treasury tax and loan accounts.

3. Other Monetary Assets
Gold

Gold is valued at market for fiscal 1995 and 1994. The market value represents the price reported for gold on the London fixing and is based on 261,734,796.787 and 261,806,237.617 fine troy ounces as of September 30, 1995 and 1994, respectively (as reported in Treasury's general ledger). The statutory price of gold is $42.222 per troy ounce.

Special Drawing Rights

The value of special drawing rights is based on a weighted average of exchange rates for the currencies of selected member countries. The value of a special drawing right was $1.5063 and $1.467 as of September 30, 1995 and 1994, respectively.

4. Accounts and Loans Receivable
Summary of Accounts and Loans Receivable Due from the Public

The federal government is the nation's largest source of credit and underwriter of risk. The Debt Collection Act of 1982 (31 U.S.C. 3719) requires agencies to prepare and transmit a report summarizing any outstanding receivables on their books.

Agencies are required to submit those reports to the OMB and the Department of the Treasury. The federal government uses the data in these reports to improve the quality of its debt collection methods.

In 1990, the Credit Reform Act was enacted to improve the government's budgeting and management of credit programs. The primary focus of the act is to provide an accurate measure of the long-term costs of both direct loans and loan guarantees and to include these costs at the time of loan origination. Most direct loans obligated and loan guarantees committed after September 30, 1991, are reported on present value basis.

5. Inventories and Related Properties

Inventories and related properties consist of several categories. Inventory held for sale is tangible personal property that is either (a) being held for sale, (b) in the process of production for sale, or (c) to be consumed in the production of goods for sale or in the provision of services for a fee. Operating materials and supplies are tangible personal property to be consumed in normal operation. Stockpiled materials are strategic and critical materials held due to statutory requirements or for use in national defense, conservation or national emergencies. Other includes forfeited property, foreclosed property, commodities and other. For amounts, see the table to the right.

Agencies use a wide variety of methods to value inventories (e.g., first-in-first-out, last-in-first-out, latest acquisition cost and weighted or moving averages). The Department of Defense uses the latest acquisition method to value its inventories. The Department of Energy uses the lower of cost or market to value its inventories.

6. Property, Plant and Equipment

Property, plant and equipment includes land, buildings, structures and facilities, ships and service craft, industrial equipment in plant and construction-in-progress. It also includes automated data processing software, assets under capital lease, and other fixed assets that have been capitalized.

Land purchased by the federal government is valued at historical costs. The land acquired through donation, exchange, bequest, forfeiture or judicial process is estimated at amounts the government would have paid if purchased at the date of acquisition. No value has been assigned to the Outer Continental Shelf and other offshore lands. More than 651 million acres of public domain land have been assigned a minimal value of $1 per acre and are included in the total land amount.

The accumulated depreciation reported by agencies in 1995 and 1994 was $76.5 billion and $66.8 billion, respectively. Most agencies use the straight-line method. Treasury estimates the depreciation for those agencies that do not report, using the straight-line method applied to the total of reported depreciable assets.

The useful lives for each classification of assets are as follows:
- Buildings: 50 years
- Structures and facilities: 21 years
- Ships and service craft: 13 years
- Industrial equipment in plant: 13 years
- All other assets: 13 years

The largest ownership of federal property, plant, and equipment, except for land, remains within the domain of the Department of Defense, whose major equipment items and weapons systems are valued at acquisition cost. When the acquisition cost cannot be determined, the estimated fair market value of such equipment and the costs of obtaining the equipment in the form and place to be put into use are recorded. Real and personal property are also recorded at acquisition cost.

7. Other Assets

Other assets includes receivables and other assets from banking assistance and failures, deferred retirement costs from the Postal Service and investments held by the agencies and other miscellaneous assets.

Inventories and Related Properties

As of September 30, In Billions of Dollars

Type of Inventory	1995*	1994**
Inventories held for sale	$60.3	$17.9
Operating supplies	57.0	90.9
Stockpiled materials	136.5	92.7
Other	5.3	21.4
Total inventories	**$259.1**	**$222.9**

* Some of the differences between inventory items from 1994 to 1995 are due to Defense reclassifying inventories and recognizing previously unreported inventory items.
** Amounts are restated due to Defense audit adjustments.

Source: U.S. Department of Treasury

Property, Plant and Equipment

As of September 30, In Billions of Dollars

Property/Plant/Equipment	1995	1994*
Military equipment**	$566.8	$475.1
Buildings†	253.0	267.4
Construction in process	85.7	99.8
Other equipment	115.0	102.5
Land	23.0	23.2
Other	12.2	157.8
Subtotal	$1,055.7	$1,125.8
Less accumulated depreciation	(552.3)	(549.6)
Total property, plant & equipment	**$503.4**	**$576.2**

* Amounts are restated due to Defense audit adjustments.
** Some of the differences from 1994 to 1995 are due to Defense reclassifying items such as aircraft and missiles from "other" in fiscal 1994 to military equipment for fiscal 1995.
† Includes: buildings, structures, facilities and lease-hold improvements.

Source: U.S. Department of Treasury

Other Assets

As of September 30, In Billions of Dollars

Assets	1995	1994
Funds appropriated to the President*	$54.9	$70.6
Federal Deposit Insurance Corporation**	5.9	9.9
Resolution Trust Corporation†	13.6	28.5
U.S. Postal Service	28.9	27.2
Other	6.1	14.9
Total other assets	**$109.4**	**$151.1**

* Amount reported for International Monetary Program was analyzed for the first time in fiscal 1995 and as a result the U.S. currency and dollar deposits were found to be overvalued in the prior year. Includes Executive Office to the President.
** Decrease was due to $4.2 billion write-off of advances to financial institutions.
† Decrease was due to reduction in net advances and net subrogated claims.

Source: U.S. Department of Treasury

Unearned Revenue

As of September 30, In Billions of Dollars

Revenue	1995	1994
Funds appropriated to the President*	$14.3	$14.2
Department of the Interior	3.5	3.5
Housing and Urban Development	6.8	7.0
U.S. Postal Service	3.1	2.8
Other	6.1	8.5
Total unearned revenue	$33.8	$36.0

* Includes Executive Office of the President.

Source: U.S. Department of Treasury

8. Unearned Revenue

Unearned revenue represents an obligation to provide goods or services for which payment has already been received. Examples of unearned revenue include unearned rent, unearned subscriptions, and advances from customers. Unearned revenue is summarized by agency (see table on the left).

9. Federal Debt Held by the Public

Total federal debt held by the public amounted to $3,603.3 billion and $3,432.3 billion at the end of fiscal 1995 and 1994, respectively. The two following debt tables on reflect information on borrowing to finance government operations. These tables support the Statement of Financial Position caption "Federal debt held by the public" and are shown net of intragovernmental holdings and unamortized premium or discount. Intragovernmental holdings represent that portion of the total federal debt held as investments by federal entities, including major trust funds.

Summary of Federal Debt Outstanding

As of September 30, In Billions of Dollars	1995 Debt	1995 Avg. Interest Rate	1994 Debt	1994 Avg. Interest Rate
MARKETABLE				
Bills	$742.5	5.897%	$697.3	4.735%
Notes	1,980.4	6.610	1,867.5	6.338
Bonds	522.6	9.134	511.8	9.229
Federal Financing Bank*	15.0	8.917	15.0	8.917
Total marketable debt**	$3,260.5	6.869%	$3,091.6	6.507%
NON-MARKETABLE				
Foreign series	$40.9	7.696%	$42.0	7.363%
Government account series	1,324.3	7.693	1,211.7	7.895
State and local government series	113.4	5.000	137.4	7.011
U.S. savings bonds	181.2	6.763	176.4	6.597
Other	30.4	6.570	30.5	7.927
Total non-marketable debt	$1,690.2	6.210%	$1,598.0	7.667%
Total interest-bearing debt	$4,950.7	6.517%	$4,689.6	6.897%
Non-interest-bearing debt†	23.3		3.2	
Total public debt outstanding	$4,974.0		$4,692.8	
Plus premium on public debt securities	$1.2		$1.3	
Less discount on public debt securities	(81.2)		(78.6)	
Total public debt (Treasury securities)	$4,894.0		$4,615.5	
Agency securities	26.9		28.2	
Total federal securities	$4,920.9		$4,643.7	
Less federal securities held as investments by government accounts	($1,317.6)		($1,211.4)	
TOTAL FEDERAL DEBT HELD BY THE PUBLIC	$3,603.3		$3,432.3	

* These marketable securities for 1995 were issued to the Civil Service Retirement Fund and are not currently traded in the market.

** Types of marketable securities: **Bills**—short-term obligations issued with a term of one year or less; **Notes**—medium-term obligations issued with a term of at least one year (but not more than 10 years); **Bonds**—long-term obligations of more than 10 years.

† Includes matured debt of $22.0 billion and other various non-interest-bearing debt of $1.3 billion for 1995 only.

Source: U.S. Department of Treasury

Federal Debt Held by the Public

As of September 30, In Billions of Dollars	1995 Debt	1995 Avg. Interest Rate	1994 Debt	1994 Avg. Interest Rate
PUBLIC DEBT				
Marketable	$3,260.5	6.869%	$3,091.6	6.507%
Non-marketable	1,690.2	7.500	1,598.0	7.667
Non-interest-bearing debt	23.3		3.2	
Total public debt outstanding	$4,974.0		$4,692.8	
Plus premium on public debt securities	$1.2		$1.3	
Less discount on public debt securities	81.2		78.6	
Total public debt securities	$4,894.0		$4,615.5	
AGENCY DEBT				
Tennessee Valley Authority	$24.8		$26.1	
Farm Credit System Financial Assistance Corporation	1.3		1.3	
Housing and Urban Development	0.1		0.1	
Federal Deposit Insurance Corporation; FSLIC resolution fund	0.2		0.2	
National Archives and Records Administration	0.3		0.3	
Architect of the Capitol	0.2		0.2	
Total agency securities	$26.9		$28.2	
Total federal securities	$4,920.9		$4,643.7	
Less federal securities held as investments by government accounts	$1,317.6		$1,211.4	
TOTAL FEDERAL DEBT HELD BY THE PUBLIC	$3,603.3		$3,432.3	

Source: U.S. Department of Treasury

10. Pensions and Other Actuarial Liabilities

The federal government administers more than 40 pension plans. The largest are administered by the Office of Personnel Management (OPM) for civilian employees and by the Department of Defense (DOD) for military personnel. The majority of the pension plans are defined benefit plans.

The accounting for accrued pension, retirement, disability plans and annuities is subject to several different assumptions, definitions and methods of calculation.

Civilian Employees and Military Personnel

Pension expense for the various federal pension plans is calculated for budgetary purposes by a variety of methods. For financial reporting purposes, federal pension plans report their accumulated benefit obligation (ABO) pursuant to directions under the provisions of Public Law number 95-595. The ABO is calculated with the "unit credit" actuarial cost method. The ABO is recognized as a liability in the Consolidated Statement of Financial Position. An expense is recognized equal to the annual change in the ABO. Most federal pension plans are funded with obligations issued by the Treasury pursuant to the actuarial method and funding requirements specified by the governing law. These plan assets (Treasury bonds or other debt), being obligations of the United States, were eliminated from the consolidated statements.

Civilian

The federal government has both defined benefit and defined contribution pension plans:

- **Defined benefit**. The principal plan is administered by OPM and covers approximately 90% of all federal civilian employees. It includes two components of defined benefits, the Civil Service Retirement System (CSRS) and the Federal Employees' Retirement System (FERS). The basic benefit components of the CSRS and the FERS are financed and operated through the Civil Service Retirement and Disability Fund (CSRDF), and all disbursements for both are made from the CSRDF. Most employees covered by CSRS contribute 7.0% of their basic pay, an amount fixed by statute. The FERS employees contribution is 0.8% in fiscal 1995. The valuation of the retirement program has been prepared by OPM in accordance with Financial Accounting Standard (FAS) 35.

- **Defined contribution**. The Federal Retirement Thrift Investment Board is a federal agency that operates the Thrift Savings Plan. The fund's assets are owned by federal employees and retirees, who have individual accounts. For this reason, the fund is excluded from the CFS, and the fund's holdings of federal debt are considered part of the debt held by the public rather than debt held by the government.

The Thrift Savings Plan is a defined contribution plan for eligible employees covered under the Civil Service Retirement System (CSRS) and the Federal Employees' Retirement System (FERS).

Pensions and Other Actuarial Liabilities, As of September 30*

(Billions of Dollars)	Actuarial Liabilities		Plan Assets		Unfunded Liabilities	
	1995	1994	1995	1994	1995	1994
Civilian retirement—OPM**	$722.4	$694.8	$344.3	$344.3	$378.1	$350.5
Military retirement—Defense	547.7	529.1	148.6	131.8	399.1	397.3
Veterans' compensation and benefits	266.6	213.8	--	--	266.6	213.8
Compensation programs	20.3	20.6	--	--	20.3	20.6
Other pension programs	30.8	27.9	16.2	14.9	14.6	13.0
Other benefits	40.4	40.0	35.9	32.0	4.5	8.0
Total	$1,628.2	$1,526.2	$545.0	$523.0	$1,083.2	$1,003.2

* Does not include actuarial liability for future costs of post-retirement health benefits.

** OPM's accumulated benefit obligation is presented as of the beginning of the year, under FAS 35. To make the unfunded liabilities more meaningful, plan assets are also presented at the same valuation date.

Source: U.S. Department of Treasury

FERS employees may contribute up to 10% of base pay to the plan, which is matched by the government up to 5%. CSRS employees may contribute up to 5% of base pay with no government match. An individual's total annual contribution could not exceed $9,500 in 1995.

The plan was started in April 1987 and as of September 30, 1995, the total invested was $33.1 billion. Investments consist primarily of U.S. government non-marketable certificates of $21.2 billion, which are included in "Federal debt held by public" in the Statement of Financial Position. In addition, $9.9 billion and $2.0 billion have been invested in the Common Stock Index and the Fixed Income Funds, respectively.

Military

The Department of Defense Military Retirement Fund was authorized in Public Law Number 98-94 for the accumulation of funds in order to finance liabilities of the Department of Defense under military retirement and survivor benefit programs. The fund provides retirement benefits for military personnel and their survivors.

Veterans' Compensation and Pension Benefits

Veterans or their dependents receive compensation benefits if the veteran was disabled or died from military-service-connected causes. War veterans or their dependents receive pension benefits, based on annual eligibility review, if the veterans were disabled or died from nonservice-connected causes. Certain pension benefits are subject to specific income limitations.

VA has a liability for benefits expected to be paid in future fiscal years to veterans and, if applicable, their survivors who have met or are expected to meet defined eligibility criteria. The liability of the Compensation and Pension Programs (C&P) is not currently funded, nor is there any intent to do so. Rather, payments for benefits that become due in a particular year are financed from that year's appropriation, in effect, on a pay-as-you-go basis. Payments of the liability as it becomes due rely on Congressional authorization of future tax revenues or other methods, such as public borrowing, for their financing.

The actuarial present value of the liability of C&P benefits as determined by VA on September 30, 1995 and 1994, is shown in the table to the right.

Compensation Programs

This amount represents the estimated future costs for injuries incurred to date for approved Federal Employees' Compensation Act cases and Black Lung cases.

Other Pension Programs

Other annual pension reports received from plans covered by Public Law Number 95-595 are reported in the same manner as those for military personnel and civilian employees (described earlier).

Other Benefits

Other benefits consist of various items for which the government is responsible, such as life insurance benefits for veterans and federal employees. VA insurance includes the following programs: United States Government Life Insurance; National Service Life Insurance; Veterans Insurance and Indemnities; Veterans Special Life Insurance; Veterans Reopened Insurance; Service Disabled Veterans Insurance; and Servicemen's Group Life Insurance.

The federal insurance program is the Federal Employees' Government Life Insurance. These other benefits do not include the actuarial liability for the future costs of post-retirement health benefits for retirees.

Post-Employment Benefits Other Than Pensions

The federal government operates a pay-as-you-go system for health benefits for both civilian and military retirees. The actuarial estimates on retirees' health care costs are summarized below.

Veterans' Compensation and Benefits

As of September 30, In Billions of Dollars

Compensation/Benefit	1995	1994
Compensation:		
Veterans	$169.3	$137.4
Survivors	59.7	45.2
Total compensation	$229.0	$182.6
Pension and burial benefits:		
Veterans	$23.7	$19.8
Survivors	10.3	8.8
Burial	3.6	2.6
Total pension and burial	$37.6	$31.2
Total compensation and benefits	$266.6	$213.8

Source: U.S. Department of Treasury

Civilian Employees Retiree Health Benefits

Generally, employees are eligible for post-retirement health benefits if they participated in the program for the five years immediately preceding their retirement. As a condition of participation, retirees must make contributions toward their premiums, which, for the vast majority, are deducted directly from their monthly annuity payments. Contributions for future post-retirement health benefit premiums are required neither of active employees nor their employers.

The Federal Accounting Standards Advisory Board (FASAB) has recommended standards for the calculation and reporting of a retirement health benefits obligation. These standards were promulgated in the Statement of Federal Financial Accounting Standards Number 5, (SFFAS No. 5), Accounting for Liabilities of the Federal Government, issued in December 1995.

When it is effective, the standard will require the use of the accrual method of accounting to recognize the cost of retirement health benefits over the active years of employee service. Upon the implementation of SFFAS No. 5, the program will recognize a retirement obligation (RO), which is the future cost of retirement benefits for future retirees relating to active service rendered up to the date of implementation. The program plans to adopt the standard no later than fiscal 1997, as required by SFFAS No. 5.

In computing the program's RO, an actuary will apply actuarial assumptions to historical health benefit cost information to estimate the future cost of retirement benefits for current and future retirees. This estimate will be adjusted for the time value of money (through discounts for interest) and the probability of having to pay (by means of decrements, such as those for death and withdrawal).

Although the standard has not yet been implemented by the program, the initial (or transition) RO has been calculated in accordance with methodology prescribed to be $113.4 billion on October 1, 1994, and $103.5 billion on October 1, 1993. [Note: Due to the time frame under which these statements must be prepared and audited, all of the information needed to compute the RO as of the end of the year is not available. Therefore, the RO is presented as of the beginning of the year.] The program's RO expense in 1995 would be $12.3 billion and $11.6 billion for 1994, rather than the $4.2 billion for 1995 and $3.8 billion for 1994 recognized as contributions expense (deductions from plan assets) under current accounting practice. Based on this calculation, employing agencies would have been required to recognize a 1995 retirement health benefit expense of $1,844 per enrolled employee for 1995 and $1,839 for 1994.

In these calculations, an annual rate of increase in health benefits costs and a discount rate of 7.0% were assumed. Demographic assumptions are based on the experience of the retirement program, with adjustments based on recent health benefits program trends and experience. For more information, see OPM's financial statements.

Military Retiree Health Plans

Military retirees and their dependents are entitled to health care in military medical facilities if the facility can provide the needed care. Until they reach age 65, military retirees and their dependents also are entitled to health care financed by the Civilian Health and Medical Programs of the Uniformed Services

Retiree Health Care Costs

As of September 30, In Billions of Dollars

Actuarial Estimates, Unfunded	1995	1994
Military health programs	$210.2	$203.7
Federal Employees Health Benefits Program	113.4	103.5
Total unfunded retiree health care costs	$323.6	$307.2

Source: U.S. Department of Treasury

(CHAMPUS). No premium is charged for CHAMPUS-financed care, but there are deductible and co-payment requirements.

After they reach 65 years of age, military retirees are entitled to Medicare. The Department of Defense costs for retiree health care include costs of buildings, equipment, education and training, staffing, operations, and maintenance of military medical treatment facilities. They also consist of claims paid by CHAMPUS and the administration of that program.

Costs are funded annually by direct appropriations in the year services are rendered (or, for CHAMPUS, billed). The cost of the 1994 CHAMPUS program was $3.3 billion, which includes both the benefit cost and the program administration cost. The funded cost of CHAMPUS was $3.3 billion. The estimate of the actuarial liability for military health programs for fiscal 1997 is $210.2 billion.

11. Other Liabilities

Other reported liabilities are summarized by agency in the adjacent table. Included in other liabilities are liabilities arising from loan guarantees, capital leases and contingencies. They also include checks outstanding, the liabilities incurred from bank resolution and litigation losses and other miscellaneous accrued liabilities.

12. Accumulated Position

The accumulated position, as presented in the table below, represents the excess of liabilities over assets. It does not, however, reflect the range of the government's resources, such as the sovereign power to tax, beyond the conventional assets.

13. Leases

Federal agencies were first required to provide financial information about lease commitments in 1986. Agencies are attempting to accumulate the lease information required. The future aggregate minimum rental commitments for noncancelable capital and operating leases as of September 30, 1995, are detailed in the chart below right.

The majority of these lease commitments relate to buildings, equipment and office space rental. The current portions of lease costs are included in accounts payable. The long-term portion of capital leases is reported as "other liabilities." Data for intragovernmental leasing transactions were not available at the time of publication.

14. Social Security and Medicare

A liability of $33.0 billion for Social Security is recognized in "other liabilities" for any unpaid amounts due as of the reporting date. No liability is recognized for future payment not yet due.

The Congress and the trustees of the funds prepare actuarial estimates on an "open group" basis, a financing

Other Liabilities

As of September 30, In Billions of Dollars

Liability	1995	1994
Funds appropriated to the President	$6.9	$8.7
Departments:		
Agriculture	$10.5	$10.9
Defense	1.1	5.3
Education	17.8	15.2
Energy*	214.3	58.9
Health and Human Services**	22.4	58.8
Housing and Urban Development	13.7	17.1
Labor	29.3	27.9
Treasury	34.9	22.6
Veterans Affairs	6.6	6.1
Other	68.0	20.4
Total liabilities	$425.5	$251.9

* Includes environmental cleanup cost of $196.8 billion.
** Includes SSA, which is now an independent agency.

Source: U.S. Department of Treasury

Accumulated Position

As of September 30, In Billions of Dollars

	1995	1994
Accumulated at beginning of period	($4,006.2)	($3,876.6)
Prior period adjustment*	(196.8)	--
Current period results**	(309.3)	(129.6)
Accumulated position at end of period	($4,512.3)	($4,006.2)

* In the past, the Department of Energy reported most of the environmental cleanup cost as "other contingencies." In fiscal 1995, the entire $196.8 billion cleanup cost is reported as a liability.
** For 1994, includes Defense audit adjustments.

Source: U.S. Department of Treasury

Leases for Fiscal 1996 and Beyond

(Billions of Dollars)	Operating Leases	Capital Leases
1996	$2.2	$0.2
1997	1.9	0.2
1998	1.6	0.1
1999	1.4	0.1
Thereafter	6.1	1.6
Total leases	$13.2	$2.2

Source: U.S. Department of Treasury

Social Security and Medicare

As of September 30, In Billions of Dollars

Actuarial Amounts	1995	1994
Actuarial expenditures	$21,255.9	$21,747.3
Actuarial contributions	18,423.2	18,909.2
Actuarial surplus/deficit	($2,832.7)	($2,838.1)

Source: U.S. Department of Treasury

method they regard as appropriate for social insurance programs, namely, that future workers will be covered by the program as they enter the labor force.

The present values of all contributions and expenditures are computed on the basis of economic and demographic assumptions described as "Alternative II" in the "1995 Annual Report of the Board of Trustees of the Federal Old-Age and Survivors Insurance and Disability Insurance Trust Funds." Alternative II is the "intermediate" set of assumptions and represents the trustees' "best estimates" of future economic and demographic conditions. In determining present values, total contributions and expenditures for the trust funds are estimated for a period of 75 years into the future.

The actuarial amounts in the table below, prepared by the Social Security Administration, are calculated on the basis of the preceding assumptions.

Medicare has total actuarial expenditures of $3,043.5 billion for the Federal Hospital Insurance Trust Fund (Part A), which is the present value of outlays projected between October 1, 1995, and September 30, 2020. This amount includes the present value of claims incurred to October 1, 1995, but unpaid as of that date and any administrative expenses related to those claims incurred by unpaid outlays. The Federal Hospital Insurance Program has a total deficit of $1,049.4 billion.

The $3.3 billion in Federal Supplementary Medical Insurance Trust Fund (Part B) liabilities represents the amount of unpaid benefits as of October 1, 1995, and the related administrative expenses. The Federal Supplementary Medical Insurance program has a total surplus of $17.4 billion.

The Secretary of the Department of Health and Human Services annually determines the amount to be paid by each Supplementary Medical Insurance enrollee and by the Department of the Treasury, under the authority of section 1839 of the Social Security Act.

Commitments of the U.S. Government

Years Ended September 30, In Billions of Dollars

Commitments	1995	1994
Long-term leases		
General Services Administration	$11.7	$9.7
Tennessee Valley Authority	0.5	0.6
U.S. Postal Service	1.7	1.5
Other	1.5	1.8
Subtotal	$15.4	$13.6
Undelivered orders, public		
Defense*	$94.8	$52.6
Education	30.3	24.3
Health and Human Services	36.3	36.5
Housing and Urban Development	171.7	189.8
Transportation	17.6	16.4
Other	71.9	65.4
Subtotal	$422.6	$385.0
Total commitments	$438.0	$398.6

Includes Army, Air Force and Defense agencies. Reporting is more complete.

Source: U.S. Department of Treasury

15. Commitments and Contingencies

Commitments are long-term contracts entered into by the federal government, such as leases and undelivered orders, which represent obligations.

Contingencies involve uncertainty as to a possible loss to the federal government that will be resolved when one or more future events occur. Contingencies of the federal government include loan and credit guarantees, insurance and unadjudicated claims.

In accordance with OMB Bulletin 94-01, "Form and Content of Agency Financial Statements," estimated losses for commitments and contingencies, namely, insurance, indemnity agreements, unadjudicated claims and commitments to international institutions, are reported if the amounts can be reasonably estimated and the losses are probable. OMB Bulletin 94-01 establishes guidelines for the reporting of liabilities for loan guarantees and capital leases.

OMB Bulletin 94-01 states that contingencies that do not meet all the conditions for liability recognition should be disclosed. The table to the left and the table on the following page show the face value of commitments and contingencies reported by federal agencies. The amounts reported in the commitments and contingencies table are presented without regard to the probability of occurrence and without deduction for existing and contingent assets that might be available to offset potential losses.

"Long-term leases" includes both operating and capital leases. "Government loan and credit guarantees" includes guarantees in force as well as contracts to guarantee. "Insurance" includes insurance in force, contracts to insure and indemnity agreements.

In 1993, the Congress approved the Resolution Trust Corporation Completion Act, which was signed into law by the President on December 17. The Completion Act provided for the release of up to $18.3 billion of previously appropriated funds that had been returned to the Treasury in 1992, bringing the total funds provided for resolution costs of institutions coming under the control of the Resolution Trust Corporation (RTC) to $105 billion.

The total amount of funds needed to cover losses of institutions coming under the control of the RTC cannot be fully determined until all of the RTC's assets and liabilities have been disposed of. The audited financial statements of the RTC for its final fiscal year (calendar year 1995) estimate the amount to be $87.8 billion, however. If that estimate proves correct, covering RTC losses will not require $17.1 billion of the $18.3 billion made available by the Completion Act.

The total cost of protecting depositors in insolvent thrift institutions is subject to too many unknown factors to estimate. This point has gained emphasis from the July 1, 1996, decision of the United States Supreme Court in *The United States of America v. Winstar Corporations*, affirming the ruling of the U.S. Court of Appeals for the Federal Circuit, that in changing supervisory good-will accounting by statute (FIRREA), the United States became liable for damages for breach of contract.

The Department of Energy manages one of the largest environmental programs in the world. The primary focus of the program is to reduce health and safety risks from radioactive waste and contamination resulting from production, development and testing of nuclear weapons. The Department of Energy issued in fiscal 1995 its first annual Baseline Environmental Management Report (BEMR).

The estimate of the life-cycle costs for the environmental management program ranges from $200 to $350 billion in constant 1995 dollars. The estimate begins in fiscal 1995 and ends in approximately 2070, when environmental activities are projected to be substantially completed. In fiscal 1995, the Department of Energy recorded a liability of $196.8 billion. For more information, see the Department of Energy's financial statements.

The federal government, in 1995, continued to be the nation's largest source of credit and underwriter of risk. Large portions of all non-federal credit outstanding have been assisted by federal credit programs, government-sponsored enterprises or deposit insurance. In particular, most credit for housing, agriculture and education is federally guaranteed.

Contingencies of the U.S. Government

Years Ended September 30, In Billions of Dollars

Contingencies	1995	1994
Insurance:		
FDIC Bank Insurance Fund	$1,915.3	$1,887.6
FDIC Savings Association Insurance Fund	708.6	691.1
Federal Emergency Management Agency	325.8	267.1
National Credit Union Administration	255.6	255.5
Pension Benefit Guaranty Corp.	853.0	950.0
Transportation*	2.0	578.8
Veterans Affairs	504.9	523.2
Other	58.0	43.2
Subtotal	$4,623.2	$5,196.5
Government loan and credit guarantees:		
Agriculture	$15.5	$15.6
Education	90.2	77.2
Export-Import Bank	28.9	29.2
Housing and Urban Development	438.3	408.2
Small Business Administration	28.3	24.4
Veterans Affairs	59.0	63.1
Other	24.7	21.0
Subtotal	$684.9	$638.7
Unadjudicated claims:		
Health and Human Services	$25.6	$22.9
Transportation	30.0	30.0
Other	4.1	0.6
Subtotal	$59.7	$53.5
Other contingencies:		
Defense	$26.8	$24.0
Energy**	--	180.0
Housing and Urban Development	11.9	19.4
Multilateral Development Banks	6.5	6.5
Other	6.5	6.8
Subtotal	$51.7	$236.7
Total contingencies	$5,419.5	$6,125.4

* Decrease is due to more appropriate disclosure.

** Decrease is due to recognition as a liability.

Source: U.S. Department of Treasury

PART III. SUPPLEMENTAL TABLES FOR STATE AND LOCAL GOVERNMENT

The most recent data compiled for state and local governments (1994) show that state and local governments spend close to a trillion dollars each year (the federal government spends $1.6 trillion) and ran a deficit of about $47 billion in 1994. The accumulated debt for state and local governments is $410 billion—which looks relatively small compared to the federal debt of almost $5 trillion.

State and Local Government Receipts and Current Expenditures (Fiscal Year 1994)

(Billions of Dollars)	Fiscal Year 1994
RECEIPTS	
Personal tax and non-tax receipts:	
Income taxes	$125.7
Non-taxes	23.4
Other	20.9
Total	$170.0
Corporate profits tax accruals	30.9
Indirect business tax and non-tax accruals:	
Sales taxes	$227.4
Property taxes	205.1
Other	47.4
Total	$479.9
Contributions for social insurance	$69.7
Federal grants-in-aid	$195.9
Total receipts	$946.4
EXPENDITURES	
Consumption expenditures	$651.7
Transfer payments to persons	$267.4
Net interest paid:	
Interest paid	$64.2
Less interest received by government	114.0
Total	($49.8)
Less dividends received by government	$11.4
Subsidies less current surplus of government enterprises:	
Subsidies	$0.4
Less current surplus of government enterprises	11.6
Total	($11.2)
Less wage accruals less disbursements	0.0
Total liabilities	$846.6
SURPLUS/(DEFICIT), NATIONAL INCOME AND PRODUCT ACCOUNTS	$99.7

Source: Bureau of Economic Analysis, U.S. Department of Commerce

State and Local Government Receipts, Current Expenditures and Gross Investment (Fiscal Year 1994)

(By Function, In Millions of Dollars)	Current Expenditures	Gross Investment	Total*
Central executive, legislative, and judicial activities:			
Administrative, legislative, and judicial activities	$29,540	$1,252	$30,792
Tax collection and financial management	31,940	759	32,699
Total	$61,480	$2,011	$63,491
Civilian safety:			
Police	$39,891	$1,753	$41,644
Fire	16,384	1,225	17,609
Correction	32,133	3,322	35,455
Total	$88,408	$6,300	$94,708
Education:			
Elementary and secondary	$244,719	$24,252	$268,971
Higher	54,604	9,256	63,860
Libraries	4,245	562	4,807
Other	15,277	360	15,637
Total	$318,845	$34,430	$353,275
Health and hospitals:			
Health	$21,858	$1,299	$23,157
Hospitals	2,406	3,762	6,168
Total	$24,264	$5,061	$29,325
Income support, social security, and welfare:			
Government employees retirement and disability	($7,570)	—	($7,570)
Workers' compensation and temporary disability insurance	8,648	—	8,648
Medical care	146,596	—	146,596
Welfare and social services	72,237	484	72,721
Total	$219,911	$484	$220,395
Housing and community services:			
Housing, community development, and urban renewal	$640	$4,394	$5,034
Water	(3,214)	7,868	4,654
Sewerage	(833)	10,766	9,933
Sanitation	5,173	1,355	6,528
Total	$1,766	$24,383	$26,149
Energy:			
Gas utilities	($356)	$434	$78
Electric utilities	(6,082)	5,003	(1,079)
Total	($6,438)	$5,437	($1,001)
Transportation:			
Highways	$46,370	$43,282	$89,652
Water	(125)	1,351	1,226
Air	(1,540)	4,103	2,563
Transit and railroad	12,845	5,845	18,690
Total	$57,550	$54,581	$112,131
Commercial activities:			
Publicly owned liquor store systems	($425)	$6	($419)
Government-administered lotteries and parimutuels	(10,196)	—	(10,196)
Other	(28)	275	247
Total	($10,649)	$281	($10,368)
Veterans' benefits and services	$158	$26	$184
Recreational and cultural activities	11,184	3,834	15,018
Agriculture	3,924	231	4,155
Natural resources	7,329	1,516	8,845
Economic development, regulation, and services	6,512	216	6,728
Labor training and services	5,288	144	5,432
Net interest paid**	$10,827	—	$10,827
Other and unallocable	46,275	7,708	53,983
TOTAL	$846,634	$146,643	$993,277

* Sum of current expenditures and gross investment.
** Excludes interest received by social insurance funds, which is netted against expenditures for the appropriate functions.

Source: Bureau of Economic Analysis, U.S. Department of Commerce

State Finances: Revenue, Expenditures, Debt and Taxes (Fiscal Year 1994)

(Dollars in Millions, except per capita)	Revenue	Expenditures	Debt	Per capita taxes*
Alabama	$11,599	$10,815	$3,854	$1,130
Alaska	6,203	5,752	3,585	2,047
Arizona	11,749	10,522	3,170	1,388
Arkansas	6,870	6,078	1,812	1,295
California	115,228	105,831	48,120	1,581
Colorado	10,425	8,903	3,263	1,136
Connecticut	11,993	12,964	13,599	2,073
Delaware	3,237	2,617	3,397	2,045
Florida	34,805	32,284	14,565	1,276
Georgia	18,265	16,823	5,174	1,245
Hawaii	5,698	5,806	5,146	2,539
Idaho	3,628	2,989	1,281	1,427
Illinois	31,897	29,449	20,355	1,317
Indiana	15,813	15,048	5,572	1,266
Iowa	8,961	8,101	1,990	1,460
Kansas	7,474	6,654	1,103	1,439
Kentucky	11,730	10,541	6,744	1,488
Louisiana	13,524	12,936	8,782	1,016
Maine	4,098	3,902	2,993	1,423
Maryland	15,581	14,203	9,130	1,515
Massachusetts	22,298	22,454	26,681	1,824
Michigan	31,814	29,305	11,505	1,624
Minnesota	17,182	15,278	4,351	1,894
Mississippi	7,697	6,796	2,066	1,246
Missouri	13,359	11,549	6,512	1,112
Montana	3,166	2,778	2,108	1,356
Nebraska	4,446	3,991	1,468	1,321
Nevada	4,767	4,203	1,685	1,634
New Hampshire	3,081	3,179	5,651	736
New Jersey	29,808	29,606	22,894	1,707
New Mexico	6,709	5,995	1,735	1,826
New York	82,202	76,871	65,078	1,806
North Carolina	21,051	19,040	4,538	1,488
North Dakota	2,289	2,083	757	1,387
Ohio	40,836	33,422	12,117	1,278
Oklahoma	9,184	8,493	3,873	1,308
Oregon	10,886	9,104	5,645	1,309
Pennsylvania	38,252	37,818	13,671	1,422
Rhode Island	4,131	3,745	5,544	1,440
South Carolina	11,268	11,209	4,972	1,229
South Dakota	2,041	1,826	1,680	914
Tennessee	12,725	11,940	2,627	1,108
Texas	45,035	40,967	9,378	1,059
Utah	5,907	5,132	2,103	1,266
Vermont	2,026	1,913	1,570	1,435
Virginia	17,295	15,523	7,912	1,227
Washington	19,379	19,577	8,266	1,816
West Virginia	6,349	6,190	2,525	1,402
Wisconsin	19,617	15,281	7,748	1,658
Wyoming	2,308	1,975	702	1,553
UNITED STATES	**$845,887**	**$779,459**	**$410,998**	**$1,439**

*Per capita amounts are based on population figures of the resident U.S. population (excluding the District of Columbia) as of July 1, 1994.

Source: U.S. Census Bureau, U.S. Department of Commerce

X. The Clinton Administration

President: William Jefferson Clinton
Vice President: Albert Gore, Jr.

Designates as of January 1, 1997

The White House Staff
1600 Pennsylvania Avenue, NW
Washington, D.C. 20500
(202) 456-1414
Chief of Staff — Erskine B. Bowles
Assts. to the President & Deputy Chiefs of Staff — Sylvia Matthews and John Podesta
Council of Economic Advisers — Daniel K. Tarullo, chmn.
National Economic Council — Gene Sperling, dir.
National Security Advisor — Samuel L. Berger
Central Intelligence Agency — Anthony Lake, dir.
Office of Management and Budget — Franklin D. Raines, dir.
U.S. Trade Representative — Charlene Barshefsky
Environmental Protection Agency — Carol M. Browner, admin.

Department of State
2201 C Street, NW
Washington, D.C. 20520
(202) 647-4000
Secretary of State — Madeleine K. Albright
Deputy Secretary — Strobe Talbott
Chief Delegate to the U.N. — Bill Richardson

Department of the Treasury
1500 Pennsylvania Avenue, NW
Washington, D.C. 20220
(202) 622-2000
Secretary of the Treasury — Robert E. Rubin
Deputy Secretary of the Treasury — Lawrence H. Summers

Department of Defense
The Pentagon
Washington, D.C. 20301
(703) 545-6700
Secretary of Defense — William S. Cohen
Chairman, Joint Chiefs of Staff — Gen. John Shalikashvili
Secretary of the Army — Togo West
Secretary of the Navy — John Dalton
Secretary of the Air Force — Dr. Sheila Widnall

Department of Justice
Constitution Avenue & 10th Street, NW
Washington, D.C. 20530
(202) 514-2000
Attorney General — Janet Reno
Dep. Attorney General — Jamie Gorelick
Federal Bureau of Investigation — Louis J. Freeh, dir.
Immigration & Naturalization Service — Doris Meissner

Department of the Interior
C Street, 18th & 19th Streets, NW
Washington, D.C. 20240
(202) 208-3171
Secretary of the Interior — Bruce Babbitt
Deputy Secretary — John Garamendi

Department of Agriculture
The Mall, 12th & 14th Streets
Washington, D.C. 20250
(202) 447-2791
Secretary of Agriculture — Daniel R. Glickman

Department of Commerce
14th Street, Constitution & E. Street, NW
Washington, D.C. 20230
(202) 482-2000
Secretary of Commerce — William M. Daley

Department of Labor
200 Constitution Avenue, NW
Washington, D.C. 20210
(202) 219-5000
Secretary of Labor — Alexis M. Herman
Deputy Secretary — Thomas P. Glynn
Bureau of Labor Statistics — Katharine Abraham

Department of Health and Human Services
200 Independence Avenue, SW
Washington, D.C. 20201
(202) 619-0257
Secretary of HHS — Donna E. Shalala
Social Security Adm. — Shirley Sears Chater

Department of Housing and Urban Development
451 7th Street, SW
Washington, D.C. 20410
(202) 708-1422
Secretary of Housing & Urban Development — Andrew M. Cuomo
Deputy Secretary — Terrence Duvernay

Department of Transportation
400 7th Street, SW
Washington, D.C. 20590
(202) 366-4000
Secretary of Transportation — Rodney E. Slater

Department of Energy
1000 Independence Avenue, SW
Washington, D.C. 20585
(202) 586-5000
Secretary of Energy — Federico F. Peña

Department of Education
400 Maryland Avenue, SW
Washington, D.C. 20202
(202) 708-5366
Secretary of Education — Richard W. Riley

Department of Veterans Affairs
810 Vermont Avenue, NW
Washington, D.C. 20420
(202) 273-4900
Secretary of Veterans Affairs — Jesse Brown

XI. The 105th Congress

Contacting Members of Congress

The letter is the most popular choice of communication with a member of Congress, but e-mail is becoming increasingly popular. Here are some suggestions for contacting your Congressperson:
- Your purpose for writing should be stated in the first paragraph, and each letter should pertain to a specific piece of legislation.
- Address only one issue in each letter, and if possible, keep the letter to one page.

Addressing correspondence:

To a Senator:
The Honorable (full name)
__(Rm. #)__(name of Senate office building)
United States Senate
Washington, D.C. 20510

To a Representative:
The Honorable (full name)
__(Rm. #)__(name of House office building)
United States House of Representatives
Washington, D.C. 20515

Alabama

Senators

Jeff Sessions (R)
34 Dirksen Senate Office Building
Phone: 1-202-224-4124
FAX: N/A
sessions@wrldnet.net (temporary)

Richard C. Shelby (R)
110 Hart Senate Office Building
Phone: 1-202-224-5744
FAX: 1-202-224-3416
senator@shelby.senate.gov

Representatives

H. L. Callahan (R)
(First District)
2418 Rayburn House Office Bldg.
Phone: 1-202-225-4931
FAX: 1-202-225-0562
callahan@hr.house.gov

Terry Everett (R)
(Second District)
208 Cannon Building
Phone: 1-202-225-2901
FAX: 1-202-225-8913
everett@hr.house.gov

Bob Riley (R)
(Third District)
510 Cannon Building
Phone: 1-202-225-3261
FAX: 1-202-225-9020
72074.2230@compuserv.com

Robert Aderholt (R)
(Fourth District)
1007 Longworth House Office Bldg.
Phone: 1-202-225-4876
FAX: 1-202-225-1604

Robert E. Cramer, Jr. (D)
(Fifth District)
2416 Rayburn House Office Bldg.
Phone: 1-202-225-4801
FAX: 1-202-225-4392
budmail@hr.house.gov

Spencer Bachus (R)
(Sixth District)
422 Cannon Building
Phone: 1-202-225-4921
FAX: 1-202-225-2082
sbachus@hr.house.gov

Earl F. Hilliard (D)
(Seventh District)
1314 Longworth House Office Bldg.
Phone: 1-202-225-2665
FAX: 1-202-226-0772

Alaska

Senators

Frank H. Murkowski (R)
706 Hart Senate Office Building
Phone: 1-202-224-6665
FAX: 1-202-224-5301
email@murkowski.senate.gov

Ted Stevens (R)
522 Hart Senate Office Building
Phone: 1-202-224-3004
FAX: 1-202-224-2354
Senator_Stevens@stevens.senate.gov

Representative At Large

Don Young (R)
2111 Rayburn House Office Bldg.
Phone: 1-202-225-5765
FAX: 1-202-225-0425
dyoung@hr.house.gov

Arizona

Senators

Jon Kyl (R)
702 Hart Senate Office Building
Phone: 1-202-224-4521
FAX: 1-202-228-1239
info@kyl.senate.gov

John McCain (R)
241 Russell Senate Office Building
Phone: 1-202-224-2235
FAX: 1-202-228-2862
Senator_McCain@mccain.senate.gov

Representatives

Matthew Salmon (R)
(First District)
115 Cannon Building
Phone: 1-202-225-2635
FAX: 1-202-225-3405
msalmon@hr.house.gov

Ed Pastor (D)
(Second District)
2465 Rayburn House Office Bldg.
Phone: 1-202-225-4065
FAX: 1-202-225-1655
edpastor@hr.house.gov

Robert Stump (R)
(Third District)
211 Cannon Building
Phone: 1-202-225-4576
FAX: 1-202-225-6328

John Shadegg (R)
(Fourth District)
430 Cannon Building
Phone: 1-202-225-3361
FAX: 1-202-225-3462
jshadegg@hr.house.gov

James T. Kolbe (R)
(Fifth District)
205 Cannon Building
Phone: 1-202-225-2542
FAX: 1-202-225-0378
jimkolbe@hr.house.gov

John Hayworth (R)
(Sixth District)
1023 Longworth House Office Bldg.
Phone: 1-202-225-2190
FAX: 1-202-225-8819
hayworth@hr.house.gov

Arkansas

Senators

Dale Bumpers (D)
229 Dirksen Senate Office Bldg.
Phone: 1-202-224-4843
FAX: 1-202-224-6435
senator@bumpers.senate.gov

Tim Hutchinson (R)
708 Hart Senate Office Building
Phone: 1-202-224-2353
FAX: 1-202-228-3973

Representatives

Marion Berry (D)
(First District)
1407 Longworth House Office Bldg.
Phone: 1-202-225-4076
FAX: 1-202-225-4654

Vic Snyder (D)
(Second District)
1319 Longworth House Office Bldg.
Phone: 1-202-225-2506
FAX: 1-202-225-9273

Asa Hutchinson (R)
(Third District)
1535 Longworth House Office Bldg.
Phone: 1-202-225-4301
FAX: N/A

Jay Dickey (R)
(Fourth District)
2453 Rayburn House Office Bldg.
Phone: 1-202-225-3772
FAX: 1-202-225-1314
jdickey@hr.house.gov

California

Senators

Barbara Boxer (D)
112 Hart Senate Office Building
Phone: 1-202-224-3553
FAX: 1-415-956-6701
senator@boxer.senate.gov

Dianne Feinstein (D)
331 Hart Senate Office Building
Phone: 1-202-224-3841
FAX: 1-202-228-3954
senator@feinstein.senate.gov

Representatives

Frank Riggs (R)
(First District)
1714 Longworth House Office Bldg.
Phone: 1-202-225-3311
FAX: 1-202-225-7710
repriggs@hr.house.gov

Walter W. Herger (R)
(Second District)
2433 Rayburn House Office Bldg.
Phone: 1-202-225-3076
FAX: 1-202-225-1609

Vic Fazio (D)
(Third District)
2113 Rayburn House Office Bldg.
Phone: 1-202-225-5716
FAX: 1-202-225-5141
dcaucus@hr.house.gov

John T. Doolittle (R)
(Fourth District)
1526 Longworth House Office Bldg.
Phone: 1-202-225-2511
FAX: 1-202-225-5444

Robert T. Matsui (D)
(Fifth District)
2308 Rayburn House Office Bldg.
Phone: 1-202-225-7163
FAX: 1-202-225-0566
ca05@hr.house.gov

Lynn Woolsey (D)
(Sixth District)
439 Cannon Building
Phone: 1-202-225-5161
FAX: 1-202-225-5163
woolsey@hr.house.gov

George Miller (D)
(Seventh District)
2205 Rayburn House Office Bldg.
Phone: 1-202-225-2095
FAX: 1-202-225-5609
gmiller@hr.house.gov

Nancy Pelosi (D)
(Eighth District)
2457 Rayburn House Office Bldg.
Phone: 1-202-225-4965
FAX: 1-202-225-8259
sfnancy@hr.house.gov

Ronald V. Dellums (D)
(Ninth District)
2108 Rayburn House Office Bldg.
Phone: 1-202-225-2661
FAX: 1-202-225-9817

Ellen Tauscher (D)
(Tenth District)
1440 Longworth House Office Bldg.
Phone: 1-202-225-1880
FAX: 1-202-225-1868
ellent@tauscher.com

Richard Pombo (R)
(Eleventh District)
1519 Longworth House Office Bldg.
Phone: 1-202-225-1947
FAX: 1-202-226-0861

Thomas Lantos (D)
(Twelfth District)
2217 Rayburn House Office Bldg.
Phone: 1-202-225-3531
FAX: 1-202-225-7900
talk2tom@hr.house.gov

Pete Stark (D)
(Thirteenth District)
239 Cannon Building
Phone: 1-202-225-5065
FAX: 1-202-226-3805
petemail@hr.house.gov

Anna G. Eshoo (D)
(Fourteenth District)
308 Cannon Building
Phone: 1-202-225-8104
FAX: 1-202-225-8890
annagram@hr.house.gov

Tom Campbell (R)
(Fifteenth District)
2442 Rayburn House Office Bldg.
Phone: 1-202-225-2631
FAX: 1-202-225-6788
campbell@hr.house.gov

Zoe Lofgren (D)
(Sixteenth District)
318 Cannon Building
Phone: 1-202-225-3072
FAX: 1-202-225-9460
zoegram@lofgren.house.gov

Sam Farr (D)
(Seventeenth District)
1117 Longworth House Office Bldg.
Phone: 1-202-225-2861
FAX: 1-202-225-6791
samfarr@hr.house.gov

Gary Condit (D)
(Eighteenth District)
2245 Rayburn House Office Bldg.
Phone: 1-202-225-6131
FAX: 1-202-225-0819
gcondit@hr.house.gov

George Radanovich (R)
(Nineteenth District)
213 Cannon Building
Phone: 1-202-225-4540
FAX: 1-202-225-5274
george@hr.house.gov

Calvin M. Dooley (D)
(Twentieth District)
1201 Longworth House Office Bldg.
Phone: 1-202-225-3341
FAX: 1-202-225-9308

Bill Thomas (R)
(Twenty-First District)
2208 Rayburn House Office Bldg.
Phone: 1-202-225-2915
FAX: 1-202-225-8798

Walter Capps (D)
(Twenty-Second District)
1118 Longworth House Office Bldg.
Phone: 1-202-225-3601
FAX: 1-202-225-3426

Elton Gallegly (R)
(Twenty-Third District)
2427 Rayburn House Office Bldg.
Phone: 1-202-225-5811
FAX: 1-202-225-1100

Brad Sherman (D)
(Twenty-Fourth District)
1524 Longworth House Office Bldg.
Phone: 1-202-225-5911
FAX: 1-202-225-0092

Howard P. McKeon (R)
(Twenty-Fifth District)
307 Cannon Building
Phone: 1-202-225-1956
FAX: 1-202-226-0683
tellbuck@hr.house.gov

Howard L. Berman (D)
(Twenty-Sixth District)
2330 Rayburn House Office Bldg.
Phone: 1-202-225-4695
FAX: 1-202-225-5279

James. Rogan (R)
(Twenty-Seventh District)
502 Cannon Building
Phone: 1-202-225-4176
FAX: 1-202-226-1279

David Dreier (R)
(Twenty-Eighth District)
237 Cannon Building
Phone: 1-202-225-2305
FAX: 1-202-225-7018
cyberrep@aol.com

Henry A. Waxman (D)
(Twenty-Ninth District)
2204 Rayburn House Office Bldg.
Phone: 1-202-225-3976
FAX: 1-202-225-4099

Xavier Becerra (D)
(Thirtieth District)
1119 Longworth House Office Bldg.
Phone: 1-202-225-6235
FAX: 1-202-225-2202

Matthew G. Martinez (D)
(Thirty-First District)
2234 Rayburn House Office Bldg.
Phone: 1-202-225-5464
FAX: 1-202-225-5467

Julian C. Dixon (D)
(Thirty-Second District)
2252 Rayburn House Office Bldg.
Phone: 1-202-225-7084
FAX: 1-202-225-4091

Lucille Roybal-Allard (D)
(Thirty-Third District)
2435 Rayburn House Office Bldg.
Phone: 1-202-225-1766
FAX: 1-202-226-0350

Esteban E. Torres (D)
(Thirty-Fourth District)
2269 Rayburn House Office Bldg.
Phone: 1-202-225-5256
FAX: 1-202-225-9711
arcoiris@hr.house.gov

Maxine Waters (D)
(Thirty-Fifth District)
2344 Rayburn House Office Bldg.
Phone: 1-202-225-2201
FAX: 1-202-225-7854

Jane Harman (D)
(Thirty-Sixth District)
325 Cannon Building
Phone: 1-202-225-8220
FAX: 1-202-226-0684
jharman@hr.house.gov

Juanita Millender-McDonald (D)
(Thirty-Seventh District)
419 Cannon Building
Phone: 1-202-225-7924
FAX: 1-202-225-7926

Steve Horn (R)
(Thirty-Eighth District)
438 Cannon Building
Phone: 1-202-225-6676
FAX: 1-202-226-1012
Stephen.Horn@mail.house.gov

Ed Royce (R)
(Thirty-Ninth District)
1133 Longworth House Office Bldg.
Phone: 1-202-225-4111
FAX: 1-202-226-0335

Jerry Lewis (R)
(Fortieth District)
2112 Rayburn House Office Bldg.
Phone: 1-202-225-5861
FAX: 1-202-225-6498
khuiskes@hr.house.gov

Jay C. Kim (R)
(Forty-First District)
227 Cannon Building
Phone: 1-202-225-3201
FAX: 1-202-226-1485

George E. Brown, Jr. (D)
(Forty-Second District)
2300 Rayburn House Office Bldg.
Phone: 1-202-225-6161
FAX: 1-202-225-8671
talk2geb@hr.house.gov

Ken Calvert (R)
(Forty-Third District)
1034 Longworth House Office Bldg.
Phone: 1-202-225-1986
FAX: 1-202-225-2004

Sonny Bono (R)
(Forty-Fourth District)
324 Cannon Building
Phone: 1-202-225-5330
FAX: 1-202-225-2961

Dana Rohrabacher (R)
(Forty-Fifth District)
2338 Rayburn House Office Bldg.
Phone: 1-202-225-2415
FAX: 1-202-225-0145
sjohnso4@hr.house.gov

Loretta Sanchez (D)
(Forty-Sixth District)
1529 Longworth House Office Bldg.
Phone: 1-202-225-2965
FAX: 1-202-225-2762

Christopher Cox (R)
(Forty-Seventh District)
2402 Rayburn House Office Bldg.
Phone: 1-202-225-5611
FAX: 1-202-225-9177
chriscox@hr.house.gov

Ronald Packard (R)
(Forty-Eighth District)
2372 Rayburn House Office Bldg.
Phone: 1-202-225-3906
FAX: 1-202-225-0134
rpackard@hr.house.gov

Brian Bilbray (R)
(Forty-Ninth District)
1530 Longworth House Office Bldg.
Phone: 1-202-225-2040
FAX: 1-202-225-2042
bilbray@hr.house.gov

Bob Filner (D)
(Fiftieth District)
330 Cannon Building
Phone: 1-202-225-8045
FAX: 1-202-225-9073

Randy Cunningham (R)
(Fifty-First District)
2238 Rayburn House Office Bldg.
Phone: 1-202-225-5452
FAX: 1-202-225-2558

Duncan L. Hunter (R)
(Fifty-Second District)
2265 Rayburn House Office Bldg.
Phone: 1-202-225-5672
FAX: 1-202-225-0235

Colorado

Senators
Ben N. Campbell (R)
380 Russell Senate Office Building
Phone: 1-202-224-5852
FAX: 1-202-224-1933

Wayne Allard (R)
716 Hart Senate Office Building
Phone: 1-202-224-5941
FAX: 1-202-224-6471

Representatives
Diana DeGette (D)
(First District)
1404 Longworth House Office Bldg.
Phone: 1-202-225-4431
FAX: 1-202-225-5842

David E. Skaggs (D)
(Second District)
1124 Longworth House Office Bldg.
Phone: 1-202-225-2161
FAX: 1-202-226-9127
skaggs@hr.house.gov

Scott McInnis (R)
(Third District)
215 Cannon Building
Phone: 1-202-225-4761
FAX: 1-202-226-0622

Bob Schaffer (R)
(Fourth District)
212 Cannon Building
Phone: 1-202-225-4676
FAX: 1-202-225-8630

Joel Hefley (R)
(Fifth District)
2230 Rayburn House Office Bldg.
Phone: 1-202-225-4422
FAX: 1-202-225-1942

Daniel Schaefer (R)
(Sixth District)
2160 Rayburn House Office Bldg.
Phone: 1-202-225-7882
FAX: 1-202-225-7885
schaefer@hr.house.gov

Connecticut

Senators
Christopher J. Dodd (D)
444 Russell Senate Office Building
Phone: 1-202-224-2823
FAX: 1-202-224-1083
sen_dodd@dodd.senate.gov

Joseph I. Lieberman (D)
316 Hart Senate Office Building
Phone: 1-202-224-4041
FAX: 1-202-224-9750
senator_lieberman@lieberman.senate.gov

Representatives
Barbara B. Kennelly (D)
(First District)
201 Cannon Building
Phone: 1-202-225-2265
FAX: 1-202-225-1031

Samuel Gejdenson (D)
(Second District)
1401 Longworth House Office Bldg.
Phone: 1-202-225-2076
FAX: 1-202-225-4977
bozrah@hr.house.gov

Rosa DeLauro (D)
(Third District)
436 Cannon Building
Phone: 1-202-225-3661
FAX: 1-202-225-4890

Christopher Shays (R)
(Fourth District)
1502 Longworth House Office Bldg.
Phone: 1-202-225-5541
FAX: 1-202-225-9629
cshays@hr.house.gov

Jim Maloney (D)
(Fifth District)
1213 Longworth House Office Bldg.
Phone: 1-202-225-3822
FAX: 1-202-225-5085

Nancy L. Johnson (R)
(Sixth District)
343 Cannon Building
Phone: 1-202-225-4476
FAX: 1-202-225-4488

Delaware

Senators
Joseph R. Biden, Jr. (D)
221 Russell Senate Office Building
Phone: 1-202-224-5042
FAX: 1-202-224-0139
senator@biden.senate.gov

William V. Roth, Jr. (R)
104 Hart Senate Office Building
Phone: 1-202-224-2441
FAX: 1-202-228-0354

Representative At Large
Michael N. Castle (R)
1227 Longworth House Office Bldg.
Phone: 1-202-225-4165
FAX: 1-202-225-2291
delaware@hr.house.gov

Florida

Senators
Robert Graham (D)
524 Hart Senate Office Building
Phone: 1-202-224-3041
FAX: 1-202-224-2237
bob_graham@graham.senate.gov

Connie Mack (R)
517 Hart Senate Office Building
Phone: 1-202-224-5274
FAX: 1-202-224-8022
chairman_mack@jec.senate.gov
connie@mack.senate.gov

Representatives
Joe Scarborough (R)
(First District)
127 Cannon Building
Phone: 1-202-225-4136
FAX: 1-202-225-5785
fl01@hr.house.gov

Allen Boyd (D)
(Second District)
1237 Longworth House Office Bldg.
Phone: 1-202-225-5235
FAX: 1-202-225-1586

Corrine Brown (D)
(Third District)
1610 Longworth House Office Bldg.
Phone: 1-202-225-0123
FAX: 1-202-225-2256

Tillie Fowler (R)
(Fourth District)
109 Cannon Building
Phone: 1-202-225-2501
FAX: 1-202-225-9318

Karen Thurman (D)
(Fifth District)
440 Cannon Building
Phone: 1-202-225-1002
FAX: 1-202-226-0329
kthurman@hr.house.gov

Clifford B. Stearns (R)
(Sixth District)
2352 Rayburn House Office Bldg.
Phone: 1-202-225-5744
FAX: 1-202-225-3973
cstearns@hr.house.gov

John L. Mica (R)
(Seventh District)
106 Cannon Building
Phone: 1-202-225-4035
FAX: 1-202-226-0821
mica@hr.house.gov

William McCollum (R)
(Eighth District)
2266 Rayburn House Office Bldg.
Phone: 1-202-225-2176
FAX: 1-202-225-0999

Michael Bilirakis (R)
(Ninth District)
2369 Rayburn House Office Bldg.
Phone: 1-202-225-5755
FAX: 1-202-225-4085
fl09@hr.house.gov

C. W. Young (R)
(Tenth District)
2407 Rayburn House Office Bldg.
Phone: 1-202-225-5961
FAX: 1-202-225-9764

Jim Davis (D)
(Eleventh District)
327 Cannon Building
Phone: 1-202-225-3376
FAX: 1-202-225-8016

Charles T. Canady (R)
(Twelfth District)
2432 Rayburn House Office Bldg.
Phone: 1-202-225-1252
FAX: 1-202-225-2279
canady@hr.house.gov

Dan Miller (R)
(Thirteenth District)
102 Cannon Building
Phone: 1-202-225-5015
FAX: 1-202-226-0828
miller13@hr.house.gov

Porter J. Goss (R)
(Fourteenth District)
108 Cannon Building
Phone: 1-202-225-2536
FAX: 1-202-225-6820

Dave Weldon (R)
(Fifteenth District)
216 Cannon Building
Phone: 1-202-225-3671
FAX: 1-202-225-9039
fla15@hr.house.gov

Mark Foley (R)
(Sixteenth District)
113 Cannon Building
Phone: 1-202-225-5792
FAX: 1-202-225-1860

Carrie Meek (D)
(Seventeenth District)
401 Cannon Building
Phone: 1-202-225-4506
FAX: 1-202-226-0777

Ileana Ros-Lehtinen (R)
(Eighteenth District)
2240 Rayburn House Office Bldg.
Phone: 1-202-225-3931
FAX: 1-202-225-5620

Robert Wexler (D)
(Nineteenth District)
1609 Longworth House Office Bldg.
Phone: 1-202-225-3001
FAX: 1-202-225-8791
Wexler1996@aol.com

Peter Deutsch (D)
(Twentieth District)
204 Cannon Building
Phone: 1-202-225-7931
FAX: 1-202-225-8456
pdeutsch@hr.house.gov

Lincoln Diaz-Balart (R)
(Twenty-First District)
404 Cannon Building
Phone: 1-202-225-4211
FAX: 1-202-225-8576

E. C. Shaw, Jr. (R)
(Twenty-Second District)
2408 Rayburn House Office Bldg.
Phone: 1-202-225-3026
FAX: 1-202-225-8398

Alcee L. Hastings (D)
(Twenty-Third District)
1039 Longworth House Office Bldg.
Phone: 1-202-225-1313
FAX: 1-202-226-0690
hastings@hr.house.gov

Georgia

Senators
Max Cleland (D)
4633 Dirksen Senate Office Bldg.
Phone: 1-202-224-3521
FAX: 1-202-224-0072

Paul Coverdell (R)
200 Russell Senate Office Building
Phone: 1-202-224-3643
FAX: 1-202-228-3783
senator_coverdell@coverdell.senate.gov

Representatives
Jack Kingston (R)
(First District)
1507 Longworth House Office Bldg.
Phone: 1-202-225-5831
FAX: 1-202-226-2269

Sanford Bishop (D)
(Second District)
1433 Longworth House Office Bldg.
Phone: 1-202-225-3631
FAX: 1-202-225-2203

Mac Collins (R)
(Third District)
1131 Longworth House Office Bldg.
Phone: 1-202-225-5901
FAX: 1-202-225-2515
rep3mac@hr.house.gov

Cynthia McKinney (D)
(Fourth District)
124 Cannon Building
Phone: 1-202-225-1605
FAX: 1-202-226-0691

John Lewis (D)
(Fifth District)
229 Cannon Building
Phone: 1-202-225-3801
FAX: 1-202-225-0351

Newt Gingrich (R)
(Sixth District)
2428 Rayburn House Office Bldg.
Phone: 1-202-225-4501
FAX: 1-202-225-4656
georgia6@hr.house.gov

Bob Barr (R)
(Seventh District)
1130 Longworth House Office Bldg.
Phone: 1-202-225-2931
FAX: 1-202-225-0473
bbarr@hr.house.gov

Saxby Chambliss (R)
(Eighth District)
1019 Longworth House Office Bldg.
Phone: 1-202-225-6531
FAX: 1-202-225-7719
saxby@hr.house.gov

Nathan Deal (R)
(Ninth District)
1406 Longworth House Office Bldg.
Phone: 1-202-225-5211
FAX: 1-202-225-8272

Charles Norwood (R)
(Tenth District)
1707 Longworth House Office Bldg.
Phone: 1-202-225-4101
FAX: 1-202-225-3397
ga10@hr.house.gov

John Linder (R)
(Eleventh District)
1005 Longworth House Office Bldg.
Phone: 1-202-225-4272
FAX: 1-202-225-4696
jlinder@hr.house.gov

Hawaii

Senators
Daniel K. Akaka (D)
720 Hart Senate Office Building
Phone: 1-202-224-6361
FAX: 1-202-224-2126

Daniel K. Inouye (D)
722 Hart Senate Office Building
Phone: 1-202-224-3934
FAX: 1-202-224-6747
senator@inouye.senate.gov

Representatives
Neil Abercrombie (D)
(First District)
1233 Longworth House Office Bldg.
Phone: 1-202-225-2726
FAX: 1-202-225-4580
neil@abercrombie.house.gov

Patsy T. Mink (D)
(Second District)
2135 Rayburn House Office Bldg.
Phone: 1-202-225-4906
FAX: 1-202-225-4987

Idaho

Senators
Larry E. Craig (R)
313 Hart Senate Office Building
Phone: 1-202-224-2752
FAX: 1-202-228-1067
larry_craig@craig.senate.gov

Dirk Kempthorne (R)
367 Dirksen Senate Office Bldg.
Phone: 1-202-224-6142
FAX: 1-202-224-5893
dirk_kempthorne@kempthorne.senate.gov

Representatives
Helen Chenoweth (R)
(First District)
1727 Longworth House Office Bldg.
Phone: 1-202-225-6611
FAX: 1-202-225-3029
askhelen@hr.house.gov

Michael D. Crapo (R)
(Second District)
437 Cannon Building
Phone: 1-202-225-5531
FAX: 1-202-225-8216

Illinois

Senators
Carol Moseley-Braun (D)
320 Hart Senate Office Building
Phone: 1-202-224-2854
FAX: 1-202-224-2626
senator@moseley-braun.senate.gov

Richard Durbin (D)
267 Russell Senate Office Building
Phone: 1-202-224-2152
FAX: 1-202-224-0868

Representatives
Bobby L. Rush (D)
(First District)
131 Cannon Building
Phone: 1-202-225-4372
FAX: 1-202-226-0333
brush@hr.house.gov

Jesse Jackson, Jr. (D)
(Second District)
313 Cannon Building
Phone: 1-202-225-0773
FAX: 1-202-225-0899

William O. Lipinski (D)
(Third District)
1501 Longworth House Office Bldg.
Phone: 1-202-225-5701
FAX: 1-202-225-1012

Luis V. Gutierrez (D)
(Fourth District)
2438 Rayburn House Office Bldg.
Phone: 1-202-225-8203
FAX: 1-202-225-7810
luisg@hr.house.gov

Rod Blagojevich (D)
(Fifth District)
501 Cannon Building
Phone: 1-202-225-4061
FAX: 1-202-225-3128

Henry J. Hyde (R)
(Sixth District)
2110 Rayburn House Office Bldg.
Phone: 1-202-225-4561
FAX: 1-202-225-1166

Danny Davis (D)
(Seventh District)
1218 Longworth House Office Bldg.
Phone: 1-202-225-5006
FAX: 1-202-225-8396

Philip M. Crane (R)
(Eighth District)
233 Cannon Building
Phone: 1-202-225-3711
FAX: 1-202-225-7830

Sidney R. Yates (D)
(Ninth District)
2109 Rayburn House Office Bldg.
Phone: 1-202-225-2111
FAX: 1-202-225-3493

John E. Porter (R)
(Tenth District)
2373 Longworth House Office Bldg.
Phone: 1-202-225-4835
FAX: 1-708-392-5774

Gerald Weller (R)
(Eleventh District)
130 Cannon Building
Phone: 1-202-225-3635
FAX: 1-202-225-4447
jweller@hr.house.gov

Jerry F. Costello (D)
(Twelfth District)
2454 Rayburn House Office Bldg.
Phone: 1-202-225-5661
FAX: 1-202-225-0285
jfcil12@hr.house.gov

Harris W. Fawell (R)
(Thirteenth District)
2368 Rayburn House Office Bldg.
Phone: 1-202-225-3515
FAX: 1-202-225-9420
hfawell@hr.house.gov

J. D. Hastert (R)
(Fourteenth District)
2241 Rayburn House Office Bldg.
Phone: 1-202-225-2976
FAX: 1-202-225-0697
dhastert@hr.house.gov

Thomas Ewing (R)
(Fifteenth District)
1317 Longworth House Office Bldg.
Phone: 1-202-225-2371
FAX: 1-202-225-8071

Donald Manzullo (R)
(Sixteenth District)
409 Cannon Building
Phone: 1-202-225-5676
FAX: 1-202-225-5284

Lane Evans (D)
(Seventeenth District)
2335 Rayburn House Office Bldg.
Phone: 1-202-225-5905
FAX: 1-202-225-5396

Ray LaHood (R)
(Eighteenth District)
329 Cannon Building
Phone: 1-202-225-6201
FAX: 1-202-225-9461
lahood18@hr.house.gov

Glenn Poshard (D)
(Nineteenth District)
2334 Rayburn House Office Bldg.
Phone: 1-202-225-5201
FAX: 1-202-225-1541

John Shimkus (R)
(Twentieth District)
513 Cannon Building
Phone: 1-202-225-5271
FAX: 1-202-225-0170
shimkus@midwest.net

Indiana

Senators
Daniel R. Coats (R)
404 Russell Senate Office Building
Phone: 1-202-224-5623
FAX: 1-202-228-4137

Richard G. Lugar (R)
306 Hart Senate Office Building
Phone: 1-202-224-4814
FAX: 1-202-228-3060
lugar@iquest.net

Representatives
Peter J. Visclosky (D)
(First District)
2313 Rayburn House Office Bldg.
Phone: 1-202-225-2461
FAX: 1-202-225-2493

David McIntosh (R)
(Second District)
1208 Longworth House Office Bldg.
Phone: 1-202-225-3021
FAX: 1-202-225-8140
mcintosh@hr.house.gov

Timothy Roemer (D)
(Third District)
2348 Rayburn House Office Bldg.
Phone: 1-202-225-3915
FAX: 1-202-225-6798
troemer@hr.house.gov

Mark Souder (R)
(Fourth District)
418 Cannon Building
Phone: 1-202-225-4436
FAX: 1-202-225-3479
souder@hr.house.gov

Steve Buyer (R)
(Fifth District)
326 Cannon Building
Phone: 1-202-225-5037
FAX: 1-317-454-7560

Daniel Burton (R)
(Sixth District)
2185 Rayburn House Office Bldg.
Phone: 1-202-225-2276
FAX: 1-202-225-0016

Edward Pease (R)
(Seventh District)
226 Cannon Building
Phone: 1-202-225-5805
FAX: 1-202-225-1649

John Hostettler (R)
(Eighth District)
431 Cannon Building
Phone: 1-202-225-4636
FAX: 1-202-225-4688
johnhost@hr.house.gov

Lee H. Hamilton (D)
(Ninth District)
2314 Rayburn House Office Bldg.
Phone: 1-202-225-5315
FAX: 1-202-225-1101
hamilton@hr.house.gov

Julia Carson (D)
(Tenth District)
1541 Longworth House Office Bldg.
Phone: 1-202-225-4011
FAX: 1-202-226-4093
jcarson@indy.net

Iowa

Senators
Thomas Harkin (D)
531 Hart Senate Office Building
Phone: 1-202-224-3254
FAX: 1-202-224-9369
tom_harkin@harkin.senate.gov

Charles E. Grassley (R)
135 Hart Senate Office Building
Phone: 1-202-224-3744
FAX: 1-202-224-6020
chuck_grassley@grassley.senate.gov

Representatives
James Leach (R)
(First District)
2186 Rayburn House Office Bldg.
Phone: 1-202-225-6576
FAX: 1-202-226-1278
talk2jim@hr.house.gov

James Allen Nussle (R)
(Second District)
303 Cannon Building
Phone: 1-202-225-2911
FAX: 1-202-225-9129
nussleia@hr.house.gov

Leonard Boswell (D)
(Third District)
1029 Longworth House Office Bldg.
Phone: 1-202-225-3806
FAX: 1-202-225-6973

Greg Ganske (R)
(Fourth District)
1108 Rayburn House Office Bldg.
Phone: 1-202-225-4426
FAX: 1-202-225-3193
ganske@hr.house.gov

Tom Latham (R)
(Fifth District)
516 Cannon Building
Phone: 1-202-225-5476
FAX: 1-202-225-3301
latham@hr.house.gov

Kansas

Senators
Sam Brownback (R)
141 Hart Senate Office Building
Phone: 1-202-224-6521
FAX: 1-202-224-8952

Pat Roberts (R)
116 Dirksen Senate Office Bldg.
Phone: 1-202-224-4774
FAX: 1-202-224-3514

Representatives
Jerry Moran (R)
(First District)
1217 Longworth House Office Bldg.
Phone: 1-202-225-2715
FAX: 1-202-225-5375

Jim Ryun (R)
(Second District)
511 Cannon Building
Phone: 1-202-225-6601
FAX: 1-202-225-2983

Vincent Snowbarger (R)
(Third District)
509 Cannon Building
Phone: 1-202-225-2865
FAX: 1-202-225-0554
vince@microlink.net

Todd Tiahrt (R)
(Fourth District)
428 Cannon Building
Phone: 1-202-225-6216
FAX: 1-202-225-3489
tiahrt@hr.house.gov

Kentucky

Senators
Wendell H. Ford (D)
173A Russell Senate Office Bldg.
Phone: 1-202-224-4343
FAX: 1-202-224-0046
wendell_ford@ford.senate.gov

Mitch McConnell (R)
361A Russell Senate Office Bldg.
Phone: 1-202-224-2541
FAX: 1-202-224-2499
senator@mcconnell.senate.gov

Representatives
Edward Whitfield (R)
(First District)
236 Cannon Building
Phone: 1-202-225-3115
FAX: 1-202-225-2169
edky01@hr.house.gov

Ron Lewis (R)
(Second District)
223 Cannon Building
Phone: 1-202-225-3501
FAX: 1-202-226-2019

Anne Northrup (R)
(Third District)
1004 Longworth House Office Bldg.
Phone: 1-202-225-5401
FAX: 1-202-225-3511

James Bunning (R)
(Fourth District)
2437 Rayburn House Office Bldg.
Phone: 1-202-225-3465
FAX: 1-202-225-0003
bunning4@hr.house.gov

Harold Rogers (R)
(Fifth District)
2468 Rayburn House Office Bldg.
Phone: 1-202-225-4601
FAX: 1-202-225-0940

Scotty Baesler (D)
(Sixth District)
2463 Rayburn House Office Bldg.
Phone: 1-202-225-4706
FAX: 1-202-225-2122
baesler@hr.house.gov

Louisiana

Senators
John B. Breaux (D)
516 Hart Senate Office Building
Phone: 1-202-224-4623
FAX: 1-202-224-4268
senator@breaux.senate.gov

Mary Landrieu (D)
825 Hart Senate Office Building
Phone: 1-202-224-5824
FAX: 1-202-224-2952

Representatives
Robert Livingston (R)
(First District)
2406 Rayburn House Office Bldg.
Phone: 1-202-225-3015
FAX: 1-202-225-0739

William Jefferson (D)
(Second District)
240 Cannon Building
Phone: 1-202-225-6636
FAX: 1-202-225-1988

W. J. Tauzin (R)
(Third District)
2183 Rayburn House Office Bldg.
Phone: 1-202-225-4031
FAX: 1-202-225-0563

James McCrery (R)
(Fourth District)
2104 Longworth House Office Bldg.
Phone: 1-202-225-2777
FAX: 1-202-225-8039
mccrery@hr.house.gov

John Cooksey (R)
(Fifth District)
317 Cannon Building
Phone: 1-202-225-8490
FAX: 1-202-225-8959

Richard H. Baker (R)
(Sixth District)
434 Cannon Building
Phone: 1-202-225-3901
FAX: 1-202-225-7313

Christopher John (D)
(Seventh District)
1504 Longworth House Office Bldg.
Phone: 1-202-225-2031
FAX: 1-202-225-1175

Maine

Senators
Olympia Snowe (R)
495 Russell Senate Office Building
Phone: 1-202-224-5344
FAX: 1-202-224-1946
Olympia@snowe.senate.gov

Susan Collins (R)
322 Hart Senate Office Bldg.
Phone: 1-202-224-2523
FAX: 1-202-224-2693

Representatives
Thomas Allen (D)
(First District)
1630 Longworth House Office Bldg.
Phone: 1-202-225-6116
FAX: 1-202-225-3353
TomAllen96@neis.net

John Baldacci (D)
(Second District)
1740 Longworth House Office Bldg.
Phone: 1-202-225-6306
FAX: 1-202-225-8297
baldacci@hr.house.gov

Maryland

Senators
Barbara A. Mikulski (D)
709 Hart Senate Office Building
Phone: 1-202-224-4654
FAX: 1-202-224-8858
senator@mikulski.senate.gov

Paul S. Sarbanes (D)
309 Hart Senate Office Building
Phone: 1-202-224-4524
FAX: 1-202-224-1651
senator@sarbanes.senate.gov

Representatives
Wayne T. Gilchrest (R)
(First District)
332 Cannon Building
Phone: 1-202-225-5311
FAX: 1-202-225-0254

Robert Ehrlich, Jr. (R)
(Second District)
315 Cannon Building
Phone: 1-202-225-3061
FAX: 1-202-225-4251
ehrlich@hr.house.gov

Benjamin L. Cardin (D)
(Third District)
104 Cannon Building
Phone: 1-202-225-4016
FAX: 1-202-225-9219
cardin@hr.house.gov

Albert R. Wynn (D)
(Fourth District)
407 Cannon Building
Phone: 1-202-225-8699
FAX: 1-202-225-8714
alwynn@hr.house.gov

Steny H. Hoyer (D)
(Fifth District)
1705 Longworth House Office Bldg.
Phone: 1-202-225-4131
FAX: 1-202-225-4300

Roscoe G. Bartlett (R)
(Sixth District)
322 Cannon Building
Phone: 1-202-225-2721
FAX: 1-202-225-2193

Elijah Cummings (D)
(Seventh District)
1632 Longworth House Office Bldg.
Phone: 1-202-225-4741
FAX: 1-202-225-3178

Constance Morella (R)
(Eighth District)
2228 Rayburn House Office Bldg.
Phone: 1-202-225-5341
FAX: 1-202-225-1389

Massachusetts

Senators
Edward M. Kennedy (D)
315 Russell Senate Office Building
Phone: 1-202-224-4543
FAX: 1-202-224-2417
senator@kennedy.senate.gov

John F. Kerry (D)
421 Russell Senate Office Building
Phone: 1-202-224-2742
FAX: 1-202-224-8525
john_kerry@kerry.senate.gov

Representatives
John W. Olver (D)
(First District)
1027 Longworth House Office Bldg.
Phone: 1-202-225-5335
FAX: 1-202-226-1224
olver@hr.house.gov

Richard E. Neal (D)
(Second District)
2236 Rayburn House Office Bldg.
Phone: 1-202-225-5601
FAX: 1-202-225-8112
wtranghe@hr.house.gov

Jim McGovern (D)
(Third District)
512 Cannon Building
Phone: 1-202-225-6101
FAX: 1-202-225-2217

Barney Frank (D)
(Fourth District)
2210 Rayburn House Office Bldg.
Phone: 1-202-225-5931
FAX: 1-202-225-0182

Martin T. Meehan (D)
(Fifth District)
2434 Rayburn House Office Bldg.
Phone: 1-202-225-3411
FAX: 1-202-225-0771
mtmeehan@hr.house.gov

John Tierney (D)
(Sixth District)
120 Cannon Building
Phone: 1-202-225-8020
FAX: 1-202-225-8037

Edward J. Markey (D)
(Seventh District)
2133 Rayburn House Office Bldg.
Phone: 1-202-225-2836
FAX: 1-202-226-0340

Joseph P. Kennedy II (D)
(Eighth District)
2242 Rayburn House Office Bldg.
Phone: 1-202-225-5111
FAX: 1-202-225-9322

John Joseph Moakley (D)
(Ninth District)
235 Cannon Building
Phone: 1-202-225-8273
FAX: 1-202-225-3984
jmoakley@hr.house.gov

William Delahunt (D)
(Tenth District)
1517 Longworth House Office Bldg.
Phone: 1-202-225-3111
FAX: 1-202-225-2212

Michigan

Senators
Carl Levin (D)
459 Russell Senate Office Building
Phone: 1-202-224-6221
FAX: 1-202-224-1388
senator@levin.senate.gov

Spencer Abraham (R)
245 Dirksen Senate Office Bldg.
Phone: 1-202-224-4822
FAX: 1-202-224-8834
michigan@abraham.senate.gov

Representatives
Bart Stupak (D)
(First District)
1410 Longworth House Office Bldg.
Phone: 1-202-225-4735
FAX: 1-202-225-4744
stupak@hr.house.gov

Peter Hoekstra (R)
(Second District)
1122 Longworth House Office Bldg.
Phone: 1-202-225-4401
FAX: 1-202-226-0779
tellhoek@hr.house.gov
usavoice@hr.house.gov

Vern Ehlers (R)
(Third District)
1717 Longworth House Office Bldg.
Phone: 1-202-225-3831
FAX: 1-202-225-5144
congehlr@hr.house.gov

David Lee Camp (R)
(Fourth District)
137 Cannon Building
Phone: 1-202-225-3561
FAX: 1-202-225-9679
davecamp@hr.house.gov

James A. Barcia (D)
(Fifth District)
2419 Rayburn House Office Bldg.
Phone: 1-202-225-8171
FAX: 1-202-225-2168
jbarcia@hr.house.gov

Frederick S. Upton (R)
(Sixth District)
2333 Rayburn House Office Bldg.
Phone: 1-202-225-3761
FAX: 1-202-225-4986
talk2fsu@hr.house.gov

Nick Smith (R)
(Seventh District)
306 Cannon Building
Phone: 1-202-225-6276
FAX: 1-202-225-6281
repsmith@hr.house.gov

Debbie Stabenow (D)
(Eighth District)
1516 Longworth House Office Bldg.
Phone: 1-202-225-4872
FAX: 1-202-225-3034

Dale E. Kildee (D)
(Ninth District)
2187 Rayburn House Office Bldg.
Phone: 1-202-225-3611
FAX: 1-202-225-6393
dkildee@hr.house.gov

David E. Bonior (D)
(Tenth District)
2207 Rayburn House Office Bldg.
Phone: 1-202-225-2106
FAX: 1-202-226-1169

Joe Knollenberg (R)
(Eleventh District)
1511 Longworth House Office Bldg.
Phone: 1-202-225-5802
FAX: 1-202-226-2356

Sander M. Levin (D)
(Twelfth District)
2209 Rayburn House Office Bldg.
Phone: 1-202-225-4961
FAX: 1-202-226-1033
slevin@hr.house.gov

Lynn Rivers (D)
(Thirteenth District)
1724 Longworth House Office Bldg.
Phone: 1-202-225-6261
FAX: 1-202-225-3404
lrivers@hr.house.gov

John Conyers, Jr. (D)
(Fourteenth District)
2426 Rayburn House Office Bldg.
Phone: 1-202-225-5126
FAX: 1-202-225-0072
jconyers@hr.house.gov

Carolyn Cheeks Kilpatrick (D)
(Fifteenth District)
503 Cannon Building
Phone: 1-202-225-2261
FAX: 1-202-225-6645

John D. Dingell (D)
(Sixteenth District)
2328 Rayburn House Office Bldg.
Phone: 1-202-225-4071
FAX: 1-313-846-5628

Minnesota

Senators
Paul Wellstone (D)
717 Hart Senate Office Building
Phone: 1-202-224-5641
FAX: 1-202-224-8438
senator@wellstone.senate.gov

Rod Grams (R)
261 Dirksen Senate Office Bldg.
Phone: 1-202-224-3244
FAX: 1-202-228-0956
mail_grams@grams.gov

Representatives
Gilbert Gutknecht (R)
(First District)
425 Cannon Building
Phone: 1-202-225-2472
FAX: 1-202-225-0051
gil@hr.house.gov

David Minge (D)
(Second District)
1415 Longworth House Office Bldg.
Phone: 1-202-225-2331
FAX: 1-202-226-0836
dminge@hr.house.gov

James M. Ramstad (R)
(Third District)
103 Cannon Building
Phone: 1-202-225-2871
FAX: 1-202-225-6351
mn03@hr.house.gov

Bruce F. Vento (D)
(Fourth District)
2304 Rayburn House Office Bldg.
Phone: 1-202-225-6631
FAX: 1-202-225-1968
vento@hr.house.gov

Martin O. Sabo (D)
(Fifth District)
2336 Rayburn House Office Bldg.
Phone: 1-202-225-4755
FAX: 1-202-225-4886
msabo@hr.house.gov

William Luther (D)
(Sixth District)
117 Cannon Building
Phone: 1-202-225-2271
FAX: 1-202-225-9802
tellbill@hr.house.gov

Collin C. Peterson (D)
(Seventh District)
2159 Rayburn House Office Bldg.
Phone: 1-202-225-2165
FAX: 1-202-225-1593
tocollin@hr.house.gov

James L. Oberstar (D)
(Eighth District)
2366 Rayburn House Office Bldg.
Phone: 1-202-225-6211
FAX: 1-202-225-0699
oberstar@hr.house.gov

Mississippi

Senators
Thad Cochran (R)
326 Russell Senate Office Building
Phone: 1-202-224-5054
FAX: 1-202-224-9450
senator@cochran.senate.gov

Trent Lott (R)
487 Russell Senate Office Building
Phone: 1-202-224-6253
FAX: 1-202-224-2262

Representatives
Roger Wicker (R)
(First District)
206 Cannon Building
Phone: 1-202-225-4306
FAX: N/A
rwicker@hr.house.gov

Bennie G. Thompson (D)
(Second District)
1408 Longworth House Office Bldg.
Phone: 1-202-225-5876
FAX: 1-202-225-5898
ms2nd@hr.house.gov

Charles Pickering (R)
(Third District)
427 Cannon Building
Phone: 1-202-225-5031
FAX: 1-202-225-3375

Mike Parker (R)
(Fourth District)
2445 Rayburn House Office Bldg.
Phone: 1-202-225-5865
FAX: 1-202-225-5886

Gene Taylor (D)
(Fifth District)
2447 Rayburn House Office Bldg.
Phone: 1-202-225-5772
FAX: 1-202-225-7074

Missouri

Senators
Christopher S. Bond (R)
293 Russell Senate Office Building
Phone: 1-202-224-5721
FAX: 1-202-224-8149
kit_bond@bond.senate.gov

John Ashcroft (R)
170 Russell Senate Office Building
Phone: 1-202-224-6154
FAX: 1-202-228-0998
john_ashcroft@ashcroft.senate.gov

Representatives
William L. Clay (D)
(First District)
2306 Rayburn House Office Bldg.
Phone: 1-202-225-2406
FAX: 1-202-225-1725

James M. Talent (R)
(Second District)
1022 Longworth House Office Bldg.
Phone: 1-202-225-2561
FAX: 1-202-225-2563
talentmo@hr.house.gov

Richard A. Gephardt (D)
(Third District)
1226 Longworth House Office Bldg.
Phone: 1-202-225-2671
FAX: 1-202-225-7452
gephardt@hr.house.gov

Ike Skelton (D)
(Fourth District)
2227 Rayburn House Office Bldg.
Phone: 1-202-225-2876
FAX: 1-202-225-2695

Karen McCarthy (D)
(Fifth District)
1232 Longworth House Office Bldg.
Phone: 1-202-225-4535
FAX: 1-202-225-5990

Pat Danner (D)
(Sixth District)
1207 Longworth House Office Bldg.
Phone: 1-202-225-7041
FAX: 1-202-225-8221

Roy Blunt (R)
(Seventh District)
508 Cannon Building
Phone: 1-202-225-7700
FAX: 1-202-225-6536

Jo Ann Emerson (I)
(Eighth District)
132 Cannon Building
Phone: 1-202-225-4404
FAX: N/A

Kenny Hulshof (R)
(Ninth District)
1728 Longworth House Office Bldg.
Phone: 1-202-225-2956
FAX: 1-202-225-7834

Montana

Senators

Max Baucus (D)
511 Hart Senate Office Building
Phone: 1-202-224-2651
FAX: 1-202-224-1974
max@baucus.senate.gov

Conrad R. Burns (R)
187 Dirksen Senate Office Bldg.
Phone: 1-202-224-2644
FAX: 1-202-224-8594
conrad_burns@burns.senate.gov

Representative At Large

Rick Hill (R)
1037 Longworth House Office Bldg.
Phone: 1-202-225-3211
FAX: 1-202-226-0244

Nebraska

Senators

Chuck Hagel (R)
528 Hart Senate Office Building
Phone: 1-202-224-4224
FAX: 1-202-224-5213
email@hagel96.com (temporary)

Bob Kerrey (D)
303 Hart Senate Office Building
Phone: 1-202-224-6551
FAX: 1-202-224-7645
bob@kerrey.senate.gov

Representatives

Douglas Bereuter (R)
(First District)
2184 Rayburn House Office Bldg.
Phone: 1-202-225-4806
FAX: 1-202-226-1148

Jon Christensen (R)
(Second District)
413 Cannon Building
Phone: 1-202-225-4155
FAX: 1-202-225-3032
talk2jon@hr.house.gov

William E. Barrett (R)
(Third District)
2458 Rayburn House Office Bldg.
Phone: 1-202-225-6435
FAX: 1-202-225-0207

Nevada

Senators

Richard H. Bryan (D)
364 Russell Senate Office Building
Phone: 1-202-224-6244
FAX: 1-202-224-1867
senator@bryan.senate.gov

Harry Reid (D)
324 Hart Senate Office Building
Phone: 1-202-224-3542
FAX: 1-202-224-7327
senator_reid@reid.senate.gov

Representatives

John Ensign (R)
(First District)
414 Cannon Building
Phone: 1-202-225-5965
FAX: 1-202-225-8808
ensign@hr.house.gov

Jim Gibbons (R)
(Second District)
1116 Longworth House Office Bldg.
Phone: 1-202-225-6155
FAX: 1-202-225-2319

New Hampshire

Senators

Judd Gregg (R)
393 Russell Senate Office Building
Phone: 1-202-224-3324
FAX: 1-202-224-4952
mailbox@gregg.senate.gov

Bob Smith (R)
332 Dirksen Senate Office Bldg.
Phone: 1-202-224-2841
FAX: 1-202-224-1353
opinion@smith.senate.gov

Representatives

John Sununu (R)
(First District)
1229 Longworth House Office Bldg.
Phone: 1-202-225-5456
FAX: 1-202-225-4370

Charles Bass (R)
(Second District)
218 Cannon Building
Phone: 1-202-225-5206
FAX: 1-202-225-0046
cbass@hr.house.gov

New Jersey

Senators

Robert Torricelli (D)
728 Hart Senate Office Building
Phone: 1-202-224-3224
FAX: 1-202-224-8567
torricel@torricelli.com

Frank R. Lautenberg (D)
506 Hart Senate Office Building
Phone: 1-202-224-4744
FAX: 1-202-224-9707
frank_lautenberg@lautenberg.senate.gov

Representatives

Robert E. Andrews (D)
(First District)
2439 Rayburn House Office Bldg.
Phone: 1-202-225-6501
FAX: 1-202-225-6583
randrews@hr.house.gov

Frank LoBiondo (R)
(Second District)
222 Cannon Building
Phone: 1-202-225-6572
FAX: 1-202-226-1108
lobiondo@hr.house.gov

H. James Saxton (R)
(Third District)
339 Cannon Building
Phone: 1-202-225-4765
FAX: 1-202-225-0778

Christopher Smith (R)
(Fourth District)
2370 Rayburn House Office Bldg.
Phone: 1-202-225-3765
FAX: 1-202-225-7768

Marge Roukema (R)
(Fifth District)
2469 Rayburn House Office Bldg.
Phone: 1-202-225-4465
FAX: 1-202-225-9048

Frank Pallone, Jr. (D)
(Sixth District)
420 Cannon Building
Phone: 1-202-225-4671
FAX: 1-202-225-9665

Bob Franks (R)
(Seventh District)
225 Cannon Building
Phone: 1-202-225-5361
FAX: 1-202-225-9460
franksnj@hr.house.gov

William Pascrell (D)
(Eighth District)
1722 Longworth House Office Bldg.
Phone: 1-202-225-5751
FAX: 1-202-225-3372
bill@pascrell.org

Steven Rothman (D)
(Ninth District)
1607 Longworth House Office Bldg.
Phone: 1-202-225-5061
FAX: 1-202-225-0745

Donald M. Payne (D)
(Tenth District)
2244 Rayburn House Office Bldg.
Phone: 1-202-225-3436
FAX: 1-202-225-4160

Rodney Frelinghuysen (R)
(Eleventh District)
228 Cannon Building
Phone: 1-202-225-5034
FAX: 1-202-225-0658
njeleven@hr.house.gov

Mike Pappas (R)
(Twelfth District)
1710 Longworth House Office Bldg.
Phone: 1-202-225-5801
FAX: 1-202-225-9181

Robert Menendez (D)
(Thirteenth District)
405 Cannon Building
Phone: 1-202-225-7919
FAX: 1-202-226-0792

New Mexico

Senators

Jeff Bingaman (D)
703 Hart Senate Office Building
Phone: 1-202-224-5521
FAX: 1-202-224-2852
Senator_Bingaman@bingaman.senate.gov

Pete V. Domenici (R)
328 Hart Senate Office Building
Phone: 1-202-224-6621
FAX: 1-202-224-7371
senator_domenici@domenici.senate.gov

Representatives

Steven H. Schiff (R)
(First District)
2404 Rayburn House Office Bldg.
Phone: 1-202-225-6316
FAX: 1-202-225-4975

Joseph Skeen (R)
(Second District)
2302 Rayburn House Office Bldg.
Phone: 1-202-225-2365
FAX: 1-202-225-9599

William Richardson (D)
(Third District)
2268 Rayburn House Office Bldg.
Phone: 1-202-225-6190
FAX: 1-202-226-2160
billnm03@hr.house.gov

New York

Senators

Daniel P. Moynihan (D)
464 Russell Senate Office Building
Phone: 1-202-224-4451
FAX: 1-202-228-0406
senator@dpm.senate.gov

Alfonse M. D'Amato (R)
520 Hart Senate Office Building
Phone: 1-202-224-6542
FAX: 1-202-224-5871
senator_al@damato.senate.gov

Representatives

Michael Forbes (R)
(First District)
416 Cannon Building
Phone: 1-202-225-3826
FAX: 1-202-225-3143
mpforbes@hr.house.gov

Rick A. Lazio (R)
(Second District)
2444 Rayburn House Office Bldg.
Phone: 1-202-225-3335
FAX: 1-202-225-4669
lazio@hr.house.gov

Peter T. King (R)
(Third District)
403 Cannon Building
Phone: 1-202-225-7896
FAX: 1-202-226-2279
peteking@hr.house.gov

Carolyn McCarthy (D)
(Fourth District)
1725 Longworth House Office Bldg.
Phone: 1-202-225-5516
FAX: 1-202-225-5758

Gary L. Ackerman (D)
(Fifth District)
2243 Rayburn House Office Bldg.
Phone: 1-202-225-2601
FAX: 1-202-225-1589

Floyd H. Flake (D)
(Sixth District)
1035 Longworth House Office Bldg.
Phone: 1-202-225-3461
FAX: 1-202-226-4169

Thomas J. Manton (D)
(Seventh District)
2235 Rayburn House Office Bldg.
Phone: 1-202-225-3965
FAX: 1-202-225-1909
tmanton@hr.house.gov

Jerrold Nadler (D)
(Eighth District)
2448 Rayburn House Office Bldg.
Phone: 1-202-225-5635
FAX: 1-202-225-6923
nadler@hr.house.gov

Charles E. Schumer (D)
(Ninth District)
2211 Rayburn House Office Bldg.
Phone: 1-202-225-6616
FAX: 1-202-225-4183

Edolphus Towns (D)
(Tenth District)
2232 Rayburn House Office Bldg.
Phone: 1-202-225-5936
FAX: 1-202-225-1018

Major R. Owens (D)
(Eleventh District)
2305 Rayburn House Office Bldg.
Phone: 1-202-225-6231
FAX: 1-202-226-0112

Nydia M. Velazquez (D)
(Twelfth District)
1221 Longworth House Office Bldg.
Phone: 1-202-225-2361
FAX: 1-202-226-0327

Susan Molinari (R)
(Thirteenth District)
2411 Rayburn House Office Bldg.
Phone: 1-202-225-3371
FAX: 1-202-226-1272
molinari@hr.house.gov

Carolyn B. Maloney (D)
(Fourteenth District)
1330 Longworth House Office Bldg.
Phone: 1-202-225-7944
FAX: 1-202-225-4709
cmaloney@hr.house.gov

Charles B. Rangel (D)
(Fifteenth District)
2354 Rayburn House Office Bldg.
Phone: 1-202-225-4365
FAX: 1-202-225-0816
rangel@hr.house.gov

Jose E. Serrano (D)
(Sixteenth District)
2342 Rayburn House Office Bldg.
Phone: 1-202-225-4361
FAX: 1-202-225-6001
jserrano@hr.house.gov

Eliot L. Engel (D)
(Seventeenth District)
2303 Rayburn House Office Bldg.
Phone: 1-202-225-2464
FAX: 1-202-225-5513
engeline@hr.house.gov

Nita M. Lowey (D)
(Eighteenth District)
2421 Rayburn House Office Bldg.
Phone: 1-202-225-6506
FAX: 1-202-225-0546
nitamail@hr.house.gov

Sue Kelly (R)
(Nineteenth District)
1222 Longworth House Office Bldg.
Phone: 1-202-225-5441
FAX: 1-202-225-0962
dearsue@hr.house.gov

Benjamin A. Gilman (R)
(Twentieth District)
2449 Rayburn House Office Bldg.
Phone: 1-202-225-3776
FAX: 1-202-225-2541

Michael R. McNulty (D)
(Twenty-First District)
2161 Rayburn House Office Bldg.
Phone: 1-202-225-5076
FAX: 1-202-225-5077
mmcnulty@hr.house.gov

Gerald B. Solomon (R)
(Twenty-Second District)
2206 Rayburn House Office Bldg.
Phone: 1-202-225-5614
FAX: 1-202-225-6234

Sherwood Boehlert (R)
(Twenty-Third District)
2246 Rayburn House Office Bldg.
Phone: 1-202-225-3665
FAX: 1-202-225-1891
boehlert@hr.house.gov

John M. McHugh (R)
(Twenty-Fourth District)
2441 Rayburn House Office Bldg.
Phone: 1-202-225-4611
FAX: 1-202-226-0621

James T. Walsh (R)
(Twenty-Fifth District)
2351 Rayburn House Office Bldg.
Phone: 1-202-225-3701
FAX: 1-202-225-4042
jwalsh@hr.house.gov

Maurice D. Hinchey (D)
(Twenty-Sixth District)
2431 Rayburn House Office Bldg.
Phone: 1-202-225-6335
FAX: 1-202-226-0774
hinchey@hr.house.gov

Bill Paxon (R)
(Twenty-Seventh District)
2412 Rayburn House Office Bldg.
Phone: 1-202-225-5265
FAX: 1-202-225-5910
bpaxon@hr.house.gov

Louise M. Slaughter (D)
(Twenty-Eighth District)
2347 Rayburn House Office Bldg.
Phone: 1-202-225-3615
FAX: 1-202-225-7822
louiseny@hr.house.gov

John J. LaFalce (D)
(Twenty-Ninth District)
2310 Rayburn House Office Bldg.
Phone: 1-202-225-3231
FAX: 1-202-225-8693

Jack Quinn (R)
(Thirtieth District)
331 Cannon Building
Phone: 1-202-225-3306
FAX: 1-202-226-0347

Amory Houghton (R)
(Thirty-First District)
1110 Longworth House Office Bldg.
Phone: 1-202-225-3161
FAX: 1-202-225-5574
houghton@hr.house.gov

North Carolina

Senators
D. M. Faircloth (R)
317 Hart Senate Office Building
Phone: 1-202-224-3154
FAX: 1-202-224-7406
senator@faircloth.senate.gov

Jesse Helms (R)
403 Dirksen Senate Office Bldg.
Phone: 1-202-224-6342
FAX: 1-202-224-7588
jesse_helms@helms.senate.gov

Representatives
Eva Clayton (D)
(First District)
2440 Rayburn House Office Bldg.
Phone: 1-202-225-3101
FAX: 1-202-225-3354
eclayton@hr.house.gov

Bob Etheridge (D)
(Second District)
1641 Longworth House Office Bldg.
Phone: 1-202-225-4531
FAX: 1-202-225-3191

Walter Jones (R)
(Third District)
422 Cannon Building
Phone: 1-202-225-3415
FAX: 1-202-225-0666

David Price (D)
(Fourth District)
2162 Rayburn House Office Bldg.
Phone: 1-202-225-1784
FAX: 1-202-225-3269

Richard Burr (R)
(Fifth District)
1513 Longworth House Office Bldg.
Phone: 1-202-225-2071
FAX: 1-202-225-4060
mail2nc5@hr.house.gov

Howard Coble (R)
(Sixth District)
2239 Rayburn House Office Bldg.
Phone: 1-202-225-3065
FAX: 1-202-225-8611

Mike McIntyre (D)
(Seventh District)
1605 Longworth House Office Bldg.
Phone: 1-202-225-2731
FAX: 1-202-225-0345

W. G. Hefner (D)
(Eighth District)
2470 Rayburn House Office Bldg.
Phone: 1-202-225-3715
FAX: 1-202-225-4036

Sue Myrick (R)
(Ninth District)
230 Cannon Building
Phone: 1-202-225-1976
FAX: 1-202-225-8995
myrick@hr.house.gov

Thomas C. Ballenger (R)
(Tenth District)
2182 Rayburn House Office Bldg.
Phone: 1-202-225-2576
FAX: 1-202-225-0316
cassmail@hr.house.gov

Charles Hart Taylor (R)
(Eleventh District)
231 Cannon Building
Phone: 1-202-225-6401
FAX: 1-202-226-6405
chtaylor@hr.house.gov

Melvin Watt (D)
(Twelfth District)
1230 Longworth House Office Bldg.
Phone: 1-202-225-1510
FAX: 1-202-225-1512
melmail@hr.house.gov

North Dakota

Senators
Kent Conrad (D)
724 Hart Senate Office Building
Phone: 1-202-224-2043
FAX: 1-202-224-7776
senator@conrad.senate.gov

Byron L. Dorgan (D)
713 Hart Senate Office Building
Phone: 1-202-224-2551
FAX: 1-202-224-1193
senator@dorgan.senate.gov

Representative At Large
Earl Pomeroy (D)
1533 Longworth House Office Bldg.
Phone: 1-202-225-2611
FAX: 1-202-226-0893
epomeroy@hr.house.gov

Ohio

Senators
John Glenn (D)
503 Hart Senate Office Building
Phone: 1-202-224-3353
FAX: 1-202-224-7983
senator_glenn@glenn.senate.gov

Michael DeWine (R)
140 Russell Senate Office Building
Phone: 1-202-224-2315
FAX: 1-202-224-6519
senator_dewine@dewine.senate.gov

Representatives
Steve Chabot (R)
(First District)
129 Cannon Building
Phone: 1-202-225-2216
FAX: 1-202-225-4732

Rob Portman (R)
(Second District)
238 Cannon Building
Phone: 1-202-225-3164
FAX: 1-202-225-1992
portmail@hr.house.gov

Tony P. Hall (D)
(Third District)
1432 Longworth House Office Bldg.
Phone: 1-202-225-6465
FAX: 1-202-225-6766

Michael G. Oxley (R)
(Fourth District)
2233 Rayburn House Office Bldg.
Phone: 1-202-225-2676
FAX: 1-202-226-1160
oxley@hr.house.gov

Paul E. Gillmor (R)
(Fifth District)
1203 Longworth House Office Bldg.
Phone: 1-202-225-6405
FAX: 1-202-225-1985

Ted Strickland (D)
(Sixth District)
336 Cannon Building
Phone: 1-202-225-5705
FAX: N/A

David L. Hobson (R)
(Seventh District)
1514 Longworth House Office Bldg.
Phone: 1-202-225-4324
FAX: 1-202-225-1984

John Andrew Boehner (R)
(Eighth District)
1011 Longworth House Office Bldg.
Phone: 1-202-225-6205
FAX: 1-202-225-0704

Marcy Kaptur (D)
(Ninth District)
2311 Rayburn House Office Bldg.
Phone: 1-202-225-4146
FAX: 1-202-225-7711

Dennis Kucinich (D)
(Tenth District)
1730 Longworth House Office Bldg.
Phone: 1-202-225-5871
FAX: N/A

Louis Stokes (D)
(Eleventh District)
2365 Rayburn House Office Bldg.
Phone: 1-202-225-7032
FAX: 1-202-225-1339

John R. Kasich (R)
(Twelfth District)
1111 Longworth House Office Bldg.
Phone: 1-202-225-5355
FAX: N/A
budget@hr.house.gov

Sherrod Brown (D)
(Thirteenth District)
328 Cannon Building
Phone: 1-202-225-3401
FAX: 1-202-225-2266
sherrod@hr.house.gov

Thomas C. Sawyer (D)
(Fourteenth District)
1414 Longworth House Office Bldg.
Phone: 1-202-225-5231
FAX: 1-202-225-5278

Deborah Pryce (R)
(Fifteenth District)
221 Cannon Building
Phone: 1-202-225-2015
FAX: 1-202-226-0986
pryce15@hr.house.gov

Ralph Regula (R)
(Sixteenth District)
2309 Rayburn House Office Bldg.
Phone: 1-202-225-3876
FAX: 1-202-225-3059

James Traficant, Jr. (D)
(Seventeenth District)
2446 Rayburn House Office Bldg.
Phone: 1-202-225-5261
FAX: 1-202-225-3719
telljim@hr.house.gov

Bob Ney (R)
(Eighteenth District)
1024 Longworth House Office Bldg.
Phone: 1-202-225-6265
FAX: 1-202-225-3394
bobney@hr.house.gov

Steven LaTourette (R)
(Nineteenth District)
1239 Longworth House Office Bldg.
Phone: 1-202-225-5731
FAX: 1-202-225-9114

Oklahoma

Senators
James Inhofe (R)
453 Russell Senate Office Building
Phone: 1-202-224-4721
FAX: 1-202-228-0380

Donald Nickles (R)
133 Hart Senate Office Building
Phone: 1-202-224-5754
FAX: 1-202-224-6008
senator@nickles.senate.gov

Representatives
Steve Largent (R)
(First District)
426 Cannon Building
Phone: 1-202-225-2211
FAX: 1-202-225-9187

Tom Coburn (R)
(Second District)
429 Cannon Building
Phone: 1-202-225-2701
FAX: 1-202-225-2796

Wes Watkins (R)
(Third District)
2312 Rayburn House Office Bldg.
Phone: 1-202-225-4565
FAX: 1-202-225-9029

J.C. Watts (R)
(Fourth District)
1210 Longworth House Office Bldg.
Phone: 1-202-225-6165
FAX: 1-202-225-9746

Ernest Jim Istook (R)
(Fifth District)
119 Cannon Building
Phone: 1-202-225-2132
FAX: 1-202-226-1463
istook@hr.house.gov

Frank Lucas (R)
(Sixth District)
107 Cannon Building
Phone: 1-202-225-5565
FAX: 1-202-225-8698

Oregon

Senators
Gordon Smith (R)
711 Hart Senate Office Building
Phone: 1-202-224-3753
FAX: 1-202-224-0276

Ron Wyden (D)
259 Russell Senate Office Building
Phone: 1-202-224-5244
FAX: 1-202-228-2717
senator@wyden.senate.gov

Representatives
Elizabeth Furse (D)
(First District)
316 Cannon Building
Phone: 1-202-225-0855
FAX: 1-202-225-9497
furseor1@hr.house.gov

Bob Smith (R)
(Second District)
1126 Longworth House Office Bldg.
Phone: 1-202-225-6730
FAX: 1-202-225-3046

Earl Blumenauer (D)
(Third District)
1113 Longworth House Office Bldg.
Phone: 1-202-225-4811
FAX: 1-202-225-8941

Peter A. DeFazio (D)
(Fourth District)
2134 Rayburn House Office Bldg.
Phone: 1-202-225-6416
FAX: 1-202-225-0373
pdefazio@hr.house.gov

Darlene Hooley (D)
(Fifth District)
1419 Longworth House Office Bldg.
Phone: 1-202-225-5711
FAX: 1-202-225-2994

Pennsylvania

Senators
Rick Santorum (R)
120 Russell Senate Office Building
Phone: 1-202-224-6324
FAX: 1-202-228-0604
senator@santorum.senate.gov

Arlen Specter (R)
530 Hart Senate Office Building
Phone: 1-202-224-4254
FAX: 1-202-224-1893
senator_specter@specter.senate.gov

Representatives
Thomas M. Foglietta (D)
(First District)
242 Cannon Building
Phone: 1-202-225-4731
FAX: 1-202-225-0088
mailtom@hr.house.gov

Chaka Fattah (D)
(Second District)
1205 Longworth House Office Bldg.
Phone: 1-202-225-4001
FAX: 1-202-225-7362

Robert A. Borski (D)
(Third District)
2267 Rayburn House Office Bldg.
Phone: 1-202-225-8251
FAX: 1-202-225-4628

Ron Klink (D)
(Fourth District)
125 Cannon Building
Phone: 1-202-225-2565
FAX: 1-202-226-2274

John Peterson (R)
(Fifth District)
1020 Longworth House Office Bldg.
Phone: 1-202-225-5121
FAX: 1-202-225-4681

Tim Holden (D)
(Sixth District)
1421 Longworth House Office Bldg.
Phone: 1-202-225-5546
FAX: 1-202-226-0996

Curt Weldon (R)
(Seventh District)
2452 Rayburn House Office Bldg.
Phone: 1-202-225-2011
FAX: 1-202-225-8137
curtpa7@hr.house.gov

Jim Greenwood (R)
(Eighth District)
2436 Rayburn House Office Bldg.
Phone: 1-202-225-4276
FAX: 1-202-225-9511
jim.greenwood@mail.house.gov

Bud Shuster (R)
(Ninth District)
2188 Rayburn House Office Bldg.
Phone: 1-202-225-2431
FAX: 1-202-225-2486
shuster@hr.house.gov

Joseph M. McDade (R)
(Tenth District)
2107 Rayburn House Office Bldg.
Phone: 1-202-225-3731
FAX: 1-202-225-9594

Paul E. Kanjorski (D)
(Eleventh District)
2353 Rayburn House Office Bldg.
Phone: 1-202-225-6511
FAX: 1-202-225-9024
kanjo@hr.house.gov

John P. Murtha (D)
(Twelfth District)
2423 Rayburn House Office Bldg.
Phone: 1-202-225-2065
FAX: 1-202-225-5709
murtha@hr.house.gov

Jon Fox (R)
(Thirteenth District)
435 Cannon Building
Phone: 1-202-225-6111
FAX: 1-202-225-3187
jonfox@hr.house.gov

William J. Coyne (D)
(Fourteenth District)
2455 Rayburn House Office Bldg.
Phone: 1-202-225-2301
FAX: 1-202-225-1844

Paul McHale (D)
(Fifteenth District)
217 Cannon Building
Phone: 1-202-225-6411
FAX: 1-202-225-5320
mchale@hr.house.gov

Joseph Pitts (R)
(Sixteenth District)
504 Cannon Building
Phone: 1-202-225-2411
FAX: 1-202-225-1116

George W. Gekas (R)
(Seventeenth District)
2410 Rayburn House Office Bldg.
Phone: 1-202-225-4315
FAX: 1-202-225-8440

Mike Doyle (D)
(Eighteenth District)
133 Cannon Building
Phone: 1-202-225-2135
FAX: 1-202-225-7747

William F. Goodling (R)
(Nineteenth District)
2263 Rayburn House Office Bldg.
Phone: 1-202-225-5836
FAX: 1-202-226-1000

Frank Mascara (D)
(Twentieth District)
314 Cannon Building
Phone: 1-202-225-4665
FAX: 1-202-225-3377

Phil English (R)
(Twenty-First District)
1721 Longworth House Office Bldg.
Phone: 1-202-225-5406
FAX: 1-202-225-1081

Rhode Island

Senators
Jack Reed (D)
339 Russell Senate Office Building
Phone: 1-202-224-4642
FAX: 1-202-224-4680
reed@collegehill.com

John H. Chafee (R)
505 Dirksen Senate Office Bldg.
Phone: 1-202-224-2921
FAX: 1-202-228-2853
senator_chafee@chafee.senate.gov

Representatives
Patrick Kennedy (D)
(First District)
312 Cannon Building
Phone: 1-202-225-4911
FAX: 1-202-225-4417

Robert Weygand (D)
(Second District)
507 Cannon Building
Phone: 1-202-225-2735
FAX: 1-202-225-9580

South Carolina

Senators

Ernest F. Hollings (D)
125 Russell Senate Office Building
Phone: 1-202-224-6121
FAX: 1-202-224-4293
senator@hollings.senate.gov

Strom Thurmond (R)
217 Russell Senate Office Building
Phone: 1-202-224-5972
FAX: 1-202-224-1300
senator@thurmond.senate.gov

Representatives

Mark Sanford (R)
(First District)
1223 Longworth House Office Bldg.
Phone: 1-202-225-3176
FAX: 1-202-225-3407
sanford@hr.house.gov

Floyd Spence (R)
(Second District)
2405 Rayburn House Office Bldg.
Phone: 1-202-225-2452
FAX: 1-202-225-2455

Lindsey Graham (R)
(Third District)
1429 Longworth House Office Bldg.
Phone: 1-202-225-5301
FAX: 1-202-225-5383

Bob Inglis (R)
(Fourth District)
320 Cannon Building
Phone: 1-202-225-6030
FAX: 1-202-226-1177
binglis@hr.house.gov

John M. Spratt, Jr. (D)
(Fifth District)
1536 Longworth House Office Bldg.
Phone: 1-202-225-5501
FAX: 1-202-225-0464
jspratt@hr.house.gov

James E. Clyburn (D)
(Sixth District)
319 Cannon Building
Phone: 1-202-225-3315
FAX: 1-202-225-2313
jclyburn@hr.house.gov

South Dakota

Senators

Thomas A. Daschle (D)
509 Hart Senate Office Building
Phone: 1-202-224-2321
FAX: 1-202-224-2047
tom_daschle@daschle.senate.gov

Tim Johnson (D)
528 Hart Senate Office Building
Phone: 1-202-224-5842
FAX: N/A

Representative At Large

John Thune (R)
506 Cannon Building
Phone: 1-202-225-2801
FAX: 1-202-225-2427

Tennessee

Senators

Fred Thompson (R)
523 Dirksen Senate Office Bldg.
Phone: 1-202-224-4944
FAX: 1-202-228-3679
senator_thompson@thompson.senate.gov

Bill Frist (R)
565 Dirksen Senate Office Bldg.
Phone: 1-202-224-3344
FAX: 1-202-228-1264
senator_frist@frist.senate.gov

Representatives

Bill Jenkins (R)
(First District)
1708 Longworth House Office Bldg.
Phone: 1-202-225-6356
FAX: 1-202-225-7812
bhorton@tricon.net

John J. Duncan, Jr. (R)
(Second District)
2400 Rayburn House Office Bldg.
Phone: 1-202-225-5435
FAX: 1-202-225-6440
jjduncan@hr.house.gov

Zach Wamp (R)
(Third District)
423 Cannon Building
Phone: 1-202-225-3271
FAX: 1-202-225-6974

Van Hilleary (R)
(Fourth District)
114 Cannon Building
Phone: 1-202-225-6831
FAX: 1-202-225-3272
hilleary@hr.house.gov

Robert Clement (D)
(Fifth District)
2229 Rayburn House Office Bldg.
Phone: 1-202-225-4311
FAX: 1-202-226-1035
clement@hr.house.gov

Bart Gordon (D)
(Sixth District)
2201 Rayburn House Office Bldg.
Phone: 1-202-225-4231
FAX: 1-202-225-6887
bart@hr.house.gov

Ed Bryant (R)
(Seventh District)
408 Cannon Building
Phone: 1-202-225-2811
FAX: 1-202-225-2814

John S. Tanner (D)
(Eighth District)
1127 Longworth House Office Bldg.
Phone: 1-202-225-4714
FAX: 1-202-225-1765

Harold E. Ford, Jr. (D)
(Ninth District)
1523 Longworth House Office Bldg.
Phone: 1-202-225-3265
FAX: 1-202-225-9215

Texas

Senators

Kay Bailey Hutchison (R)
283 Russell Senate Office Building
Phone: 1-202-224-5922
FAX: 1-202-224-0776
senator@hutchison.senate.gov

Phil Gramm (R)
370 Russell Senate Office Building
Phone: 1-202-224-2934
FAX: 1-202-228-2856

Representatives

Max Sandlin (D)
(First District)
214 Cannon Building
Phone: 1-202-225-3035
FAX: 1-202-225-7265

James Turner (D)
(Second District)
1508 Longworth House Office Bldg.
Phone: 1-202-225-2401
FAX: 1-202-225-1764

Sam Johnson (R)
(Third District)
1030 Longworth House Office Bldg.
Phone: 1-202-225-4201
FAX: 1-202-225-1485
samtx03@hr.house.gov

Ralph M. Hall (D)
(Fourth District)
2221 Rayburn House Office Bldg.
Phone: 1-202-225-6673
FAX: 1-202-225-3332

Pete Sessions (R)
(Fifth District)
1318 Longworth House Office Bldg.
Phone: 1-202-225-2231
FAX: 1-202-225-0327

Joseph Barton (R)
(Sixth District)
2264 Rayburn House Office Bldg.
Phone: 1-202-225-2002
FAX: 1-202-225-3052
barton06@hr.house.gov

William Archer (R)
(Seventh District)
1236 Longworth House Office Bldg.
Phone: 1-202-225-2571
FAX: 1-202-225-4381

Kevin Brady (R)
(Eighth District)
1531 Longworth House Office Bldg.
Phone: 1-202-225-4901
FAX: 1-202-225-2772

Nick Lampson (D)
(Ninth District)
417 Cannon Building
Phone: 1-202-225-6565
FAX: N/A

Lloyd Doggett (D)
(Tenth District)
126 Cannon Building
Phone: 1-202-225-4865
FAX: 1-202-225-3018
doggett@hr.house.gov

Chet Edwards (D)
(Eleventh District)
2459 Rayburn House Office Bldg.
Phone: 1-202-225-6105
FAX: 1-202-225-0350

Kay Granger (R)
(Twelfth District)
518 Cannon Building
Phone: 1-202-225-5071
FAX: 1-202-225-2786

William Thornberry (R)
(Thirteenth District)
412 Cannon Building
Phone: 1-202-225-3706
FAX: 1-202-225-3486

Ron Paul (R)
(Fourteenth District)
203 Cannon Building
Phone: 1-202-225-2831
FAX: 1-202-225-1108

Ruben Hinojosa (D)
(Fifteenth District)
1032 Longworth House Office Bldg.
Phone: 1-202-225-2531
FAX: 1-202-225-2534

Silvestre Reyes (D)
(Sixteenth District)
514 Cannon Building
Phone: 1-202-225-4831
FAX: 1-202-225-4825

Charles W. Stenholm (D)
(Seventeenth District)
1211 Longworth House Office Bldg.
Phone: 1-202-225-6605
FAX: 1-202-225-2234
texas17@hr.house.gov

Sheila Jackson-Lee (D)
(Eighteenth District)
410 Cannon Building
Phone: 1-202-225-3816
FAX: 1-202-225-3317

Larry Combest (R)
(Nineteenth District)
1026 Longworth House Office Bldg.
Phone: 1-202-225-4005
FAX: 1-202-225-9615

Henry B. Gonzalez (D)
(Twentieth District)
2413 Rayburn House Office Bldg.
Phone: 1-202-225-3236
FAX: 1-202-225-1915
bnkgdems@hr.house.gov

Lamar S. Smith (R)
(Twenty-First District)
2231 Rayburn House Office Bldg.
Phone: 1-202-225-4236
FAX: 1-202-225-8628
lamars@hr.house.gov

Thomas DeLay (R)
(Twenty-Second District)
341 Cannon Building
Phone: 1-202-225-5951
FAX: 1-202-225-5241
thewhip@mail.house.gov

Henry Bonilla (R)
(Twenty-Third District)
1427 Longworth House Office Bldg.
Phone: 1-202-225-4511
FAX: 1-202-225-2237

Martin Frost (D)
(Twenty-Fourth District)
2256 Rayburn House Office Bldg.
Phone: 1-202-225-3605
FAX: 1-202-225-4951
frost@hr.house.gov

Ken Bentsen (D)
(Twenty-Fifth District)
128 Cannon Building
Phone: 1-202-225-7508
FAX: 1-202-225-2947
bentsen@hr.house.gov

Richard K. Armey (R)
(Twenty-Sixth District)
301 Cannon Building
Phone: 1-202-225-7772
FAX: 1-202-225-7614

Solomon P. Ortiz (D)
(Twenty-Seventh District)
2136 Rayburn House Office Bldg.
Phone: 1-202-225-7742
FAX: 1-202-226-1134

Frank Tejeda (D)
(Twenty-Eighth District)
323 Cannon Building
Phone: 1-202-225-1640
FAX: 1-202-225-1641

Gene Green (D)
(Twenty-Ninth District)
2429 Rayburn House Office Bldg.
Phone: 1-202-225-1688
FAX: 1-202-225-9903
ggreen@hr.house.gov

Eddie Bernice Johnson (D)
(Thirtieth District)
1123 Longworth House Office Bldg.
Phone: 1-202-225-8885
FAX: 1-202-226-1477

Utah

Senators
Robert Bennett (R)
431 Dirksen Senate Office Bldg.
Phone: 1-202-224-5444
FAX: 1-202-224-4908
senator@bennett.senate.gov

Orrin G. Hatch (R)
131 Russell Senate Office Building
Phone: 1-202-224-5251
FAX: 1-202-224-6331
senator_hatch@hatch.senate.gov

Representatives
James V. Hansen (R)
(First District)
2466 Rayburn House Office Bldg.
Phone: 1-202-225-0453
FAX: 1-202-225-5857

Merrill Cook (R)
(Second District)
1431 Longworth House Office Bldg.
Phone: 1-202-225-3011
FAX: 1-202-225-3491

Christopher Cannon (R)
(Third District)
118 Cannon Building
Phone: 1-202-225-7751
FAX: 1-202-226-7683

Vermont

Senators
Patrick J. Leahy (D)
433 Russell Senate Office Building
Phone: 1-202-224-4242
FAX: 1-202-224-3595
senator_leahy@leahy.senate.gov

James M. Jeffords (R)
513 Hart Senate Office Building
Phone: 1-202-224-5141
FAX: N/A
vermont@jeffords.senate.gov

Representative At Large
Bernard Sanders (I)
2202 Rayburn House Office Bldg.
Phone: 1-202-225-4115
FAX: 1-202-225-6790
bsanders@hr.house.gov

Virginia

Senators
Charles S. Robb (D)
154 Russell Senate Office Building
Phone: 1-202-224-4024
FAX: 1-202-224-8689
Senator_Robb@robb.senate.gov
vascr@CapAccess.org

John W. Warner (R)
225 Russell Senate Office Building
Phone: 1-202-224-2023
FAX: 1-202-224-6079
senator@warner.senate.gov

Representatives
Herbert H. Bateman (R)
(First District)
2350 Rayburn House Office Bldg.
Phone: 1-202-225-4261
FAX: 1-202-225-4382

Owen B. Pickett (D)
(Second District)
2430 Rayburn House Office Bldg.
Phone: 1-202-225-4215
FAX: 1-202-225-4218
opickett@hr.house.gov

Robert C. Scott (D)
(Third District)
2464 Rayburn House Office Bldg.
Phone: 1-202-225-8351
FAX: 1-202-225-8354

Norman Sisisky (D)
(Fourth District)
2371 Rayburn House Office Bldg.
Phone: 1-202-225-6365
FAX: 1-202-226-1170

Virgil Goode (D)
(Fifth District)
1520 Longworth House Office Bldg.
Phone: 1-202-225-4711
FAX: 1-202-226-1147

Robert W. Goodlatte (R)
(Sixth District)
123 Cannon Building
Phone: 1-202-225-5431
FAX: 1-202-225-9681
talk2bob@hr.house.gov

Thomas J. Bliley, Jr. (R)
(Seventh District)
2409 Rayburn House Office Bldg.
Phone: 1-202-225-2815
FAX: 1-202-225-0011

James P. Moran, Jr. (D)
(Eighth District)
1214 Longworth House Office Bldg.
Phone: 1-202-225-4376
FAX: 1-202-225-0017
repmoran@hr.house.gov

Rick Boucher (D)
(Ninth District)
2329 Rayburn House Office Bldg.
Phone: 1-202-225-3861
FAX: 1-202-225-0442
ninthnet@hr.house.gov

Frank R. Wolf (R)
(Tenth District)
241 Cannon Building
Phone: 1-202-225-5136
FAX: 1-202-225-0437

Thomas Davis (R)
(Eleventh District)
224 Cannon Building
Phone: 1-202-225-1492
FAX: 1-202-225-2274
tomdavis@hr.house.gov

Washington

Senators
Patty Murray (D)
111 Russell Senate Office Building
Phone: 1-202-224-2621
FAX: 1-202-224-0238
senator_murray@murray.senate.gov

Slade Gorton (R)
730 Hart Senate Office Building
Phone: 1-202-224-3441
FAX: 1-202-224-9393
Senator_Gorton@gorton.senate.gov

Representatives
Rick White (R)
(First District)
116 Cannon Building
Phone: 1-202-225-6311
FAX: 1-202-225-3524
repwhite@mail.house.gov

Jack Metcalf (R)
(Second District)
1510 Longworth House Office Bldg.
Phone: 1-202-225-2605
FAX: 1-202-225-4420

Linda Smith (R)
(Third District)
1317 Longworth House Office Bldg.
Phone: 1-202-225-3536
FAX: 1-202-225-3478
asklinda@hr.house.gov

Doc Hastings (R)
(Fourth District)
1323 Longworth House Office Bldg.
Phone: 1-202-225-5816
FAX: 1-202-225-3251

George Nethercutt (R)
(Fifth District)
1527 Longworth House Office Bldg.
Phone: 1-202-225-2006
FAX: 1-202-225-3392
grnwa05@hr.house.gov

Norman D. Dicks (D)
(Sixth District)
2467 Rayburn House Office Bldg.
Phone: 1-202-225-5916
FAX: 1-202-226-1176

James A. McDermott (D)
(Seventh District)
2349 Rayburn House Office Bldg.
Phone: 1-202-225-3106
FAX: 1-206-553-7175

Jennifer Dunn (R)
(Eighth District)
432 Cannon Building
Phone: 1-202-225-7761
FAX: 1-202-225-8673
dunnwa08@hr.house.gov

Adam Smith (D)
(Ninth District)
1505 Longworth House Office Bldg.
Phone: 1-202-225-8901
FAX: 1-202-225-3484

West Virginia

Senators
Robert C. Byrd (D)
311 Hart Senate Office Building
Phone: 1-202-224-3954
FAX: 1-202-228-0002
senator_byrd@byrd.senate.gov

John D. Rockefeller (D)
109 Hart Senate Office Building
Phone: 1-202-224-6472
FAX: 1-202-224-7665
senator@rockefeller.senate.gov

Representatives
Alan B. Mollohan (D)
(First District)
2346 Rayburn House Office Bldg.
Phone: 1-202-225-4172
FAX: 1-202-225-7564

Robert E. Wise, Jr. (D)
(Second District)
2367 Rayburn House Office Bldg.
Phone: 1-202-225-2711
FAX: 1-202-225-7856
bobwise@hr.house.gov

Nick Joe Rahall II (D)
(Third District)
2307 Rayburn House Office Bldg.
Phone: 1-202-225-3452
FAX: 1-202-225-9061
nrahall@hr.house.gov

Wisconsin

Senators
Russell Feingold (D)
502 Hart Senate Office Building
Phone: 1-202-224-5323
FAX: 1-202-224-2725
russell_feingold@feingold.senate.gov

Herbert H. Kohl (D)
330 Hart Senate Office Building
Phone: 1-202-224-5653
FAX: 1-202-224-9787
senator_kohl@kohl.senate.gov

Representatives
Mark Neumann (R)
(First District)
415 Cannon Building
Phone: 1-202-225-3031
FAX: 1-202-225-3393
mneumann@hr.house.gov

Scott Klug (R)
(Second District)
2331 Rayburn House Office Bldg.
Phone: 1-202-225-2906
FAX: 1-202-225-6942
badger02@hr.house.gov

Ron Kind (D)
(Third District)
1713 Longworth House Office Bldg.
Phone: 1-202-225-5506
FAX: 1-202-225-6195

Gerald D. Kleczka (D)
(Fourth District)
2301 Rayburn House Office Bldg.
Phone: 1-202-225-4572
FAX: 1-202-225-8135
jerry4wi@hr.house.gov

Thomas M. Barrett (D)
(Fifth District)
1224 Longworth House Office Bldg.
Phone: 1-202-225-3571
FAX: 1-202-225-2185
telltom@hr.house.gov

Thomas E. Petri (R)
(Sixth District)
2262 Rayburn House Office Bldg.
Phone: 1-202-225-2476
FAX: 1-202-225-0561
tompetri@hr.house.gov

David R. Obey (D)
(Seventh District)
2462 Rayburn House Office Bldg.
Phone: 1-202-225-3365
FAX: 1-202-225-3240

Jay Johnson (D)
(Eighth District)
1313 Longworth House Office Bldg.
Phone: 1-202-225-5665
FAX: 1-202-225-0087

F. J. Sensenbrenner (R)
(Ninth District)
2332 Rayburn House Office Bldg.
Phone: 1-202-225-5101
FAX: 1-202-225-3190
sensen09@hr.house.gov

Wyoming

Senators
Michael Enzi (R)
116 Dirksen Senate Office Bldg.
Phone: 1-202-224-3424
FAX: 1-202-228-0350
mike@enzi.senate.gov

Craig Thomas (R)
302 Hart Senate Office Building
Phone: 1-202-224-6441
FAX: 1-202-224-1724
craig@thomas.senate.gov

Representative At Large
Barbara Cubin (R)
1114 Longworth House Office Bldg.
Phone: 1-202-225-2311
FAX: 1-202-225-3057

Author's Note:

As a citizen of the United States, you should always feel free to write or call any member of the government, especially those who represent you directly in Congress.

This is why we have provided you with the names and addresses of the Administration and all members of the U.S. Congress.

Your representatives and others serving in the government want to hear from you and learn how you feel about issues that face this nation and your particular area of the country.

One letter or call can make a difference in the way a U.S. Senator or U.S. Representative votes in Washington, D.C.

Your representatives in Washington, D.C. also have offices in their states. You are encouraged to visit your representatives in person with your questions and comments.

Public and school libraries have references explaining how to effectively communicate with our leaders.

XII. Notable Supreme Court Decisions

The Supreme Court

The Supreme Court term that began Oct. 2, 1995, and ended July 1, 1996, marked William H. Rehnquist's 10th year as Chief Justice. The Court issued signed opinions in only 75 cases, seven fewer than in 1994-95 and its lightest caseload in more than 40 years. The full Court ruled unanimously in 34 cases, or 45% of the total; 12 cases, or 16%, were decided by a 5-4 vote.

Two moderate conservatives, Justices Sandra Day O'Connor and Anthony M. Kennedy, held the balance of power. O'Connor dissented only six times, Kennedy five; each voted with the majority in 75% of the 5-4 decisions. Justice John Paul Stevens, a moderate liberal, was the Court's most frequent dissenter, siding with the minority in 19 of the 41 cases where the Court did not reach a unanimous verdict. The Court's most conservative member, Justice Antonin Scalia, also dissented frequently.

Notable Decisions from 1995 to 1996

Banking and Commerce

- **U.S. v. Winstar**, July 1: In a ruling that could cost U.S. taxpayers up to $10 billion, the Court held, 7-2, that the federal government had breached its contract with savings and loan institutions when Congress changed accounting rules and, in effect, pushed many S&Ls into insolvency.

- **Smiley v. Citicorp**, June 3: A 9-0 ruling upheld the right of banks to charge late fees on out-of state credit card accounts even when cardholders' home states ban or limit such fees.

- **BMW v. Gore**, May 20: The Court, 5-4, struck down as "grossly excessive" a $4 million punitive-damage award for a car sold as new that had been repainted.

Confidentiality

- **Jaffee v. Redmond**, June 13: By a 7-2 vote, the Court held that mental health professionals, including clinical social workers, may not be compelled to reveal details of counseling sessions with patients.

Criminal Law

The Court strengthened the hand of law-enforcement officials against drug traffickers by upholding the government's right both to seek criminal penalties against a defendant and to seize the same person's property.

- **U.S. v. Ursery**, June 24: Writing for an 8-1 majority, Chief Justice Rehnquist maintained that such civil forfeiture did not violate the constitutional ban on double jeopardy.

- **U.S. v. Armstrong**, May 13: Another important 8-1 decision ruled out purely statistical claims that the federal government's prosecution of crack-cocaine cases was racially biased.

- **Whren v. U.S.**, June 10: The Court was unanimous in granting the police wide latitude to use even a minor traffic violation as a reason for stopping a vehicle and searching it for drugs.

Death Penalty

- **Loving v. U.S.**, June 3: The Court unanimously upheld the use of capital punishment by the military justice system.

- **Felker v. Turpin**, June 28: The Court unanimously upheld a federal law restricting appeals by death-row inmates.

Notable Decisions from 1995 to 1996 (continued)

Equal Rights

- *Romer v. Evans*, May 20: The Court struck down, 6-3, a controversial state constitutional amendment in Colorado that specifically excluded homosexuals from civil rights protections.

- *U.S. v. Virginia*, June 26: The Court ruled, 7-1, that women cannot be barred from a state-supported military college. The majority opinion by Justice Ruth Bader Ginsburg applied the standard of "skeptical scrutiny" to government actions treating men and women differently. Justice Clarence Thomas did not participate because his son attended Virginia Military Institute, the college in question.

- *O'Connor v. Consolidated Coin Caterers*, Apr. 1: The Court held unanimously that a worker may sue for age discrimination even if replaced by someone also over 40 years old.

Federal Authority and States' Rights

- *Seminole Tribe v. Florida*, Mar. 27: A 5-4 decision curtailed the power of Congress to pass laws allowing states to be sued in federal court.

- *Wisconsin v. New York*, Mar. 20: The Court unanimously upheld the results of the 1990 Census against a challenge by New York and other large cities that sought a statistical adjustment for undercounting.

First Amendment

- *Colorado Republican Federal Campaign Committee v. Federal Election Commission*, June 26: A divided Court underscored the primacy of political speech by holding that political parties may spend as much as they want to support candidates, as long as such spending is "independent" of the candidates' campaigns. Four justices said they would be willing to outlaw all limitations on political parties' campaign spending.

- *Board of County Commissions v. Umbehr* and *O'Hare Truck Services v. City of Northlake*, June 28: In two patronage cases, the Court ruled, 7-2, that the First Amendment protects government contractors from losing business because they supported a particular candidate, party or political position. In a stinging dissent, Justice Scalia wrote: "The Court must be living in another world. Day by day, case by case, it is busy designing a Constitution for a country I do not recognize."

- *Denver Area Consortium v. Federal Communications Commission*, June 28: In a fragmented ruling that involved six separate opinions, the Court held that certain provisions of a 1992 law that allowed cable television providers to decide whether to show sexually explicit programs violated free-speech guarantees.

- *44 Liquormart v. Rhode Island*, May 13: The Court strengthened commercial speech rights when it unanimously overturned a state law that banned advertising liquor prices.

Voting Rights

- *Shaw v. Hunt* and *Bush v. Vera*, June 13: In parallel 5-4 rulings, the Court invalidated one majority black Congressional district in North Carolina and three majority black and Hispanic districts in Texas as the product of race-based gerrymandering. In her plurality opinion in the Texas case, Justice O'Connor argued that the 14th Amendment required "a commitment to eliminate unnecessary and excessive governmental use and reinforcement of racial stereotypes."

Source: *The World Almanac* and K-III Reference Corporation

XIII. Major Actions of the 104th Congress

The 104th Congress

When the 104th Congress convened Jan. 4, 1995, Republicans controlled both the House and the Senate for the first time in 40 years. Newt Gingrich (R, Georgia) was sworn in as House speaker and Bob Dole (R, Kansas) Senate majority leader. The agenda for most of 1995 was dominated by the "Contract With America," a legislative program endorsed by most GOP House candidates during the 1994 campaign. A budget deadlock between Congress and the White House led to two partial shutdowns of the federal government, Nov. 14 through 20, 1995, and Dec. 16, 1995 through Jan. 4, 1996.

On June 11, 1996, Mr. Dole gave up his Senate seat and majority leadership post to run for President full-time. Trent Lott (R, Mississippi) was elected Senate majority leader June 12. Congress adjourned for the 1996 elections Oct. 4.

The following is a summary of major actions of the 104th Congress during Bill Clinton's third and fourth years as President. Measures that have become law are followed by the Public Law (PL) number.

Selected Important Actions of the 104th Congress

1995

Congressional Accountability Act The first law passed by the 104th Congress, as called for in the "Contract With America." Extends to Congressional employees various civil rights and employment protections that already covered most Americans. Passed by the House Jan. 17, 390-0; passed by the Senate Jan. 11, 98-1; signed by Pres. Clinton Jan. 23 (PL 104-1).

Balanced Budget Amendment Would have amended the Constitution to require a balanced federal budget. Passed the House Jan. 26, 300-132; in the Senate received 65-35 vote Mar. 2, short of the two-thirds vote needed for passage; also failed in the Senate, 64-35, on June 6.

Unfunded Mandate Reform Act Bars Congress from imposing new requirements on states and localities without providing funds to implement them. Passed by the House Mar. 16, 394-28; passed by the Senate Mar. 15, 91-9; signed by Pres. Clinton Mar. 22 (PL 104-4).

Congressional Term Limits Would have amended the Constitution to limit the number of terms served by Senate and House members. Four term-limit proposals all rejected by the House, Mar. 29.

Interstate Commerce Commission Congress abolished the 108-year-old Interstate Commerce Commission as of Jan. 1, 1996. Its remaining responsibilities were transferred to the U.S. Department of Transportation. Passed by the House Nov. 14, 417-8; passed the Senate Nov. 28 by voice vote; signed by Pres. Clinton Dec. 29 (PL 104-88).

Speed Limits A provision of the National Highway System Designation Act repeals national highway speed limits. Passed unanimously by the House Nov. 18; passed by the Senate Nov. 17, 80-16; signed by Pres. Clinton Nov. 28 (PL 104-59).

Lobbying Disclosure Act Toughens regulations on lobbyists. Requires more lobbyists to register with Congress and to report whom they represent and how much they are paid. Passed the House by voice vote Nov. 29; passed by the Senate July 25, 98-0; signed by Pres. Clinton Dec. 19 (PL 104-65).

Source: *The World Almanac* and K-III Reference Corporation

Selected Important Actions of the 104th Congress (continued)

1996

Telecommunications Reform Act   Landmark measure deregulates telephone, mobile phone and cable TV service. Provides for installation in new TV sets of the V-chip, permitting objectionable material to be blocked electronically. Seeks to halt transmission of "indecent" materials via the Internet. Passed by the House Feb. 1, 414-16; passed by the Senate Feb. 1, 91-5; signed by Pres. Clinton Feb. 8 (PL 104-104).

Abortion   Measure would have banned an abortion method as late-term or partial-birth abortion. Passed by the House Mar. 27, 286-129; passed by the Senate Dec. 7, 1995, 54-44; vetoed by Pres. Clinton Apr. 10; motion to override passed the House Sept. 19, 285-137; failed in the Senate Sept. 26, 58-40 (a two-thirds majority is required).

National Debt   Congress raised the public debt limit to $5.5 trillion. Passed by the House Mar. 28, 328-91; passed the Senate Mar. 28 by unanimous consent; signed by Pres. Clinton Mar. 29 (PL 104-121).

Line-Item Veto   Authorizes the President to eliminate specific items in spending and tax bills, subject to Congressional override. Exempts major entitlement programs, such as Social Security, and tax breaks affecting more than 100 taxpayers. Passed by the House Mar. 28 without objection; passed by the Senate Mar. 27, 69-31; signed by Pres. Clinton Apr. 9 (PL 104-130).

Freedom to Farm Act   Ends government controls over which crops may be planted and how much land must be left idle. Replaces subsidies with "transition payments" that decline over seven years. Passed by the House Mar. 29, 318-89; passed by the Senate Mar. 28, 74-26; signed by Pres. Clinton Apr. 4 (PL 104-127).

Product Liability   Legislation would have limited damage awards in product liability lawsuits. Passed by the House Mar. 29, 259-158; passed by the Senate Mar. 21, 59-40; vetoed by Pres. Clinton May 2; motion to override failed in the House May 9, 258-163.

Defense of Marriage Act   Frees states and localities from any obligation to recognize same-sex marriages accepted in other jurisdictions. Passed by the House July 12, 342-67; passed by the Senate Sept. 10, 85-14; signed by Pres. Clinton Sept. 21 (PL 104-199).

Welfare   Landmark welfare-reform legislation. Authorizes states to establish their own welfare programs using block grants from the federal government. Requires most adult recipients to find work within two years. Establishes a lifetime limit of five years on welfare. Abolishes Federal Aid to Families with Dependent Children (AFDC), effectively ending welfare as an entitlement program. Authorizes cuts in benefits to non-citizens. Passed by the House July 31, 328-101; passed by the Senate Aug. 1, 78-21; signed by Pres. Clinton Aug. 22 (PL 104-193).

Health Insurance Portability and Accountability Act   Formerly known as the Kennedy-Kassebaum bill. Allows workers who change jobs to maintain coverage. Prevents insurers from withholding coverage from people with pre-existing medical conditions. Passed by the House Aug. 1, 421-2; passed by the Senate Aug. 2, 98-0; signed by Pres. Clinton Aug. 21 (PL 104-191).

Safe Drinking Water   Requires municipal water systems to report on levels of contaminants. Establishes fund for upgrading water systems. Passed by the House Aug. 2, 392-30; passed by the Senate Aug. 2, 98-0; signed by Pres. Clinton Aug. 6 (PL 104-182).

Minimum Wage   Raises the hourly minimum wage for most employees from $4.25 to $4.75 as of Oct. 1, 1996, and to $5.15 as of Sept. 1, 1997. Passed by the House Aug. 2, 354-72; passed by the Senate Aug. 2, 76-22; signed by Pres. Clinton Aug. 20 (PL 104-188).

Omnibus Consolidated Appropriations Act   Comprehensive measure enacted just before adjournment, averting another government shutdown. Appropriates $244 billion for defense and $356 billion for non-military programs for the 1997 fiscal year. Intensifies U.S. efforts against illegal immigration. Provides $1.1 billion for new anti-terrorism measures. Boosts funding for education programs. Bars anyone convicted of domestic violence from owning a handgun. Passed by the House Sept. 28, 370-37; passed by the Senate Sept. 30 by voice vote; signed by Pres. Clinton Sept. 30 (PL 104-208).

Source: *The World Almanac* and K-III Reference Corporation

XIV. Suggested Reading and Sources

Amos, Jr., Orley M. *Economic Literacy*. Career Press: New Jersey, 1994.

Bagby, Wesley M. *Introduction to Social Science and Contemporary Issues*. Nelson-Hall: Chicago, 1995.

Bannock, Graham, R.E. Baxter and Evan Davis. *Dictionary of Economics*. Penguin: London, 1987.

Baumol, William J. and Alan S. Blinder. *Economics Principles and Policy*. Harcourt Brace Jovanovich: San Diego, 1991.

Bennett, William J. *The Index of Leading Cultural Indicators*. Simon & Schuster: New York, 1994.

Blaug, Mark. *Great Economists Since Keynes*. Cambridge University Press: Cambridge, 1985.

Bork, Robert H. *Slouching Towards Gomorrah*. HarperCollins: New York, 1996.

Budget of the United States Government. Executive Office of the President of the United States. Fiscal Year 1997.

Calleo, David. *The Bankrupting of America*. Avon Books: New York, 1992.

Cane, Michael Allan. *Guide to Federal Income Taxes*. Dell: New York, 1995.

Caplan, Richard and John Fetter. *State of the Union 1994*. Westview Press: Boulder, 1994.

Caves, Richard E., Jeffrey A. Frankel and Ronald W. Jones. *World Trade and Payments*. HarperCollins: New York, 1993.

Chideya, Farai. *Don't Believe the Hype*. Plume: New York, 1995.

Choate, Pat. *Agents of Influence*. Simon and Schuster: New York, 1990.

Christian, Spencer. *Electing Our Government*. St. Martin's Griffin: New York, 1996.

Clinton, William J. *Between Hope and History*. Random House: New York, 1996.

Clinton, Hillary Rodham. *It Takes a Village*. Simon & Schuster: New York, 1996.

Collins, James C. and Jerry I. Porras. *Built to Last*. HarperBusiness: New York, 1994.

Contract With America. Random House: New York, 1994.

Colson, Chuck. *Why America Doesn't Work*. Word Publishing: Dallas, 1991.

Dornbusch, Rudiger and F. Leslie Helmers. *The Open Economy*. Oxford University Press: New York, 1988.

Downes, John and Jordan Elliot Goodman. *Finance & Investment Handbook*. Barron's Educational Series, Inc.: New York, 1990.

Duffy, Paula Barker. *The Relevance of A Decade*. Harvard Business School Press: Boston, 1994.

Economic Report of the President 1996. National Council of Economic Advisors: Transmitted to the Congress of the United States.

Economic Report of the President 1995. National Council of Economic Advisors: Transmitted to the Congress of the United States.

Eisner, Robert. *The Misunderstood Economy: What Counts and How to Count It*. Harvard Business School Press: Boston, 1994.

Feldstein, Martin. *American Economic Policy in the 1980s*. National Bureau of Economic Research: Cambridge, 1994.

Feldstein, Martin. *The Risk of Economic Crisis*. University of Chicago Press: Chicago, 1991.

Figgie, Harry E. *Bankruptcy 1995*. Little, Brown and Company: Boston, 1992.

Fischer, Stanley, Rudiger Dornbusch and Richard Schmalensee. *Economics*. McGraw-Hill: New York, 1988.

Friedman, Milton. *Capitalism and Freedom*. University of Chicago Press: Chicago, 1982.

Fuchs, Lawrence H. *The American Kaleidoscope*. University Press of New England: New Hampshire, 1990.

Fukuyama, Francis. *Trust*. Free Press: New York, 1996.

Gaebler, Ted and David Osborne. *Reinventing Government*. Penguin: New York, 1993.

Galbraith, John Kenneth. *The Good Society*. Houghton Mifflin Company: Boston, 1996.

Galbraith, John Kenneth. *Whence It Came, Where It Went*. Houghton Mifflin Company: Boston, 1995.

Gore, Al. *The Best Kept Secrets in Government*. Random House: New York, 1996.

Heilbroner, Robert and Lester Thurow. *Economics Explained*. Simon & Schuster: New York, 1994.

Information Almanac 1997. Houghton Mifflin: Boston, 1997.

Jackson, Rev. Jesse. *Legal Lynching*. Marlowe & Company: New York, 1996.

Kennedy, Paul. *Preparing For The Twenty-First Century*. Random House: New York, 1993.

Krugman, Paul. *Peddling Prosperity*. W.W. Norton & Company: New York, 1994.

Krugman, Paul R. and Maurice Obstfeld. *International Economics*. HarperCollins: New York, 1991.

Mankiw, Gregory N. *Macroeconomics*. Worth Publishers: New York, 1992.

Moore, Stephen. *Restoring The Dream*. Time Books: New York, 1995.

Moore, Stephen. *Government: America's #1 Growth Industry*. Institute for Policy Innovation: Texas, 1995.

Morgan, Ivan W. *Deficit Government*. Ivan R. Dee: Chicago, 1995.

Nixon, Richard. *Beyond Peace*. Random House: New York, 1994.

Nye, Joseph S. *Bound to Lead*. Basic Books: New York, 1991.

Perot, H. Ross. *Intensive Care*. HarperCollins: New York, 1995.

Perot, H. Ross, with Pat Choate. *Save Your Job, Save Our Country*. Hyperion: New York, 1993.

Peterson, Peter G. *Facing Up*. Simon & Schuster: New York, 1994.

Peterson, Peter G. *Will America Grow Up Before It Grows Old?* Random House: New York, 1996.

Phillips, Kevin. *Politics of the Rich and Poor*. HarperCollins: New York, 1989.

Pindyck, Robert S. and Daniel L. Rubinfeld. *Microeconomics*. Macmillan: New York, 1992.

Porter, Michael E. *Competitive Advantage of Nations*. Free Press: New York, 1990.

Reich, Robert B. *The Work of Nations*. Alfred A. Knopf, Inc.: New York, 1991.

Rosen, Harvey S. *Public Finance*. Irwin: Chicago, 1995.

Sachs, Jeffrey D. and Felipe, Larrain B. *Macroeconomics in the Global Economy*. Prentice Hall: New Jersey, 1993.

Schlesinger, Arthur M. *The Disuniting of America*. W.W. Norton and Company: New York, 1992.

Social Security Administration. "Understanding Social Security." April 1995.

The New York Times. The Downsizing of America. Random House: New York, 1996.

The 1996 Information Please Almanac. Houghton Mifflin Company: Boston, 1996.

The 1997 Information Please Almanac. Houghton Mifflin Company: Boston, 1997.

The World Almanac of U.S. Politics, 1993-1995. Funk & Wagnalls: New Jersey, 1993.

Thurow, Lester. *Head to Head*. Time Warner: New York, 1993.

Varian, Hal. R. *Intermediate Microeconomics: A Modern Approach*. W.W. Norton & Company: New York, 1990.

West, Cornel. *Race Matters*. Random House: New York, 1994.

World Almanac and Book of Facts 1997. K-III Reference Corporation: New Jersey, 1997.